Building Community

SOCIAL SCIENCE IN ACTION

Building Community

SOCIAL SCIENCE IN ACTION

Philip Nyden
Loyola University Chicago

Anne Figert
Loyola University Chicago

Mark Shibley
Loyola University Chicago

Darryl Burrows
Neighborhood Progress Incorporated, Cleveland

PINE FORGE PRESS
Thousands Oaks, California
London ■ *New Delhi*

Copyright © 1997 by Pine Forge Press

For information, address:

 Pine Forge Press
A Sage Publications Company
2455 Teller Road
Thousand Oaks, California 91320
(805) 499-4224
E-mail: sales@pfp.sagepub.com

Sage Publications Ltd.
6 Bonhill Street
London EC2A 4PU
United Kingdom

Sage Publications India Pvt. Ltd.
M-32 Market
Greater Kailash I
New Delhi 110 048 India

Production: Melanie Field, Strawberry Field Publishing
Copy Editor: Judith Brown
Interior Designer: Lisa Mirski Devenish
Typesetter: Christi Payne, Book Arts
Cover Designer: Marnie Deacon Kenney
Production Management: Scratchgravel Publishing Services
Print Buyer: Anna Chin

Printed in the United States of America
97 98 99 00 01 10 9 8 7 6 5 4 3 2 1

Library of Congress Cataloging-in-Publication Data
Building community : social science in action / edited by Phil Nyden
. . . [et al.].
    p.   cm.
  Includes bibliographical references and index.
  ISBN 0-8039-9093-6 (pbk. : alk. paper)
  1. Community and college—United States—Case studies.
 2. Community development—United States—Case studies.
 3. Universities and colleges—United States—Public service—Case
studies. 4. Public relations—Universities and colleges—United
States—Case studies. 5. Evaluation research (Social action
programs)—United States. I. Nyden, Philip W.
LC238.B85 1997

                                          96-45369
                                            CIP

About the Editors

Philip Nyden
Currently Professor of Sociology and Director of the Center for Urban Research and Learning (CURL) at Loyola University Chicago. In the late 1980s, he helped to establish the Policy Research and Action Group (PRAG)—a group of Chicago-based community leaders and university-based researchers that has been building a collaborative network to bring community knowledge and perspectives to the research process. Books authored or co-authored include *Challenging Uneven Development: An Urban Agenda for the 1990s* (Rutgers University Press, 1991) and *Chicago: Race, Class, and the Response to Urban Decline* (Temple University Press, 1987).

Anne Figert
Assistant Professor of Sociology at Loyola University Chicago. Her research and teaching interests are in the sociology of science, medicine, and gender. Her own effort at collaborative research with community groups is contained in this volume. She is the author of *Women and the Ownership of PMS: The Structuring of a Psychiatric Disorder* (Aldine de Gruyter, 1996).

Mark Shibley
Assistant Professor of Sociology at Loyola University Chicago. His research and teaching interests are in the sociology of religion and the sociology of the environment. He is the author of *Resurgent Evangelicalism in the United States: Mapping Cultural Change Since 1970* (University of South Carolina Press, 1996) and numerous book chapters and articles.

Darryl Burrows
Received his graduate training in political science and sociology at the University of Chicago. He is currently Vice President of Neighborhood Progress, Inc. of Cleveland, Ohio. Neighborhood Progress is a local support intermediary for Cleveland's community development industry. He previously served as Executive Director of the Citizens Service and before that as Senior Vice President of Bethel New Life in Chicago. He has written a number of research reports—most recently, *Understanding the Causes of Child Abuse* (1996) for the Department of Children and Family Services for the State of Illinois.

About the Publisher

Pine Forge Press is a new educational publisher, dedicated to publishing innovative books and software throughout the social sciences. On this and any other of our publications, we welcome your comments.

Please call or write us at:

Pine Forge Press
A Sage Publications Company
2455 Teller Road
Thousand Oaks, CA 91320
Phone: (805) 499-4224
E-mail: sales@pfp.sagepub.com

Visit our new World Wide Web site, your direct link to a multitude of on-line resources:

http://www.sagepub.com/pineforge

Contents

Introduction

Why Collaborate and Models of How To / 1

CHAPTER ONE
**University-Community Collaborative Research:
Adding Chairs at the Research Table / 3**

Although, traditionally, there have been tensions between community-based organizations and university-based researchers, these two forces can join to create new capacities for finding solutions to pressing problems. Community and university can become true partners at all stages of research. While all research is "political" in some way, in the case of collaborative projects, rigorous research practices can be maintained and communities can be given increased capacity to shape and influence policy research.

CHAPTER TWO
Effective Models of Collaboration / 14

As both community-based organizations and universities face declining resources, new models of community-university collaborative research are emerging. These models draw on capacities, skills, and experience inside and outside the university. Representing a variation on already developed research traditions, such as participatory action research, this new research methodology is being used in more and more communities. A detailed discussion of an eight-year-old collaborative project, the Policy Research Action Group (PRAG), is provided, along with lessons from collaborative research experiences.

Part I

Racial, Ethnic, and Economic Diversity: Pipe Dream of the Politically Correct or Are There Working Models? / 29

CASE STUDY 1
Creating and Sustaining Racially and Ethnically Diverse Communities / 32

Philip Nyden, Loyola University Chicago
Joanne Adams, Loyola University Chicago
Kim Zalent, Organization of the NorthEast

In a six-year partnership, community organizers and university-based researchers work side-by-side in seeking ways to strengthen links across different racial, ethnic, and income groups in two of the most diverse communities in the United States. Reports from this project have focused on housing, business development, interreligious cooperation, and the needs of youth. The work has been used successfully to shape local social services as well as to put pressure on political leaders—from the mayor of Chicago to the president of the United States.

CASE STUDY 2
University-Community Collaboration in Low-Income Housing Projects and Neighborhood Revitalization in Louisville, Kentucky / 42

John Gilderbloom
R. L. Mullins, Jr.
Russ N. Sims
Mark T. Wright
La tondra R. Jones

A collaboration between a university, local government, business, and community organizations has revitalized a low-income neighborhood in Louisville, Kentucky. The Russell Partnership has used the coordinating capacities as well as the database analysis skills of various departments in a university to design and implement a holistic approach to community revitalization.

CASE STUDY 3
Collaborative, Policy-Related Research in the Area of Fair Housing and Community Development / 47

John Lukehart, Leadership Council for Metropolitan Open Communities

One of the premier regional fair housing advocate agencies in the United States, the Leadership Council participated in an innovative researcher-practitioner research project in 1986. With a $50,000 grant from the U.S. Department of Housing and

Urban Development, nine separate research action projects were developed examining mortgage lending practices, counseling services, mid-census estimates of racial patterns, trends in housing prices, and experiences of African American "pioneers" in previously all-white suburbs.

This coalition between a university and local community leaders demonstrates how data analysis by university researchers can combine with community group capacity to influence government regulatory practices. The result is watchdogging of existing legislation that bans discrimination in lending practices on the part of local banks.

Demonstrating that collaborations can start in an uncomplicated way, a graduate student and a community leader found common ground, establishing a productive research and action relationship. This provides a model that can be used by other students and community leaders in getting partnerships started.

Part II

In working with an African American community in suburban Houston, a university professor and his students gained experience on the front lines of a national movement confronting environmental racism—the practice of locating industrial plants that produce hazardous chemicals or toxic waste dumps in minority communities. The impact of research like this on national policy is documented.

**Conclusion: Collaboration Gives Hope and Voice
in an Age of Disenchantment / 240**

Changing the academic mind-set from thinking about "social problems" to instead putting energies into seeking "social solutions" is an outcome of the collaborative experience. University-community partnerships have the potential for enhancing the quality of students' educational experience at the same time that they strengthen the voice of community organizations and increase their capacity to address serious social issues.

Appendix / 243

References / 250

Index / 257

Preface

As with many books, the title of this one has many nuances. The collaborative work described in the subsequent chapters is truly activity that *builds* on an *existing* foundation of knowledge, social networks, organizational capacity, and grassroots energy. We do not intend to perpetuate a myth that academia has all the answers, any more than we would say that community activists, social service practitioners, or political leaders have all the answers. *Building Community* means building stronger relationships among all of these forces that have traditionally been separated or, worse, at odds with one another and unwilling to work together.

Building Community pays particular attention to strengthening the relationship between the university and the broader communities within which we all live and work—neighborhoods, the workplace, and non-geographically-based communities of "interest" (for example, gays and lesbians, women, those discriminated against, children, and immigrant workers). The capacity realized and the excitement unleashed by partnerships between previously isolated groups and individuals are impressive. All of us who have been involved in university-community collaborations have experienced those exciting moments when new approaches to persistent community problems have emerged in the course of collaborative research discussions where there is a new mix of minds and perspectives. Also, the trust and respect that emerge from such productive collaborative work invariably produce new relationships and networks that live beyond the initial project.

Building Community is about increasing capacity. The community experiences increased capacity by gaining access to the research and knowledge inside academia and inside the maze of disciplines housed in universities. But this is only half of the picture. Increasing community capacity by "giving" our knowledge from academia to those outside academia is more along the lines of the traditional view of university-community relationships. In this traditional relationship, university "experts" impart their knowledge and help the "dependent" community. In contrast to this, the collaborations described in this book are aimed not at perpetuating dependency on universities, but rather at increasing communities' ability to understand the research process so that they have equal footing in setting the direction of social science research.

Collaboration increases the capacity of the university as well. Books, ideas, theories, and datasets are all abstractions. Community-university partnerships enable faculty and students to gain an understanding of the world around them. Direct experience in the community can provide the real hook on which to hang a theory. Some of us learn better by seeing real examples rather than by just reading about them. Community-based research can be more exciting than just reading about it. Although it can be very messy and complicated at times, such research—particularly with action components aimed at social change—can provide the excitement that motivates students not just to learn, but to choose what directions they want to take in pursuing careers and life after college.

Building Community also assumes that research is not done in a vacuum, nor is it done just to put more books on the shelves of libraries. It is done to improve the quality of life; there is an action component to it. You cannot *build* a house by just reading the instructions or by just knowing the mathematics of load-bearing walls or the quality of materials. To build a house you have to actively participate in the construction project. In building community you may have to confront employers, elected officials, other entrenched community leaders, or even university officials. You *experience* the research and *experience* the process of putting it into place. Although there is a need to distinguish between the rigorous research and the effective social action stages of building community, to see these as two totally separate processes that should not be connected is just plain wrong.

This is an optimistic book. The activists and researchers writing and described in this book could not summon the energy to move ahead with their work if they did not think positive social change was within their reach. We need to recognize but not wallow in social problems. We are in the business of looking for solutions that address the needs of all members of our society.

We prepared the cases and commentaries in *Building Community* so that they could be useful to students, researchers, and community activitists. In addition to being useful in courses specifically devoted to the study of communities, urban sociology, urban politics, or social policy, this book can serve as a supplementary text in research methods or community organizer training. We hope that the broad variety of cases as well as the discussion of how social science research techniques can be used in a multitude of settings will make this book a valuable asset inside and outside the classroom for those interested in shaping positive community change.

Thank you to the following reviewers: Jose Calderon, Pitzer College; Jess Enns, University of Nebraska; Susan Brown Eve, University of North Texas; David Hartman, University of North Texas; Wilfred Holton, Northeastern University; Stan Ingman, University of North Texas; and Roland Liebert, University of Illinois, Urbana–Champaign.

To provide a more dynamic textbook, we invite you to explore recent developments in collaborative research and action networks. You can visit the Loyola University Chicago Center for Urban Research and Learning World Wide Web Home Page at http://www.luc.edu/depts/curl and the Policy Research Action Group WWW Home Page at http://www.luc.edu/depts/curl/prag. If you are interested in participating in a listserve to talk with others about collaborative research and teaching collaborative research methods, contact us via e-mail at curlcomm@luc.edu.

Philip Nyden
Anne Figert
Mark Shibley
Darryl Burrows

Foreword

Government plays an important role in our lives. It provides resources and funding to address problems that would otherwise go unnoticed. Government also makes a positive impact on the most disadvantaged in our society. A government that can reach out and help people is one which Americans need and want.

Building Community: Social Science in Action tells us how government is making a difference in the United States today and how we can do better. Through partnerships between universities and communities, government has been able to help researchers, community activists, and government employees form solutions to the social and economic problems affecting our diverse communities.

It is not surprising that *Building Community* focuses on urban communities. They are generally the most afflicted by problems of illiteracy, crime, gang violence, and racism. Urban communities often are the most likely to benefit from government, community, and university collaboration. With knowledge and dedication, urban communities can make such a partnership a success.

If we can get universities and communities to work together, we will be able to have new and better resources to use in the 21st century. With declining resources at the university and federal government levels, partnerships such as these will be needed in the future even more.

Both in my current position as a U.S. Senator and in my next post-Senate career in academia, I hope to profit from *Building Community*'s message: attacking issues with the cooperation of the government, universities, and our communities.

Paul Simon
U.S. Senator (Illinois, 1985–1997)
Washington, D.C.

Foreword

Research about social systems, individual behavior, and social policies can greatly improve the effectiveness of policy making and help solve societal problems. But to incorporate research findings into the day-to-day routines of organizations or apply knowledge gained through academic research to the lives of real people is extremely difficult. *Building Community: Social Science in Action* presents a wealth of case studies that show how research can be effectively applied in practice.

These cases, moreover, underscore the importance and value of collaboration—among researchers, practitioners, and community members. Community organizations discover the utility of systematic study in analyzing problems, identifying solutions, and promoting public action. Researchers find new ways to use their skills, gain insights into problems, and contribute to public well-being. Universities develop stronger relationships with their surrounding communities. And, most important, progress is made toward finding solutions to real community problems.

The experience of groups like the Policy Research Action Group, a collaborative effort of Chicago-based academics and community organizations, shows that rigorous research practices can be maintained even as communities increase their role in shaping policy research. PRAG-sponsored research has tackled issues of vital concern, including adult education and workforce preparation, residential stability in diverse neighborhoods, citizen participation and empowerment, community economic development, and lead poisoning among children.

By engaging university researchers and community organizations in collaborations aimed at changing social policy, the work profiled in *Building Community* has helped take social science beyond the identification of social problems toward the discovery of sustainable social solutions.

Adele Simmons
President, The John D. and Catherine T.
MacArthur Foundation

Foreword

Community groups and organizations are no less dependent on accurate data than any corporation or university. In order to ensure successful outcomes for their constituents, community activists must have a clear and accurate understanding of the needs in their community. That understanding cannot be acquired through osmosis or serendipity, but rather through careful observation and analysis. Community leaders have an obligation to do a thorough assessment of needs and to do diligent research to identify solutions.

Community groups too often lack the appropriate resources to do quality research. As the authors correctly point out, funding is almost always the primary obstacle. Consequently, community leaders must improvise to obtain the data they need, sometimes at the expense of accuracy or completeness. As a result, they are hampered in their ability to do the very best for their constituents.

Collaboration between university and community is essential. Universities have the resources for quality research that community groups lack. In exchange, the community provides the university with a fertile setting in which to do mutually meaningful research. I know from personal experience how highly significant this union can be.

I direct a housing advocacy organization on behalf of Chicago's Latino community. We knew that our community had minimal access to publicly assisted housing resources, but we did not know the extent of our under-representation, and did not have the resources with which to do a thorough analysis. We established a relationship with the Policy Research Action Group (PRAG), a network of universities and community organizations, which provided us with graduate students as research associates. In short order, we were able to document that Chicago has 110,000 units of publicly assisted housing units and that less than 3 percent of these units housed Latino families, even though Latinos comprise 25 percent of the eligible population. Realizing that an accurate inventory of assisted housing did not exist, not even at the U.S. Department of Housing and Urban Development (HUD) from which all of the subsidies derive, we developed the most comprehensive accounting of assisted housing in Chicago. This data augmented our findings that the Chicago Housing Authority (CHA) had engaged in policies and practices that were discriminatory against Latinos.

Latinos United, along with four other community organizations and five community residents, filed and won a class action lawsuit against HUD and CHA. The net result is the elimination of these discriminatory policies and practices, and an estimated $210 million in housing resources for eligible Latino families over the next 10 years.

Building Community: Social Science in Action masterfully documents that grassroots victories such as these are no mere accident, but rather the inevitable result when two highly committed and capable partners, university and community, join forces to do what is right for society.

Carlos R. DeJesús
Executive Director, Latinos United

Introduction

*Why Collaborate and
Models of How To*

CHAPTER ONE

University-Community Collaborative Research

Adding Chairs at the Research Table

Saul Alinsky, one of America's best known community organizers, once said, "the word academic is synonymous for irrelevant" (Alinsky 1969, ix). Alinsky felt that community organizations themselves needed to collect information to be used in their battles with aldermen, mayors, bank executives, and large companies. With their emphasis on scientific methods, objectivity, and desire to stay above the political fray, in Alinsky's eyes academics could not produce the kind of information needed. Community organizers saw academics as more concerned with the advancement of their respective disciplines than with social change. While the founder of "in-your-face" organizing tactics may have been overstating the issue to maximize the shock value of his statement, there is some basis to this comment. Traditional academic-based research does not always have the betterment of a particular community in mind, nor is it consistently concerned with finding ways to improve the quality of life for those in society who do not have a fair share of their nation's wealth. Rather, to the traditional academic researcher, it is the advancement of knowledge *within* the discipline that is of utmost importance.

Speaking to Nyden's graduate sociology field methods class in the early 1970s, sociologist Erving Goffman said that furthering sociological theory and research took priority in the research enterprise. Contributions to the quality of life in our society were not specific goals of his sociological research. In fact Goffman argued that even violation of accepted norms was acceptable if it facilitated the collection of data; when a student asked if "sleeping with the wife of a key player in the organization you are studying to get critical information could be justified," Goffman answered yes, if it furthered research.

Like Alinsky, Goffman may have been overstating the case to make his point. However, the revered community organizer and the internationally known sociologist represent opposite ends of the research spectrum. While both recognize the importance of data and analysis of that data, one prefers to use it for the betterment of the less powerful, and the other prefers to use it for the advancement of his discipline. These opposing orientations to research have traditionally created a barrier to community-based leaders and academics working together.

The purpose of this book is to present an alternative route to gaining a better understanding of the world around us. We do this by providing more than 25 case studies of collaborative university-community research. The collaborative model discussed and illustrated in this book represents a research approach whereby community activists and academic researchers work together during *all* phases of the research process. On the one hand it explores the neutral territory between the community[1] and the university—a territory where both community and academia feel comfortable. On the other hand, it seeks to use the tensions between community leaders and university researchers to strengthen the research. It recognizes that different perspectives on the same social issue can lead to more productive and rigorous research.

In the collaborative research model, academics and nonacademics work together in identifying the research issue, developing the research design, collecting the data, analyzing the data, writing up the results, and even working with policy makers and practitioners in designing programs and policies. While the amount of collaboration at each level varies in the case studies presented in this book, the spirit of cooperation exists in all examples. Because the research projects described here are shaped by both practitioners and researchers, the end results are more likely to have relevance in solving pressing problems in today's society—problems ranging from meeting the need for more affordable housing in urban neighborhoods to making sure that information on AIDS/HIV prevention gets into the hands of the populations most at risk. This research is also more actionable—that is, the end result of the research project is more likely to be immediately usable to community activists, government policy makers, and other organizational leaders.

---

[1]We use the term *community* broadly in this book. It can refer to geographic communities, such as specific city neighborhoods, or to nongeographic communities of interest, such as women, children, the working poor, Latinos, immigrants, gays and lesbians, or people with disabilities.

Adding Chairs at the Research Table and Accepting a New Set of Critics

In essence, we are suggesting adding chairs to the research table. A central part of all academic research has been a process of talking with colleagues about your research. Within universities, informal meetings, seminars, colloquia, or brown-bag lunches have all been used as settings where research ideas or research in progress can be shared with colleagues. Annual professional conventions serve as more formal settings, where researchers present their ideas to colleagues not only to inform them of research findings but also to get critical feedback on the work. It is during discussion at such gatherings that ideas are tested, weaknesses are pointed out, and strengths are complimented. Often, discussion helps to identify past research or new perspectives that the researcher did not initially see, but may find useful in the present project. This scrutiny of research by colleagues in the discipline is at the heart of academic research. While our model recognizes the value of peer review and constructive criticism by colleagues, we are suggesting that the definition of peers and colleagues be expanded to include members of the community outside the university.

The invitation of community leaders to the research table brings a valuable set of experiences and perspectives into the research process. Community leaders may not speak the language of academics or have the depth of knowledge of research methodologies, bodies of research, or theoretical perspectives held by academic researchers, but they still do have much to add. A community leader's general knowledge of day-to-day life in a community or specific information about the people being studied is valuable in both framing the research and in analyzing data coming out of the research. Nonacademics also bring a fresh, critical perspective to the research table; naivety about well-established theories in the social science field may be an advantage rather than a hindrance. All of us tend to become immersed in our areas of expertise and do not always see the weaknesses or the strengths of our theories or ideas. It sometimes takes an outsider to see them and point them out to us.

Likewise, academic researchers can bring similar critical perspectives to the community. Community leaders who are frequently trying to deal with very pressing day-to-day problems cannot always see the forest for the trees. Because they are removed from everyday concerns and pressures, researchers may see trends and patterns that are not immediately apparent to community leaders. As sociologist Herbert Blumer states in his classic book, *Symbolic Interactionism*, the task of the sociologist is to "lift the veils that cover . . . group life" (Blumer 1969, 39). In *Invitation to Sociology*, Peter Berger talks about the ability of the trained sociologist to step back from his or her own involvement in society and look at those social forces that affect our lives:

> We see the puppets dancing on their miniature stage, moving up and down as the strings pull them around, following the prescribed course of their various little parts. We learn to understand the logic of this theater and we find ourselves in society and thus recognize our own position as we hang from its subtle strings. For a moment we see ourselves as puppets indeed. But then we grasp a decisive difference between the puppet theater and our own drama. Unlike the puppets, we have the possibility of stopping in our movements, looking up and perceiving the machinery by which we have been moved. In this act lies the first step towards freedom. And in this same act we

find the conclusive justification of sociology as a humanist discipline. (Berger 1963, 176)

Community activists and researchers alike have "blinders" on that keep them from seeing social phenomena even when they are right in front of them. It often takes someone with a different background to ask the questions and point out the blind spots. Collaborative research helps to provide these new sets of perspectives needed to eliminate the blind spots.

Because an important part of collaborative research is the willingness of both sides to accept criticism and respect the input of others, the relationship takes time to develop. Successful collaborative projects typically have at their foundation a working relationship that has been built up over time. In research on important elements of 20 collaborative projects in Chicago, "trust" was one of the common threads mentioned by both academic researchers and community leaders. This is trust that the researcher will incorporate community input into the research, and trust that he or she will not just use the research for publications but will give something back to the community in terms of a final report, assistance in planning, or continued discussion with community leaders about policy issues. This is also trust that the community leader will respect the research standards of the academic and understand the pressure on the researcher to publish the research in his or her own field in addition to publishing it in a more popular form of use to the community. Trust is not something both sides sign off on in a contract; it is something that emerges as a working relationship develops. Collaborative relationships are not instantly created from the top down. They usually involve a number of steps that start with smaller, limited projects to test the waters and then build into larger research projects.

Effective Communication: Getting Beyond Community-Speak and Academic Jargon

Communication between the collaborative partners as well as clear communication of research results to the general public are also critical elements in the research discussed in this book. All concerned need to share information on a regular basis. There is also a need to communicate in a language that is understood by all. Community organizations can easily fall into the "community-speak" of their particular area. For example, those involved in housing issues may talk about "Section 8 units," "HUD prepayment buildings," or "LIHPRHA." Names and acronyms of other community organizations may fly by fast and furious in community conversations, making academic researchers feel a bit lost. At the same time, academia has been notorious for its development of specialized languages that only the anointed inside a discipline can understand.

Academic disciplines often fall into their own little worlds of concepts and jargon. This produces an illusion of complexity and profundity that is as much a way of keeping out the uninitiated as it is useful in understanding the social problems under study. For example, in the abstract of a recent *American Journal of Sociology* article examining theoretical trends in the sociology of education, the author writes:

> The article argues that the 'immanentism'—the practice of asserting a necessary movement of history that concerns subordinate groups with objective interests in radical change—of critical approaches is the source of theoretical difference and that the trajectory of critical theories reflects shifting conceptions of how this change will occur. (Davies 1995)

To the uninitiated, even after reading the sentence three times, the idea is barely intelligible. Admittedly even among sociologists, only a few would find themselves quickly engaged in this article. Collaborative research assumes that much of this kind of jargon can and should be eliminated. Concepts should be made understandable to people outside the discipline. Unless obscurity or irrelevance is one of the goals of academic researchers, they need to work at clearer communication with the world outside of the academy.

We do not mean to imply that research in the social sciences is of little use to community leaders. On the contrary, the vast majority of research in the social sciences does have direct relevance to many contemporary community initiatives. The reader can easily see the pertinence that articles in recent issues of the *American Sociological Review* would have to community leaders and policy makers interested in support for single mothers, greater involvement in community struggles, and racism in the community: "Mother's Occupational Status and Children's Schooling" (April 1994); "Economic Inequality: New Methods for New Trends" (April 1994); "Why Social Movement Sympathizers Don't Participate" (October 1994); and "The Continuing Significance of Race: Antiblack Discrimination in Public Places" (February 1991).

Although some articles may be titled or written in ways not as understandable to the layreader as they are to the seasoned social scientist, the links to public policy research are there. It is up to the collaborative researcher to serve as translator of much of this work. For example, two articles in a recent issue of the *American Sociological Review* (August 1994) might seem obscure to nonsociologists: "Imbalanced Structures, Unfair Strategies: Power and Justice in Social Exchange" and "Gender, Legitimate Authority, and Leader-Subordinate Conversations." On the other hand, the research material contained in these articles would be invaluable to a community leader seeking to increase the voice of women in community organizations and in guiding the direction of grassroots organizing.

As much as we would like to see social science research written in plain English (or Spanish, or whatever language is spoken and read by the people consuming the research), we also recognize that we cannot change the academic world completely. Therefore, one of the functions of collaborative researchers is to provide a bridge between the more obscure parts of academic research and the practical questions under study. Good collaborative researchers not only know how to work with community leaders, but they also know how to _translate_ useful research inside their field so that it can be understood and applied by those outside of their field. Without this translation function, relevant research reports may continue to gather dust on library shelves, read only by a few graduate students collecting more references for their dissertation bibliographies.

Research Done *with* the Community, Not *to* It

Another reason why community organizations see research as alien to their needs is the history of negative experiences with research. Research is a dirty word in some community circles. One kind—evaluation research—is common. With this kind, community organizations and social service agencies see researchers come in and judge how well they have been performing their jobs. Usually required by government or private foundation funders to see if their money is being used effectively, these evaluation projects are seen as judgmental—organizations or projects are given the "thumbs up" or "thumbs down" by outside evaluators. Continued funding may be on the line in such cases. Although more and more "formative" evaluation is being done today—evaluation that works with community organizations to improve existing programs and services—the history of outside review has certainly affected the community's view of research.

A second kind of research has been the more independent research done by professors or their students who come into the community to collect data, sometimes including interviews with residents and leaders, only to disappear and never give back any information to the community. This research can be likened to scientific expeditions into exotic lands to collect information and artifacts that are brought back to the university for analysis. Just like colonial anthropologists, the applied researcher may keep the artifacts or knowledge, share them with colleagues, but never return them to the community. Research is seen as a series of forays into the community to collect data. A common complaint that we hear from community leaders is that they helped a faculty member or student collect information on their community or their organization and never saw the results of the research—not even the student's final paper. Given the limited staff and scarce resources of most community organizations and social service agencies, helping university researchers is often viewed as a drain on organizational resources. With each successive experience, community leaders become more and more reluctant to assist in research.

In contrast, the collaborative research we illustrate in this book is research done *with* the community and not *to* the community. From the beginning, project accountability to the community is built into the process. The sharing of results is part of the research model. Humanist sociologist Alfred McClung Lee explains that

> The great challenge of social science is the development and wide dissemination of social wisdom and social action techniques that will enable more and more people to participate in the control and guidance of their groups and their society. In meeting this challenge, social science stimulates and nurtures the fuller development of individual potential. (Lee 1973, 6)

Collaborative research is aimed at stopping the "expedition" approach to community research. Involving community leaders from the beginning of the research project helps to assure the usefulness of the final product. Community perspectives as well as academic perspectives are put on the table as the research is designed, data collected, and results analyzed. The research will be relevant to both academics and community leaders. Community leaders' interest in the research is also increased because they have a voice in the project. The involvement of community leaders with no "research" credentials should not be construed as producing less rigorous research that compromises accepted standards for the sake of "helping out" a community.

Maintaining Rigorous Research

Research is only useful to a community if it is accurate and provides information that is an honest representation of the issue being studied. Quality collaborative research does not abandon accepted research practices in sociology, psychology, anthropology, political science, chemistry, epidemiology, or any other science. As with any other research, careful study needs to be given to negative results—for example, evaluation research results that show that a community organization's program is not doing what it says it is doing. If the research is done well, it should point the organization and community toward more effective alternatives to current strategies. Positive results—for example, results showing that a community organization's program *is* successful in addressing a pressing social issue—are useful only insofar as the research that has come to this conclusion was done in a rigorous manner. Positive research outcomes will not only document that an organization is doing something right, but will provide the useful analysis that can be applied by other organizations in communities or cities in effectively addressing problems in their neighborhoods. Research results, whether positive or negative, are only useful insofar as they are shared with a broad audience that can act on them.

There are two major categories of collaborative research. One is evaluation research, which examines the effectiveness of a particular program or the impact of an organization's strategies. This research is of particular use in strengthening or adjusting components of existing programs. For example, an organization might want to know if its job counseling program has been more effective in helping women get jobs than just letting women look on their own. The other type of research is broader policy research—an analysis of community needs and potential ways of addressing those needs. This research is often used by community organizations as ammunition in policy battles at local, state, or national levels. For instance, it might be used in making the case that welfare-to-work programs need to include GED programs, drug abuse counseling, or day care options if they are to work well.

There is overlap between the two types of research. Evaluation research can be used in making the case for replication of a program to other areas. Similarly, policy research does have implications for the specific day-to-day workings of various programs. It is easy to see that in both cases, research is a political process, since it can make or break future support for a program or can be used to develop new initiatives.

Research Is Political

In thinking about collaborative research it is critical that the political aspect of research be understood and addressed up front. We use the term *political* here to refer to processes that affect the distribution of power and resources in our society. Anyone who claims that good research is not political is just plain wrong. The mere choice of what to research is a political decision. Research that examines male and female differences in car buying behavior will be of great interest to automobile companies in increasing their sales. On the other hand, a researcher who decides to examine how to increase the efficiency of public transportation systems is doing research that will strengthen alternatives to car usage and help that portion of the population who cannot afford cars. Research can be political in two ways. First, it can be related to the *external* political process; the decision to research a certain issue will potentially influence public policy debates in broader society. Second, there are *internal* political processes within the research process itself. The relationship between the researcher and the organization or people to be researched is also a political relationship.

The internal politics of research is of prime concern in constructing effective collaborative relationships. In large part this is an outgrowth of the resource imbalance in our society. One reason you are more likely to see collaborative research relationships develop in the community organization, nonprofit organization, and grassroots movement world is that most of these groups or movements lack the resources

to "buy" researchers outright. In the corporate world, businesses often have enough money to hire full-time research staff or hire researchers on a consulting basis. Since it is "their" money, corporations call the shots and typically have researchers sign contracts that give the company total ownership of the researcher's results and prohibit public distribution of the results without corporate permission. This is the way the corporate world deals with the liabilities of negative research results. They can decide to use or not to use, publish or not publish, the research results as they see fit.

Nonprofit organizations typically do not have the luxury of this kind of control. The initial motivation to pursue collaborative research has to do with getting research at a discount price, or at no cost at all. When you can't afford to do it yourself, or pay for it yourself, collaboration is a reasonable avenue. Although researcher-community activist relationships often grow beyond this expedient basis for their relationship, it is important to note that the first impetus for collaboration may be primarily financial. In the development of collaborative research under these circumstances, the community organization typically gets to help define the research issue, but the researcher typically gets to publish the research. The community is not in total control over how the research is used and published.

This is where many collaborative relationships are made or broken. What happens when research results make your collaborator's program or organizing strategies look bad? What happens when your research questions the basis of what has been seen as an important program? These are issues that need to be addressed early in the collaborative research relationship. In well-established collaborative relationships, a familiarity with each others' working styles and a trust develops. However, this takes time.

In some cases, before this working relationship or trust is fully developed, an up-front written agreement can be helpful. The function of this contract is not only to have a formal agreement, but to provide an opportunity for both researcher and practitioner to think about and discuss their relationship before a research project is under way. Many of the collaborative projects described in this book are not the first cooperative efforts between researchers and activists. Projects often develop after the waters have been tested with smaller cooperative efforts. Each partner gains an understanding of the other and builds trust. This trust extends to a comfort with how the results—particularly negative results—can be used. In other cases, negative research results can be kept "in-house" to be used to modify and adjust a community program. Researchers who may want to use the negative case for published analysis within academic journals can usually do so without identifying the specific organization involved.

Recognition of the political character of research is important in explicitly addressing some of the land mines on the road to collaboration at the same time that it is important in understanding why people collaborate. It would be wrong to make the cynical assumption that the only reason to collaborate has to do with self-interest—the researcher getting an opportunity to collect data for another article or the community organization getting some cheap research labor. Collaborations are formed and held together because people share the same values. In the research case studies in this book, both sides consistently recognize the potential of research in helping to bring about positive social change for various groups of people, whether it be low-income families seeking better quality housing or community leaders trying to clean up toxic chemicals in

their community. What drives the collaborative research we are describing is not just a desire to add to our understanding of the world around us, but also a desire to identify the tools needed to change the world around us. In the information age, data and research outcomes are political commodities. As one community organization leader explained, the collaborative research project in which his organization was involved gave him a "pocket full of factoids" that he could use in confronting leaders of government agencies and elected officials. It gave him bits of information with which to counter developers in media debates over the need for more affordable housing versus the advantages of gentrification. This action component brings up the issue of "objectivity" and research.

One of the pitfalls of collaborative research is the potential of transgressing into ideological justifications for existing community action projects instead of rigorously assessing community needs or evaluating the merits of existing strategies. There is no miracle formula to avoid this trap. One safeguard is an awareness of this danger. Inattention to rigorous research methods can undermine the credibility of the research. Also, if the community truly wants to find out what works and what does not work so that it can most efficiently use its limited resources in addressing pressing problems, it is in its best interests to use solid research techniques.

Thus, objectivity in collaborative research does not mean consciously ignoring how the research might be used to a particular end, such as improving the quality of AIDS/HIV prevention education, increasing public acceptance of group homes for delinquent youth, or improving race relations in a community. Objectivity means exposing collaborative research to as much of the critical standards of social science research as possible.

What Keeps Collaborative Relationships Going and What Are the Lasting Contributions?

We have talked about some of the initial motivations of partners in collaborative research, but what are some of the lasting benefits of this relationship to both sides? What makes them want to come back for more after the first encounter? The impact of collaborative research goes beyond the immediate practical value of the research. The research broadens the perspective of both community leaders and university researchers.

For community activists, collaborative research brings them into the research process. It is exciting and empowering to be at the table with people who share different perspectives on problems that you have been addressing in the community for years. New ideas that come out of this amalgam of community and academic perspectives hold within them the potential to bring about change. It is arrogant of academics to think that the world is divided into "thinkers" like themselves—those able to step back from day-to-day issues and study the broad implications and theoretical links between the various pieces of the puzzles—and those only able to see immediate problems—those who do applied work. Community activists are equally competent in the "thinking" game. The only difference is that they are constrained by the day-to-day realities of community life. They are constrained by the urgencies of hunger, violence, poor housing, and poor education. These problems are not abstractions to the community leader; they have the real faces of the homeless mother who is seeking shelter; the 8-year-old who just saw his brother shot to death; the family that wants to get out of a rat-infested building; and the inner-city high school student who wants to go to college but is reading at fifth grade level.

By bringing these realities to the research table, community activists provide the materials for the needed acid test of academic theories. To talk and debate with academic researchers who have been able to step back from the numbing effect of urgent, pressing problems can be productive and invigorating. Individuals who seek to solve the practical problems of urban communities are no less creative than those who look at the connections between academic-discipline-based theories and new research results. Together they represent the coherent theoretical and practical machinery needed to bring about change. Apart they represent only the scattered pieces of the engine needed to drive the policy development process.

The collaborative research process has lasting effects for the community because it provides a better understanding of the workings of research. In a collaboration, community activists may not become expert in all the ins and outs of survey research, but they may gain a better understanding of the steps in questionnaire design, sampling, data collection, data entry, and computer analysis. They may gain an understanding of the resources needed to complete a survey and where to get those resources. Community leaders become informed consumers in the collaborative process.

Similarly, collaborative research involves researchers in the "real" world with the opportunity to see their research efforts used by communities to improve the quality of life of its members. Hardly a day goes by when we don't pick up the *Chicago Tribune* and see stories about groups we have worked with and issues that we have researched. For faculty and students, this is an exciting and empowering process. You feel that you are part of something and not just on the sidelines watching the world go by. Collaborative research demystifies the political process by allowing faculty and students to understand how decisions are influenced and made. It reduces cynicism and apathy; while community activists may point out the difficulties of bringing about social change, by definition they recognize that changes can be made if their information, their organizing efforts, and their strategies are carefully chosen. This optimism is a wonderful antidote to the tendency of academic researchers to study problem after problem without attention to possible solutions.

When collaborative research involves undergraduate and graduate students as part of the research team, it produces memorable experiences for students. After graduation they remember their involvement in that community survey or that report that was ultimately featured in the local newspaper. When students think about urban issues they no longer pull up some fuzzy abstract image in their mind; they see real communities and real faces. For professor and student, collaborative research provides another method of learning. Practical experiences give everyone a real "hook" on which to hang theories and more abstract concepts. Practical experiences with all their complexities help faculty and students guard against oversimplification. Watching elementary school students in an after-school program on the Westside of Chicago take turns being the "dead person" when they play funeral certainly gives students pause in trying to understand how childhood in inner-city neighborhoods differs from childhood in most suburbs. It provides a better grasp on the complexities of policy development; for example, it shows that standard suburban educational practices are not necessarily the answers to the city's educational crisis.

Collaborative projects leave behind strengthened academic-community networks. Even after a project is completed, interpersonal and interorganizational relationships remain. When a question arises, help may be only a phone call away, whereas before, there was no efficient way to find an answer. Community leaders who, in the past, found universities to be unapproachable, complicated bureaucracies, now know some of the insiders who can help them find the right "expert," the student intern, or the existing data. Similarly, researchers who have questions about developments in community-based programs related to their research can get up-to-date information and insights from community activist friends. For students, there are also lasting relationships and experiences. Not only are they plugged into policy and action projects, but like the brick mason who drives by a building and can say, "I helped to build that apartment building," so too can the student say, "I had a part in the development of that new affordable housing program."

We are not suggesting that collaborative research should be *the* research method within the social sciences, nor are we suggesting that involving students in community-based, collaborative research is the only way of teaching. We are presenting a case for strengthening this area as an additional approach to research and an additional way of teaching in the university. It is not easy, it is messy, and it does not always go as you have planned. There are safer routes for professors and students. Junior professors can get tenure by developing careers in collaborative research, but sometimes they have to work a bit harder to do that. Teachers can develop collaborative research projects involving community organizations, but it often takes more time, and the work does not always stop at the end of the semester. Success in collaborative research usually means more requests from the community and more projects for the willing academic. For students, it involves more time to go out to communities, to go beyond the boundaries of the university library in doing research.

However, collaborative research is an enjoyable, exciting process. It gives you a free membership in the community of social change agents. You are invited in to commiserate over the failures and celebrate the successes. You are recognized as being part of the solution and not part of the problem. Just as social science can "lift the veils" that obscure social processes, so too can collaborative research open windows on entirely new experiences for professors, students, and community activists.

CHAPTER TWO

Effective Models of Collaboration

The first chapter outlined the traditional tensions between academics and community activists as well as the additional capacity that can be realized when collaborative relationships are established. We would like to describe a new collaborative model of university-community research that is emerging in the United States today. Like any other "new" model, it is really an amalgam of old and new elements that have developed in response new political, economic, and social realities in the country today. We are going to draw heavily on the experiences of the Chicago-based Policy Research Action Group (PRAG) as well as other policy research and action organizations around the country. Austerity and budget cutbacks in the academy and in community settings have produced the need for more cooperation between universities and communities as a way of using limited resources more efficiently. In this vein, private foundations and government agencies have encouraged collaboration by making interinstitutional cooperation a precondition to some grants. The response has been the emergence of a new model of collaboration. Before looking at the nuts and bolts of university-community collaborative programs, we will take a brief look at the factors producing this major growth of collaborative models today.

The New Austerity Hits the University and the Community

Although there has always been a network of university-based researchers and community activists who have worked together, the envi-ronment today is even more hospitable to supporting such collaborations. Ironically, this new "hospitable" environment is emerging in a period of austerity that has reduced total resources available to both the university and the community. The new environment is partially driven by funders—private foundations and government agencies—that are giving preference to collaborations. A rationale behind this new prioritization is the increased need for more effective and efficient coordination of policy research activities, which means more effective and efficient use of foundation and government dollars.

The need to be more efficient with money is the result of the leveling of, or decline in, government and foundation support for such activity. Unlike the growth mode during much of the post-World War II era, the 1990s is the age of austerity. Tax revolts in the late 1970s and 1980s have had their impact on local, state, and federal budgets. Funding for research and social programs is not as plentiful as it once was. As government funding for social programs declines, former recipients of government funding (social service agencies, universities, and community-based organizations) are now seeking support from private foundations. This has increased competition in this sector. The size of the pie is shrinking and the funding world is getting more competitive.

This austerity in research support is happening at a time when there is an even larger crisis in American communities and workplaces. As resources to support innovative community-based policy research activity have become tighter, the need for such activity has increased. Part of this crisis is related to the current era of downsizing and severed connections between citizen and community institutions or between worker and employer. Today, on a regular basis the American public reads of the latest corporate downsizing, job cuts measured in the thousands, and the fallout that this has on communities. In 1996 the *New York Times* ran a series entitled the "Downsizing of America"—looking at a broad range of institutions from corporations to communities (*New York Times* 1996a). The debate it set off had less to do with whether or not we are downsizing, but more to do with how we react to it. One corporate leader referred to this new era as one in which workers will be "jobless, but not workless"; he sees people laid off from one firm moving to another as needed (Leana 1996, 15). The level of commitment to workers by companies is declining.

In a related trend, inequality is on the rise in America. Wealth and income is more concentrated in the hands of fewer people than has been the case anytime since the 1930s.[1] Between 1977 and 1989, *94 percent* of the total increase in after-tax income of American families (adjusted for inflation) went to the top 20 percent of American families. Only *6 percent* of income gains during this 12-year period went to the remaining 80 percent of American families. Looking at this another way, the top 1 percent of income-earning families (with an average 1989 income of $559,800) saw their buying power increase by 77 percent. At the same time, each of the two bottom fifths of American families (with average 1989 incomes of $20,100 and $8,400, respectively) experienced 1 percent and 9 percent declines in buying power, respectively (*New York Times*, 1996b). The consequence is the emergence of a dual society in our cities, where the bottom 80 percent of the population waits on, cleans up after, cares for the children of, and in other ways serves the top 20 percent of the population. This dual society is divided along race and ethnic lines as well as class lines (Hacker 1992; Mollenkopf & Castells 1991).

The uncertainties of the economy and the trend toward downsizing has not left universities untouched. Despite promises of increased enrollment as the children of the baby boom generation reach college age in the late 1990s, universities are looking at ways to cut costs and use existing resources more efficiently. Some of the strategies considered and implemented have involved downsizing of administrative workers and faculty.[2] Among other things, these economic strains have increased pressure on universities to demonstrate how they contribute to society in general and to their local communities in particular. Aside from the obvious role in educating new workers in an increasingly information-based society, universities are looking at how they contribute to the community around them. This is particularly the case with public universities that annually must justify appropriations provided by state legislatures. Given heightened antispending sentiment in most corners of government, this

[1]Two federal studies document this. One dealing with income distribution was completed by the Congressional Budget Office (*New York Times* 1992). Another study scrutinizing changing distribution of American wealth was completed by the Federal Reserve and the Internal Revenue Service (*New York Times* 1992).

[2]Faculty tenure is under attack as a vestige of a university of time past (*Newsweek* 1996). Tenure is seen as an impediment to universities wanting to respond to social and economic changes by reconfiguring disciplines, department sizes, and faculty activities.

has upped the political ante for universities. Although it does not manifest itself as directly, private universities also are feeling pressures to demonstrate their role in maintaining and improving the economic and social health of the world around them. More and more, private benefactors as well as public and private granting agencies are looking for these accountabilities. This has made universities more receptive to modifying their teaching and research practices.

The increased competition for funding and increased scrutiny of how universities are serving the broader community bring an opportunity to explore new university-community relationships. As always, *successful* relationships depend on a willingness on the part of universities to partner with and cooperate with the community rather than try to control the relationship. Similarly, the community has to want to partner with universities. As mentioned in the first chapter, community organizations are more sophisticated today than in the past. Leaders are more savvy when it comes to understanding research and the policy formation process. While the more effective community organizations are much less likely to accept a subservient role to the university, they are more likely to see the usefulness of policy research in increasing their effectiveness in serving the community around them.

From the university side there is also a new generation of administrators—many of whom were involved in the social movements of the 1960s and who are more sensitive to community demands. These new administrators are more open to a redefined university-community relationship. Responsive to the cries for relevance and recognizing the need for addressing inequities and other persistent social problems, this new generation of uni-

versity leaders is opening doors for faculty researcher-community activist collaborations. This represents a contrast to 30 years ago, when during the turmoil of the sixties, students were battling with resistant university administrators over a variety of campus reforms.

This is not to say that *all* universities are now amenable to developing stronger programs with community partners. It is not the elite universities, but rather the second tier of universities and new non-university think tanks that now are more amenable to getting involved in partnerships with community organizations. Elite universities are still very much wedded to discipline-defined and generated research agendas; community social change is not what drives this research. In a presentation to an international conference on "Urban Universities and Their Cities," New York University historian of university development Thomas Bender observed that

> It is astonishing how few social scientists (outside of professional schools) at New York's two great research universities, NYU and Columbia, are studying the issues on everyone's minds—the delivery of health care, poverty and inequality, race relations, education, urban politics, the parties and the electoral system, the environment, and others one could name. (Bender 1996, 11–12)

As a consequence of the absence of a willingness by elite universities to address issues identified by the world around them, new networks of knowledge production are growing outside the university setting—from community-based research institutes to the high-tech think tanks in Silicon Valley (Gibbons 1994, 6). Bender notes the irony that "just when the notion of a 'knowledge society' and the economic value of knowledge is being widely accepted, the university is losing its putative monopoly on knowledge" (1996, 7–8). However, the historian does go on to admonish academics, stating that "metropolitan academics ought not work so hard at keeping the city at bay: it is a source of energy, of wonderfully complex intellectual problems, and of non-academic intellectuals who have much to offer" (13).

However, the flat-footedness of elite universities in responding to this new environment has left the door open to other universities who are ready to participate. For example, in Chicago it is Loyola University Chicago, DePaul, and the University of Illinois Chicago that have developed centers emphasizing this new model. The traditional elite universities, such as Northwestern and University of Chicago, are not as heavily involved in community-based projects. This is not to say that there are not faculty at the elite universities doing community-oriented research, but it is to say that such research is not receiving the institutional support that we see growing at the next tier of universities. This differentiation between first- and second-tier universities was also noted by U.S. and European participants at the international conference on Urban Universities and Their Cities.[3] What are the collaborative models that we see emerging and how are they different from past models?

Collaborative Research Models

As noted in Chapter 1, the models of collaborative research discussed in this book are different from traditional academic models because they recognize that it is important to tap knowledge in academia *and* in the community. Furthermore, it is recognized that community can

play a role in defining the research agenda. The traditional view inside the academy of "objective" and "unbiased" research rejects the interference of outside organizations in directing the research agenda. Such outside intervention is seen as tainting the research enterprise with political concerns. However, this disconnection from research involving a community perspective is itself a "political" decision. The assumption that academics can be more objective about a social issue and hence can produce more accurate knowledge than a collaborative or community-driven process is open to debate. Reacting to the biases of academic-driven research, the model of "participatory action research" (PAR)—emphasizing the community role in research—has emerged in recent decades.

Largely growing out of grassroots movements in Third World countries—particularly Latin America—PAR aims at empowering the community by giving it the tools to do its own research and not be beholden to universities or university professors to complete the work. Most notable among the international leaders of the PAR movement is Paulo Freire, who wrote *Pedagogy of the Oppressed* in 1970.[4] PAR focuses on the building of research capacity in the community independent from any university ties. Peter Park, a sociologist and president of the Center for Community Education and Action, explains that "participatory research provides a framework in which people seeking to overcome oppressive situations can come to understand the social forces in operation and gain strength through collective action" (Park 1993, 3). PAR is not just the collection of data or

---

[3]The Urban Universities and Their Cities Conference was held at the University of Amsterdam, Amsterdam, Netherlands, March 1996.

[4]Kurt Lewin is credited with developing the concept of action research—research linked to social action—earlier (Lewin 1946). PAR carries this model a step further by seeing the community as necessarily playing the central role in the development of knowledge for social change.

---

information; at its heart is the recognition that knowledge and information is power. To bring about greater equality and participation in decision making, this needs to be controlled by the community. As Park continues,

> The social and political significance of participatory research, however, does not lie only in the production of narrowly technical knowledge for the control of the physical and social realities. Theorists and practitioners of participatory research have used terms like *empowerment, critical consciousness, transformation, conscientization, dialogue, social action*, and similar terms, as well as *participation*, to characterize different aspects of participatory research. (Park 1993, 4)

PAR is not a model that universities as institutions can fit into easily. As Bud Hall, the former secretary-general of the International Participatory Research Network, states, "I do . . . deeply believe that university or similarly accredited researchers are not necessary to a participatory research process" (Hall 1993, xx). The dilemma this produces for faculty or students in colleges and universities does not go unnoticed by many theorists of PAR who are themselves university faculty. John Gaventa, a sociologist at the University of Tennessee and long-time associate of the Highlander Center—a community-based social action training and education center serving Appalachia—points to the possible middle road in university "expert" involvement in PAR:

> Obviously, to clone the expert in every person, or even in every oppressed group, is not the only response to expert domination. Alternatives would include forms of democratic participation and control in defining the problems to be studied, in setting the research priorities, and in determining the ends to which the results are to be used. They would recognize the importance of the production of scientific knowledge by scientists as one type of knowledge production that is not inherently supe-

rior to others. Such strategies would insist . . . on having laypersons involved in deciding about the production of knowledge if not actually doing it, for example, through the development of popularly controlled research centers. (Gaventa 1993, 39)

In thinking about capacity building to bring about progressive social change, it would be a serious mistake to dismiss any potential role of universities. Without discounting the validity of the PAR approach, the models presented in this book recognize, as does Gaventa, the importance of the skills held by university faculty and students as well as the knowledge that has been produced by university-based disciplines.[5] While many PAR projects involve university or university-trained researchers, the goal is typically to produce a research and action capacity independent from universities. However, we feel that the development of separate university and community research enterprises can be a mistake. It can fragment what limited progressive research resources we have available to us. Rather than seeing further separation between university and community, we argue that tensions and differences in perspectives need to be addressed and better *connections* between university and community forged. Hence the approach taken in this book and by most of the contributors recognizes that need to develop improved models of university-community cooperation—models that can increase community research capacity and community research involvement. Given the crises in our society, balkanizing what

[5]We do not want to oversimplify the character of participatory action research. There are various threads of PAR, some of which have involved academics more than others. Further discussion of PAR can be found in Whyte (1991). PARnet also maintains a World Wide Web home page with articles, bibliographies, and information on a variety of PAR projects (http://munex.arme.cornell.edu/parnet/home.htm).

limited resources we have to collect information and develop solutions is not a productive avenue.

While the expertise present inside the university could conceivably be transferred to or "bought" by outside organizations, given the limited resources available to grassroots community groups, there will be no 100 percent transfer or complete control. Corporations may be able to afford to buy the top experts, but communities do not have those kinds of resources. Given this reality and the opportunity to partner with universities in getting access to this knowledge at little or no cost, collaboration is a more productive avenue for communities.

The central point in negotiating relationships and minimizing dependency of communities on universities is to figure out what knowledge can be transferred and what specialized knowledge is best left to the universities to provide when needed. The expertise within universities—often developed after years of training—is not always something that can be easily transferred. For example, detailed knowledge of how to select a sample for a major survey or development of survey questions is not something that can be transferred to a community in afternoon workshops. On the other hand, knowledge of how to organize and train community members to do door-to-door interviews is something that a community organization can develop. Therefore, collaboration means understanding how to efficiently structure the research division of labor, letting the university do what it does well and increasing the capacity of the community to do research tasks that it could do, but typically has not done in the past.

As a way of illustrating how university and community can partner in creating knowledge of use to the community to bring about pro-gressive social change, we would like to take a detailed look at the development of the Policy Research Action Group (PRAG), which developed in the Chicago metropolitan area over the past seven years. While not blind to the shortcomings of exclusively university-controlled research (for example, the use of technical terms and language that make understanding research reports difficult or the study of topics that have no direct relevance to pressing community problems), PRAG has worked to bring the university's enormous capacity to bear on persistent community problems. It has done this through a new model of university-community partnership; one that does not seek to eliminate the traditional tensions but rather to harness them.[6]

The Policy Research Action Group: A New Kind of Network

We are seeing increased involvement in collaborative research by universities and colleges. In essence this represents an institutionalization of elements of the participatory action model. While it may not always be as radical as some of the PAR research, it does represent a significant departure from academic business as usual.

The best way of illustrating this model is to describe the development of the Policy Research Action Group (PRAG)—a network of 4 universities and 15 community organizations in the Chicago metropolitan area—that has been supporting grassroots research projects since 1989. Support for community-based research has been primarily in the form of providing interns (graduate and undergraduate

[6]An earlier discussion of this idea of harnessing community-university tensions is included in Nyden and Wiewel (1992).

students working for four to eight months); research assistants (more advanced graduate students); and apprentices (community organization staff or volunteers) to work on research projects developed by community organizations. Only projects that involve community-university collaboration are supported. Research projects identified by university faculty alone are not funded; instead PRAG puts such researchers in touch with relevant community organizations for development of collaborative projects. The PRAG model or a variation of it has been or is being replicated in other areas—in Minneapolis, Philadelphia, and statewide in Ohio. A discussion of PRAG's development can serve as a model for creating similar large or small collaborative projects in other communities or cities.

The idea for PRAG emerged at a meeting at the John D. and Catherine T. MacArthur Foundation in 1988. The MacArthur Foundation, based in Chicago and one of the 10 largest foundations in the United States, was concerned about direct and indirect criticisms of its neighborhood organization funding policies appearing in a series of articles in the *Chicago Tribune* (McCarron 1988). Through its Community Initiatives Program, the MacArthur Foundation had been supporting a wide range of programs in Chicago's neighborhoods. Underlying their funding decisions was a concern that direct support for neighborhood initiatives was critical and that money invested in big, downtown, central business district projects did not "trickle down" to the neighborhoods. The *Tribune* series, "Chicago On Hold," primarily targeted the progressive, pro-neighborhood policies of Harold Washington, Chicago's first black mayor, who had successfully challenged the entrenched "machine" in the nation's third largest city. The MacArthur Foundation's pro-neighborhood funding policies were also implicitly criticized by the author of the series, which promoted the view that downtown investment should be a priority and neighborhood investment was often misused, misdirected, or ineffective in helping the economic health of the city. This pro-growth view sees downtown business development, job growth, tax revenue generation, and image building as central to the future of the city and de-emphasizes the social and economic conditions in the neighborhoods around the city.[7]

In the discussion at the Foundation over how to address this criticism, two approaches were considered. Should a large, one-time, city-wide information gathering project be developed to collect data documenting project effectiveness? Or should a series of much smaller projects, involving collaboration between university researchers and community activists, be supported with the intention of documenting small but effective alternative approaches to persistent urban problems? The smaller projects would have the potential of identifying new models that could be replicated in other communities—in Chicago or elsewhere—while increasing community members' capacity to look at urban policy and how it affects their particular neighborhood. The larger project would have the advantage of fitting into the traditional policy research mold: have academic researchers produce reports and numbers that are seen as legitimate in the eyes of the media and government officials. However, this would do little to increase the communities' capacities to become players in policy development.

The Foundation decided to provide a small planning grant to fund a series of meetings

---

[7]The conflict between pro-growth and even-growth policies has been well documented. For more background on this, you may want to see Logan and Molotch 1987; Nyden and Wiewel 1991; Squires et al. 1987.

involving a group of community-based organization activists, government officials, city-wide civic association directors, labor leaders, and university-based researchers who were geographically, racially, ethnically, and gender diverse. The object was to identify the top policy issues confronting Chicago at the time. After three half-day meetings in early 1989, the planning project—coordinated by Phil Nyden (Loyola University Chicago) and Wim Wiewel (University of Illinois Chicago)—commissioned "state-of-the-art" papers in the top 10 areas. The papers, written by both academic-based researchers and community or government-based researchers, reported on what we knew about each issue, what policy "tool kit" we had available to solve problems in that area, and what tools we still needed to develop.

The papers were then presented at a city-wide conference in September 1989. Topics included community intervention efforts to oppose gentrification; preservation of racially diverse communities; the role of residential credit in community economies; the development effects of property assessments and taxes; the employment potential of new service industries; the role of government in land development; and effective strategies in community economic development. All the papers generated significant interest among the 130 people attending the conference.

However, it was a panel on the relationship between community activists and university researchers that stole the show. The panelists—all of whom had experience working on cooperative projects between community organizations and university-based researchers—touched on many of the points of tension outlined in the first chapter of this book. Demonstrating frustration with academics' training to be critical of everything, one community leader talked about how academics are people who do

not just walk through the door that has been opened for them, but prefer to come through "kicking, screaming, and fighting every inch of the way." On the other hand, university researchers talked of the lack of understanding sometimes demonstrated by community organizations when research protocols are followed or when careful research practices mean that the research cannot be completed quickly. The debate and reactions kicked off by this afternoon panel underscored the need to address community-university research action issues if constructive working relationships were to be forged.

With this in mind, two collaborative "think tanks" were developed following the conference. Both were co-chaired by a community leader and a university researcher. Each group consisted of 24 individuals drawn from community organizations and universities, and each focused on one problem area identified by the conference. One examined gentrification, displacement, and racial diversity, and the other focused on the employment and economic development contributions of the new service sector.

Less important than the specific topics was the process that emerged. The purpose of the groups—which were each funded with $20,000 grants from the MacArthur Foundation—was to study their respective topics by commissioning papers and developing action agendas from the research. During this process, a more powerful relationship between university and community was developing. Participants in the groups increasingly recognized the usefulness of having different perspectives around the table—community and academic views. The two groups represented neutral territory, where academics respected community perspectives and community activists respected academic work. We even rotated the meetings between community locations and university locations so that we were not seen as meeting exclusively inside the university walls or out in the community. The groups functioned neither on "community turf" nor "in the university," but rather occupied a "free space," to use Sara Evans and Harry Boyte's term (Evans and Boyte 1986). Over the months of working together, a trust emerged between some participants that allowed them to criticize each other without feeling threatened or under attack by "anti-community" or "anti-university" sentiment. It was in this environment that the next step in PRAG's development took place.

As the groups were successful in completing policy research that communities could use in addressing a variety of issues, there was increased discussion in one of the groups about how to enhance the community's capacity to influence existing policy research and develop its own research projects. The idea of supporting internships with a nontraditional twist emerged. Through a new round of funding from the MacArthur Foundation, one of the think tanks solicited research ideas from community organizations around the metropolitan area. From over 50 responses to the "requests for proposals," 12 projects were "funded" in the form of undergraduate and graduate student interns. These were nontraditional in the sense that community organizations were driving the research process. Each project had community organization staff and university professors mentoring the interns.

The outcomes from these projects were very positive. One project supported by the Chicago Legal Clinic—an environmental law clinic—developed a manual that instructed nonprofit organizations how to avoid liabilities of receiving "donated" property with toxic problems, such as unseen underground gasoline storage tanks or older buildings with sub-stantial amounts of asbestos around pipes or in insulation. The manual, entitled *Not-for-Profits Beware* is now in its second printing and was used by Congress to modify federal legislation a few years ago. Another project helped to do the groundwork to save an old blues club on the Southside of Chicago by creating a blues/jazz historic cultural district. This innovative project recognized that communities do not live by bricks and mortar alone; economic development needs to include cultural development to preserve the soul of the community. The community supervisor of this project said that it allowed his organization to "take the box off the shelf" and let the intern complete a project that was two-thirds completed but was stalled because no one in the organization had time to complete it. A selected list of PRAG projects is included in the Appendix.

This first round of projects allowed participants to gain the experience in supporting university-community collaborative research. PRAG demonstrated that research did not have to be something esoteric that was completed only to gather dust on a library shelf; they showed a direct relevance of data gathering and analysis to key community concerns. In the course of doing all of this, PRAG was building relationships between universities and community organizations. A community organization could call the PRAG office to find out who in the university community was doing work in a particular area or who might be interested in sitting down with a community group to examine a problem. PRAG enabled professors and students to find research projects that allowed them to use their knowledge and skills at the same time they were developing policy projects that would have a real impact on families and communities. While community and academic participants within PRAG and within the research projects maintained a healthy ability to agree to disagree, the dysfunctional stereotypes that each "side" had of the other started to crumble.

PRAG's "Structure"

With this experience under its belt, PRAG had a working model and the credibility to attract additional funding to expand the project. Since 1993, PRAG has received more than $4 million in funding from the U.S. Department of Education and the MacArthur Foundation to continue its work.[8] This has provided support for a small staff consisting of a director (20 percent time of a university faculty member), project coordinator (which has varied from full-time to two-thirds time), a research outreach coordinator to help community groups develop stronger research projects (two-thirds time), and a secretary. However, the bulk of this money has been used to support interns, research assistants, and apprentices on many collaborative projects. Since 1991 PRAG has supported more than 130 projects.

PRAG has consciously walked the thin line between enough *structure* to get things done efficiently and enough *flexibility* so that it can be responsive to changing needs and to new ideas that emerge in the research and action process. The "Core Group"—consisting of approximately 24 members from universities, citywide organizations, and community-based organizations—discusses and sets policies governing PRAG's activities. While there are about 10 individuals who have been with PRAG for more than four years, some members have moved out of the Core Group as time pressures and career developments have changed priorities. In most cases PRAG continues to work with these individuals, but on specific projects. At the heart of PRAG's flexibility is the recognition that we all experience changes in our priorities, work demands, and interests. The Core Group is more the center of a series of concentric rings, from intense involvement at the center to less intense involvement at the periphery (but still connected to PRAG). An executive committee of co-chairs consisting of representatives from each of the four participating universities (Loyola University Chicago, University of Illinois Chicago, DePaul University, and Chicago State University) and four additional community representatives functions in between bimonthly Core Group meetings.

The following are some of the current projects PRAG is working on.

- *Support for collaborative research and action projects in the form of interns, research assistants, and apprentices.* Research is identified by community needs and is geared toward producing "actionable" research—research that can document new models for addressing pressing needs or helping to bring about changes in communities. This is still at the heart of PRAG's activity.

- *Working groups.* While PRAG still "casts the net" to identify new community policy research needs through the RFP process, PRAG recognizes the need to support more focused research and action activity in

[8]Throughout the development of PRAG, Loyola University Chicago has served as its fiscal agent. This means that grant money comes to Loyola and is dispersed to the various community organizations, universities, interns, graduate students, and apprentices. Because Loyola has been willing to serve this function and receive only a modest amount of indirect expenses, community groups and other partners have been comfortable with this arrangement. By using the existing university organizational structure—for example, a budget office, human resources office, purchasing office, accounting office, and a grants and contracts office—PRAG has been able to minimize the costs of setting up a new entity. Consequently, more money has flowed into the community-based projects.

subject and geographic areas that have emerged in the course of the 130 projects already supported. Each working group has two co-chairs who represent either the research or action sides of policy issues. Five working groups have been established around one of the following issues: furthering adult education and workforce preparation; creating residential stability in racially and ethnically diverse urban neighborhoods; enhancing citizen participation and empowerment; mapping strategies to eliminate lead poisoning among children in low-income neighborhoods; and examining alternative community economic development models.

■ *University-community partnerships.* Each of the four cooperating universities has developed ongoing partnerships with organizations in its respective surrounding communities. All involve equal resources going to community organizations and universities. This is aimed at "institutionalizing" collaboration at each of the universities.[9]

■ *On-line internship clearinghouse.* A searchable database of more than 1,500 internships has been put on-line and made available to the public. The original focus was on providing community organizations and prospective student interns with a way of locating each other and finding the right match, but the clearinghouse is

also accessible to the general public. Computers at public libraries and university libraries, as well as individual home computers, all provide access to this system. This has been developed in cooperation with United Way/Crusade of Mercy in Chicago.

■ *Access to routine research tools.* Through some of its participating universities, PRAG has been providing computer accounts and library privileges to community partners in collaborative research. There has been much discussion of inequities in access to the new information superhighway (Alkalimat, Gills, and Williams 1995; Sclove 1995); this is one way in which a local network can increase community organization access to the tools available to university-based researchers. PRAG has also provided ongoing technical assistance to organizations in the form of interns going out to the organization and setting up hardware and software to access Internet accounts.[10]

■ *Policy breakfasts with local government officials.* Through a formal agreement with the city of Chicago Office of the Mayor, PRAG is sponsoring policy breakfasts that brief city commissioners, city staff, and alderpersons on completed research projects. Although PRAG also sponsors meetings where community organizations are provided with this information, this is

---

[9]With increased cooperation between universities, an "Urban University Collaborative" of urban center directors from all metropolitan area universities and colleges has been formed in the past two years. Information on research projects, some of which involve university-community collaborations, is exchanged in quarterly meetings. This also has improved communications between the universities.

[10]PRAG completed a study that determined that most small to midsize community-based organizations (5–10 staff members) had the computer hardware needed to access and function efficiently on the World Wide Web. However, lack of knowledge of how to access WWW, as well as constraints that limited time available to study manuals and straighten out the inevitable bugs, have inhibited this access. This was the basis for creating an intern position to help connect community organizations to the Net.

another way to make sure that research products get into the hands of decision makers.[11]

Lessons from Collaborations

The experience of PRAG and other collaborations, including those you will read about in this book, has produced a number of lessons that we summarize here.

- *Collaboration takes time to develop.* Collaborative research is not the fastest way to get research done, but it does develop strong commitment by participants in the long run. Given the historic tensions between university and community, collaboration does not develop overnight. However, when it is successful it produces stronger and longer-lasting relationships that are valuable to both university and community.

- *Collaborative research is more enjoyable for most students, researchers and community members.* In an era when observers have lamented the loss of community and the impersonal ways in which we all relate to each other, collaborative research represents an antidote. Working with others in the course of developing and completing community-based research has intrinsic

[11]PRAG recognizes that informing a government official of research does not mean that a policy will be adopted. Community pressure on government to continue successful existing programs and implement new programs is still the primary currency in the policy implementation process. However, this process gets research that has involved the communities themselves into the hands of elected officials. Because it includes implicit input from voters and political actors relevant to elected representatives, research by constituents *and* university researchers has a different ring than research by university-based researchers alone.

social rewards. Also, particularly for students, being part of a process that brings about positive changes in community is exciting.

- *Collaborative policy research demystifies the policy research process.* In the process of bringing community "experts" and university "experts" to the research table, all participants start getting a clearer picture of the whole process—from research to political action—in bringing about new policies. The policy formation process changes from something that happens "up there" at the national level in the big policy think tanks to something accessible to all. Individuals who thought they could not have a role in shaping the future of their community now see that they can be involved. Participants feel they are a part of something bigger than themselves.

- *Flexibility is important.* A willingness to modify work relationships as the research progresses and, particularly in long-term projects, a recognition that the mixture of those involved in the research will change over time, is important. Collaborative research is not something that fits easily into formulas; it is a dynamic process that changes and modifies itself, just like the changing social world it is studying.

- *A lasting network is put in place.* The energy that goes into developing a collaboration is not lost. Even after the project is over, the relationships and trust remain. This helps to build other projects and bring new people into the process.

- *Collaboration creates an environment welcoming to new participants.* Collaboration challenges the "lone ranger" mode of research in which individuals protect their turf and do not want to share the limelight with others. In the process of working with others, researchers and activists realize that they can accomplish more collectively than separately. There is enough to go around for everyone. In fact, the more people you get involved in the process, the more likely it is to be successful. Also, when a welcoming environment is created, participants feel more attached to the project.

- *Collaboration "grows" new collaborative researchers.* Related to the preceding point, participation in a collaborative process trains new researchers with an understanding of and attachment to the collaborative process. This produces new collaborative researchers on both the community and university sides of this relationship.

- *Success attracts attention and new participants.* As collaboratives demonstrate that they can be successful, they attract attention. Institutional players, such as universities and other community organizations, want to become part of this success. It opens the door for institutions, particularly universities, to commit more resources to this successful process. Success also validates the work of academics who have been doing collaborative work but have never received attention for it within the traditional reward systems of the university.

- *Existing resources are used more effectively.* Part of the success of collaborations is their ability to use scarce resources more effectively. As noted earlier, the era of austerity has produced an environment more hospitable to collaboration. From the community side, this gives access to research capacity that they would otherwise not have. From the university side, this provides additional opportunities to do research and an easier entry into the community.

- *Collaboration builds capacity in the community.* Participation in collaborative research is an effective way of training members of the community how to do research. Skills and knowledge are transferred in the process of working together on a research project. When certain skills may be too complex to transfer in even a long-term collaborative project, participants become aware of what parts of the research process they can complete themselves and what parts they may need outside help in completing. The community becomes a more effective manager of policy research; it no longer is the exclusive domain of universities or research organizations.

- *Collaboration offers an alternative to top-down policy development.* Related to the preceding point, grassroots-based collaborative research provides an alternative to policy research and development by national organizations with minimal connections to local communities. By anchoring this research in community-based organizations, the research is shaped by the needs of individuals and organizations facing the issues on a daily basis. This puts a "face" on the research and does not treat the community as an abstract data set.

- *Local-to-local networks in policy development become possible.* With the greater availability of computers, decentralized policy research connecting a community project in one city with a community project in another city is possible. This also builds capacity because it reduces the role of the "middleman"—typically the national research organization that coordinates the research. Similarly, communities within the same city can find it easier to communicate with each other and share information. This also increases community capacity.

As you read the case studies that follow, you will see rich illustrations of these lessons of collaboration. You will also see how university and community partnerships have linked the thinkers and doers to increase capacity to bring about social change. In these collaborations you can see ideas blossom and tangible change take place.

Organization of the Case Studies

Following are 27 case studies of university-community collaborations. As you will see, the nature of the collaboration ranges from a new relationship developed by an individual graduate student and a community organization to ongoing institutional arrangements between universities and communities that have lasted for more than 10 years. The case studies are taken from cities around the country; one study looks at microeconomic development in El Salvador. We have organized these around substantive policy issues. Although we have an obvious interest in the process of evaluation, the driving force behind all of these cooperative arrangements is the particular policy issue addressed in the project.

The five areas we have selected represent key topics for much of the collaborative work taking place in the United States today. In the wake of the Los Angeles riots, the O. J. Simpson trial, and debate over immigration issues, racial, ethnic, economic diversity, and tensions are unquestionably central policy matters in our country today. The United States is becoming more diverse, and it is in city neighborhoods where this diversity is playing itself out. In Part I we look at case studies in Chicago, Louisville, Milwaukee, and Cleveland.

The cases in Part II have a focus that reflects the maturing of the environmental movement. Since Rachel Carson wrote her book, *Silent Spring*, the importance of protecting the environment has been on the policy radar screen in this country. The "environment" does not just mean preserving virgin forests and exotic wildlife. The environment also means cleaning up city neighborhoods after years of indiscriminate polluting or use of toxic chemicals and materials. It means protecting workers from chemical hazards in the workplace. These environmental issues also disproportionately affect low-income neighborhoods and people of color. These are stories of collaborations that have empowered urban communities and addressed serious toxic hazards of the 1990s.

The third part, education, covers a variety of topics. Because teaching and learning are very much a part of the process of collaboration, this part provides insights into the different ways in which universities and community groups can work with each other. One case is about a university providing scientific literacy education in a local community. In other cases, leadership training and parent training are the focus. Other cases give details on using university classes in working with local community organizations on policy and action projects.

Health care is clearly of central concern today. From the continued need for health care reform to the AIDS crisis, we have everyday reminders of how this affects all of our lives. The cases in Part IV examine nontraditional issues or approaches, such as problems of cancer in the lesbian community or violence as a health epidemic. In all cases it is clear that research results are ammunition for the ongoing political battles surrounding health care policy.

Our final section on community control and voice presents a range of case studies aimed at strengthening the position of geographic communities and communities of interest in various policy debates. Community safety and community policing are hot topics in established political circles today. What do these initiatives really mean for improving the quality of life in urban neighborhoods? The new federal empowerment zone process has its supporters and detractors. How have researchers and activists contributed to the development of the Empowerment Zone (EZ) process as it has unfolded in Chicago? How can universities work with local organizations in the community planning process? Although the case study of microenterprises in El Salvador may seem out of place in this collection of case studies, there are remarkable lessons to be learned from the Third World in understanding policy struggles in low-income neighborhoods in our own cities. Finally, the East St. Louis case represents an exciting, dynamic model for university-community cooperation that has shaken the roots of established interests in this struggling former industrial city.

Each part starts with an overview. After each case study we highlight its contribution to our understanding of the collaborative process and of the particular policy research issue. As a whole, the case studies provide a tool kit that can be used in different communities to address issues of primary concern to residents and grassroots organizations. They also demonstrate a new dimension to university research and education. These are not neat, clean, and predictable projects. They provide the dead ends, the twists, the turns, and the rewards that are the hallmarks of life in a changing society of the late 20th century.

Part I

*Racial, Ethnic, and Economic
Diversity: Pipe Dream of
the Politically Correct or
Are There Working Models?*

Racial, ethnic, and economic conflict are not new to American society or to societies throughout history. That does not mean that conflict is inevitable and part of human nature. This part contains five case studies of university: community collaborations that have worked to overcome conflict and forge cooperation between different racial, ethnic, and economic groups. For the United States, it is more important than ever to address racial divisions within our society. As pointed out in the first case, American society is becoming more diverse. Demographers predict that by the middle of the 21st century, over half of the U.S. population will be "minority." Will we become a society of even more insulated communities that are racially, ethnically, and economically segregated? Or will we see the emergence of models of cooperation and constructive interaction between different groups?

The various cases approach this question differently. The first case examines the effort of a community organization in an already diverse community to turn conflict into cooperation. The primary goal of the project between Loyola University Chicago and the Organization of the NorthEast has been to preserve affordable housing in this northern lakefront Chicago community. The maintenance of opportunities for *all* economic groups is closely related to providing equal opportunity for *all* racial and ethnic groups, since racial and ethnic minorities are often disproportionately represented in lower-income groups in our cities. The second case carries this same theme forward, examining university involvement in the planning and rehabilitation of affordable housing in Louisville. More than some cases examined, this also involved top levels of the university administration and local government officials.

The Fair Housing project described by John Lukehart, vice president of the Leadership Council for Metropolitan Open Communities, is an example of a multiuniversity and multicommunity organization collaboration. The Leadership Council— founded as a result of Martin Luther King's marches against discriminatory housing practices in Chicago's white neighborhoods in the 1960s—led this project along with Gary Orfield—a noted national policy researcher on school and housing integration. Gregory Squires' and Dan Willett's description of research on discriminatory lending practices in Milwaukee is a similar story. Involving fair housing advocates and university researchers, the Fair Lending Coalition has successfully pressured local elected officials to join them in getting banks to invest in low-income and minority communities. Finally, the article by Janet Smith and Bobbie Reichtell describes how a graduate student researcher can assist a "white-ethnic" neighborhood in understanding racial change. In an effort to work with a community organization to avoid the familiar pattern of racial resegregation, Smith and Reichtell look at ways in which the community can construct a new, more diverse image of itself.

Creating and Sustaining Racially and Ethnically Diverse Communities

Philip Nyden and *Joanne Adams, Loyola University Chicago,* and *Kim Zalent, Organization of the NorthEast*

Loyola University and the Organization of the NorthEast (ONE)—an umbrella organization for a number of community-based organizations on Chicago's northern lakefront—collaborated on a six-year project that was aimed at strengthening cooperation among the area's diverse racial, ethnic, and economic groups. By working to establish a stable, mixed neighborhood, ONE and other community organizations could demonstrate that low-income residents as well as racial and ethnic "minorities" need not be displaced as community reinvestment occurs. The goal was to produce a *stably* diverse neighborhood and demonstrate that not all diverse neighborhoods are neighborhoods in transition. This would also reassure middle-class white homeowners that diversity was not the prelude to an all-"minority," low-income neighborhood experiencing declining property values. This collaborative project was only one of many ongoing community efforts to maintain a stable diverse community in Uptown and Edgewater, but it has been a factor in the continued stability of these communities. Since 1990, teams of Loyola faculty, graduate research assistants, and undergraduate students have worked with organizers and board members of ONE to produce policy research reports and provide data that could be used in organizing in a community that is one of the most diverse in the nation.

Uptown and Edgewater—two community areas, each with a population of about 60,000—are potential models of future urban diversity. As the United States heads into the 21st century, demographers are projecting that over 50 percent of the country's population will be "minority" by the year 2050. With this as the backdrop, we could say that wherever American urban communities are going, Uptown and Edgewater are going to get there first.[1] Just south of Loyola University's main undergraduate campus, Edgewater and Uptown have been ports of entry for new immigrant groups as well as home for established families.

This has produced an impressive diversity. For example, the local public high school has students from families speaking 65 different languages. Slightly less than 50 percent non-Hispanic white, the population of these two community areas includes about 20 percent African American, 20 percent Hispanic, and 10 percent Asian. Ethnic groups include Vietnamese, Cambodian, Filipino, Chinese, Korean,

[1]This is a paraphrasing of Mayor Kenneth Gibson's comment about Newark, New Jersey, in the 1960s: "Wherever American cities are going Newark is going to get there first."

Asian Indian, Tibetan, Ethiopian, Nigerian, Cuban, Mexican, Puerto Rican, Irish, Swedish, Romanian, and Bosnian. Until very recently Chicago's primary Native American Cultural Center was located in Uptown. Within a few blocks you can move from a neighborhood with large homes occupied by politicians, radio talk show hosts, and corporate lawyers to one with homeless shelters, single-room occupancy hotels, and AIDS clinics.

Organization of the NorthEast

Founded in 1973 by residents, concerned community organizations, and a cross section of religious congregations in Chicago's Uptown and Edgewater neighborhoods, ONE has a commitment to develop a stable, multiethnic, and economically diverse community. ONE is an organization of organizations, governed by a 15-member board of directors, who are elected annually from the 61 dues-paying member organizations. The membership includes Catholic, Baptist, Methodist, and Evangelical congregations; banks; chambers of commerce; low-income tenant and housing organizations; colleges and universities; and ethnic mutual aid associations.

Since 1991, ONE advocacy campaigns have been organized by "Strategy Teams" addressing the issues of housing, youth and family support, education, jobs and economic development, and cultural diversity. It is an Alinsky-style organization that does not shy away from confrontational tactics with landlords, elected officials, and any institution that is perceived as not being responsive to the needs of *all* of Uptown and Edgewater's residents. Friends and opponents alike recognize that ONE has become a powerful force in improving the quality of life in these northern lakefront communities.

How the Loyola-ONE Collaboration Started

Josh Hoyt, who was then the executive director of ONE, and Phil Nyden, a professor of sociology at Loyola, were brought together by an acquaintance (a former city assistant commissioner) who was familiar with their mutual interest in combining research and action. Nyden had experience doing social change-oriented research on a variety of issues. He was also personally involved in community organizations and school board politics in Evanston, a suburb just north of Chicago. This gave him an activist orientation toward research and direct experience with community organizing that contributed to an understanding of the relationship between research and community-based social change.

Hoyt was aware of the importance of credible research in a community organization's efforts to pressure elected officials for change. He used to talk of needing a "pocket full of factoids" that he could throw at officials and use when presenting his organization's side on issues to the media. While holding on to an obvious willingness to criticize academic research, he recognized the usefulness of the right research at the right time.

After a couple of productive meetings, Hoyt and Nyden decided to develop a "testing the waters" project. As noted in the second chapter of this book, building trust is a key part of any collaboration. Gaining an understanding of how easily each side can work with each other, how responsive each party is to the other's needs, and how the research results can be useful to the community is an important part of building a solid researcher-community relationship. With ONE's input, Nyden involved a graduate sociology qualitative methods class in studying race and ethnic relations in three subsidized high-rise buildings in Uptown.[2]

In 1990, ONE was just starting to organize tenants in 10 U.S. Department of Housing and Urban Development–financed "prepayment buildings." These are high-rise apartment buildings that were built and managed by private developers with HUD low-interest loans on the condition that they provide below-market-rate housing to low-income families. The owners of these buildings had found a loophole in their mortgages that would allow them to buy out the mortgages and turn their buildings into very profitable, market-rate apartments. Over 11,000 people out of Uptown's 60,000 lived in these buildings. ONE was concerned that this would displace thousands of residents from these relatively decent-quality, affordable housing units.

ONE felt that documentation of the positive race and ethnic relations in these buildings would strengthen their case for preserving these buildings as affordable housing. Community efforts were already under way to have tenants and/or community economic development corporations (on behalf of the tenants) buy, rehab, and manage the buildings. This would effectively lock in affordable housing in Uptown, protecting low-income residents from displacement in any subsequent gentrification of the area.

In the spring 1990 semester, the eight graduate students, faculty member, and graduate research assistant completed 43 in-depth interviews with a sample of tenants along with developing a pilot telephone survey.[3] The research examined (1) attitudes toward racial,

ethnic, and religious diversity among residents, (2) the importance of affordable housing in providing a stable foundation for residents in the buildings, and (3) the role of affordable housing in maintaining stable racial and ethnic diversity in Uptown. The research project gained even greater credibility when, through ONE's efforts, the city of Chicago Commissioner of Human Relations and Executive Director of the Human Relations Foundation provided $500 for research expenses and printing costs of a final report. The Loyola research team and ONE published a report of this work, entitled *Racial, Ethnic, and Economic Diversity in Uptown's Subsidized Housing: A Case Study of Its Present Character and Future Possibilities* (Nyden et al. 1990).

Principal among the findings were that the affordable housing provided families and individuals with the financial and social foundation upon which to build self-sufficiency. Another key finding was that residents were attracted to Uptown's diversity and found it a comfortable place to live because of the community's acceptance of different ethnic and racial groups. Community institutions—ranging from churches to community-based organizations—played a role in increasing interaction between the various groups, nurturing intergroup cooperation. However, the research did find some tensions that needed attention—tensions between renters and middle-income homeowners, between single adult families and families with children, and between African Americans and recently arrived Africans.

The working relationship and trust that the Loyola researchers and ONE leaders established through this project built the foundation for an expanded collaborative research effort. The fact that we had produced a significant research report with minimal outside funding

---

[2]A more detailed discussion of using graduate qualitative methods classes in community-based research projects is included in an article in *Teaching Sociology* (Nyden 1991).

[3]Most tenants had telephones. This survey was the basis for a face-to-face survey instrument that was used a year later in expanded research throughout the whole community.

gave us significant credibility in the eyes of potential foundation funders. When we went to Chicago Community Trust for funding for a multiyear collaborative research and action project, having a previous research product that we could show them gave us an edge over the pool of other grant applications that they regularly review. Over the next five years we received $240,000 in funding for expanded research. This money was split evenly between ONE and Loyola.

A Longer-Term Collaborative Project

With this funding, ONE and Loyola worked over the next five years to complete three major reports and a smaller think piece on religion and diversity. The needs identified by ONE set the topic for the reports. The Loyola researchers also provided data to ONE when the need arose in their organizing efforts; the researchers were an on-call research arm of the organization. The bulk of the funding went to support two thirds of an organizer's salary at ONE and two thirds of a graduate student researcher's salary at Loyola (Joanne Adams).[4] Over the next five years, this core staff worked with a changing team of graduate and undergraduate students.

There were various levels to this research process. The Loyola research team, consisting of Phil Nyden, Joanne Adams, graduate research assistants, and undergraduate interns, met on a regular basis to discuss the progress of research and talk about the findings to date. During the peak of research activity these meetings took place every week; as production

of the reports wound down, the frequency also became less. The two primary Loyola researchers then also regularly met with the ONE executive director and the organizer assigned to the project. These meetings were held on a monthly basis at first, but the frequency did decline as transitions within ONE (the appointment of a new executive director and new demands on the organizer) pulled ONE staff away from a closer relation to the research project.

An advisory committee consisting of university and community representatives knowledgeable in the subject area of the reports was also established and met two or three times during the research and writing of each report. The members of the committee, agreed upon by ONE staff and the Loyola researchers, were roughly two thirds community representative and one third university representative. Because we were looking for strong input from the community, the community bias was established; at the same time, as researchers, we always had relatively easy access to colleagues inside the university at any time.

We produced three 50–60 page reports over the next five years. Although the Loyola researchers did the bulk of the research and writing of the reports, the leaders and staff of ONE developed the focus of the reports. Recommendations contained in the report were made only after considerable discussion over the previous months about research findings as they were developed. The first report, *Our Hope for the Future: Youth, Family, and Diversity in the Edgewater and Uptown Communities* (Nyden, Adams, and Mason 1992), was well received. Although 500 copies were distributed initially, another 500 were printed to accommodate additional requests as word got out in the community that we had done the report. Requests came from community organization

---

[4]As they do with most graduate students funded by outside grants, Loyola provided free tuition for the graduate students as a match from the university, which also helped to convince the funder that the university had a strong commitment to this type of research project.

leaders, social service agency staff, elected officials, and residents. Some of these people used the information for organizational planning and grant writing; others were simply interested in a report done on the community in which they worked or lived.

The second report focuses on the nature of business in a diverse community, *Diversity and Opportunity in a Local Economy: Community Business in Edgewater and Uptown* (Nyden, Bennett, and Adams 1993). The purpose of this report was to look at the connection between a diverse residential base and business development. Were there particular types of businesses that did well in this diverse market? Were there gaps in the types of businesses that needed to be filled as a way of strengthening the neighborhood economy?

The third report, which proved to be the longest to research and produce, looks at the stories of the 10 HUD-subsidized, affordable-rent buildings in Uptown that were threatened with buyout and conversion to market-rate housing. Unlike the other reports, which were printed and spiral-bound in a more conventional manner, *Saving Our Homes: The Lessons of Community Struggles to Preserve Affordable Housing in Chicago's Uptown* (Nyden and Adams 1996) was produced in a newsletter format. Because tenant leaders played a much greater role in developing the content and giving editorial comments on this report, production time was longer. However, the feeling of collective ownership over this report has been greater.

Our Hope for the Future examines how the well-being of children parallels the general social and economic health of a community. Children serve as significant points of contact between different racial, ethnic, and economic groups. We found that families with children are more tuned into key community issues, such as the quality of education, and are more

likely to use businesses and services in the local community. However, households with children are twice as likely as households without children to say that they will move out of the neighborhood in the next year in search of better living conditions. The recommendations include the need to consciously develop programs to support children of immigrants in their "ambassador" function in the local community; maintain quality services to lower-income families and youth; provide more resources per capita for social services because of the complexity of functioning in a diverse community with different cultures and languages; and foster the understanding among community institutions that fundamental changes in family structure need to be met with fundamental changes in how services are delivered (for example, more night and weekend hours to accommodate single-parent households).

Diversity and Opportunity in a Local Economy studies the relationship between a diverse residential base and business development. It points to the lack of understanding of how businesses function in a diverse community. The research found a mixed economy that provides substantial benefits to lower-income residents who have access to a broader range of more reasonably priced stores than what you typically find in an exclusively low-income community. We made a number of recommendations: aggressively market the diversity of businesses; examine how banks can better serve low-income residents; examine ways to increase the number of African American businesses; form small business incubators; establish bridges between large institutions and community-oriented economic development; and explore the possibility of developing an arts and entertainment district that would reflect the ethnic, racial, and economic diversity present in the two communities. As we did with *Our Hope for the Future*, ONE set up a forum in which the researchers presented the findings to business leaders, alderpersons, community organization leaders, and other university researchers.

Saving Our Homes, the report about tenant organizing in the 10 HUD prepayment buildings, is intended not only to document what had happened, but also to provide an analysis that will be valuable to community leaders in Chicago and elsewhere. This report was written in newsletter format to make it more accessible to a larger audience. It allowed us to print different stories that would be of varying appeal to readers, which would include the tenants themselves, elected city officials, community organization leaders, and leaders outside the Chicago area. Drew Astolfi, a ONE organizer involved in this project, pointed out that a valuable contribution of research is to provide a written history and analysis of community organizing—a history that often gets lost because the community typically does not have the time or money to complete such histories. *Saving Our Homes* contains sections on the affordable housing crisis; Loyola and ONE working together; lessons learned from organizing in the 10 buildings; the history of each of the buildings; why tenants became involved; organizing in a diverse community; the role of women in tenant organizing; and the top 10 tips for multicultural organizing. Sidebars highlight a number of the tenant leaders. One of the leaders was so touched by seeing her accomplishments documented in print that she had a hard time expressing her appreciation through her tears.

Impact on Policy

Our research had an impact on local policy in a number of ways. First, it provided documentation of the ways in which different racial and ethnic groups were already cooperating and the areas where community organization intervention could improve relations. This allowed ONE and other community organizations in Uptown and Edgewater to convince funders and government agencies that time and money spent in their communities would be well spent. This provided evidence that intergroup cooperation is possible in diverse urban neighborhoods. Our research was the subject of numerous newspaper articles. Because policy debates are carried out more and more in the media, press coverage is very helpful to the community. The mayor's office was aware of our research; at one meeting unrelated to Uptown/Edgewater issues, an assistant to Mayor Daley commented that ONE's and Loyola's collaborative research was having a noticeable, positive impact on the communities. Other community organizations used our research as a basis for further research.

The reports also enhanced the capacity of the community to use research for its own benefit. Over our six years of collaborative research activity, not only did ONE recognize the usefulness of research in supporting changes in the community, but other community-based organizations saw the benefits of a positive cooperative relationship with researchers. For example, many organizations used our first report on families and children to shape their funding requests and document need to outside private and public funders. Also, by participating in various facets of the research process, such as selection of samples, developing interview schedules, and analysis of census data, the ONE staff gained more of an understanding of the nuances of research. Although they do not have the capacity to do all the research themselves, they are more aware of the various steps to the research and the time and resources needed to complete them. Similarly, the university-based researchers have a better sense of how research should be framed to be useful to the community.

A third facet of the impact of the research was the actual documentation of community organization struggles and the analysis of the effectiveness of these struggles. Community organizations are constantly struggling to gather sufficient resources to continue their efforts. Even when they have sufficient resources, they are generally in the midst of some political fray in the community that requires them to spend long hours focusing their resources to bring about a success. These organizations always need things yesterday. University researchers bring a longer-term perspective to the table and also have an ability to step back from an issue and look at connections to other related issues. The stepping-back process produces an intellectual engagement that is central to activities in the university—whether it be in the classroom or in research—but which is often a luxury in the community. A few months ago, when organizers and researchers on this project spent a couple hours to reflect, Kim Zalent commented that she does not get a chance to read on general issues anymore and that our project reports and related discussions helped to counter some of the frustration of feeling intellectually isolated.

Reflections on the Collaborative Relationship

To many academic researchers, collaborative research brings relevance and enjoyment to the research project. Your research will not merely be cataloged and placed on a library shelf only to gather dust; it will be used by community organizations and other researchers. Because the issues are defined as important to the com-munity, the collaborative process produces *actionable* research—research that can be used as the informational basis for social change.

There is also an excitement to doing community-based research. One of the attractions of teaching and research is the unpredictability of it all. As with any research, community-based research is full of challenges. However, more than most research projects, the emergence of new ideas and the constant challenges of the community's practical concerns produce an especially lively research environment.

Watching the community organization use your research is also enjoyable. Irreverence for the status quo provides a common bond between many an academic and community organizer. Watching ONE go after former U.S. Department of Housing and Urban Development Secretary Jack Kemp for not responding to their requests for a meeting on the HUD prepayment buildings was exciting if not downright entertaining. After ONE-inspired editorials in Chicago's newspapers, a unanimous vote of support by Chicago City Council, and numerous calls from Chicago congressmen, Kemp refused to meet with community representatives to discuss how to prevent HUD-funded housing in Uptown from turning market rate and potentially displacing thousands of low-income families. This is when it got interesting. Feeling that they had been patient long enough, ONE sent a man dressed up as a chicken to present a singing telegram at a HUD-sponsored event in Boston. Singing "Jack the Giant Windbag" to the tune of "Puff the Magic Dragon," the chicken entertained the audience and infuriated Secretary Kemp and his staff. In the context of doing research, academics cannot engage in such clearly partisan political acts. However, watching a community organization do this is as entertaining as it is educational. It is also quite a heady experience to see a local community organization exert enough political strength to get a member of the U.S. president's cabinet to finally listen to them and support their demands.

It would be incorrect to say that six years of collaboration passed without any bumps in the road. The intensity of the relationship fluctuated, depending on the stage of the research and writing process and depending on other priorities that may have been placed above the ongoing research project. If ONE was focusing on a particular community event or political action, the research may not have taken front seat for a while. At busy times during the academic year, particularly at the end of semesters, ONE could not expect quick responses from the research team. Turnover in the staff of ONE, including a new executive director and two different organizers during the research process, did result in the adjustment of priorities and a new understanding of working relationships. Such turnover is typical in community organizations and needs to be taken into consideration when planning long collaborative relationships. Because both the community organization and the university entered this relationship knowing the potential land mines, many potential tensions were avoided. At the beginning of the process we developed and signed a contract outlining our responsibilities to each other. A key aspect of this was ONE's willingness not to edit or veto recommendations or analysis completed by the researchers. At the same time, ONE had the right to review all written material. When there were disagreements—which were about interpretation of results and not concerns over any negative political implications of the findings—modifications incorporating the community perspective strengthened the research reports.

Demystifying Research and the Policy-Making Process

By combining expertise and experience on both the community organizing and research sides of an issue, participants get a much better picture of what it takes to bring about changes in the community. "Research" can be an intimidating concept to students who assume that it always follows the nice, neat, logical pattern that they read about in journal articles. The collaborative nature of the research also provides students with the chance to see "living" research—research that has immediate policy implications. On a number of occasions during the project, articles appeared in the *Chicago Tribune* or the local neighborhood newspaper reporting on the research. This is not something students normally experience in the average college class. Students also got a chance to meet city officials and other community leaders, demystifying the process of how community pressure groups work and how decisions are made.

Trust and Respect

The two key ingredients that made our project work were trust and respect. Researchers had to gain the trust of the community organization and the community. They had to demonstrate that they were not just going to do another research project *on* the community. The contact that organizations and residents in low-income or mixed-income communities have with research is frequently related to documentation of the plethora of social problems with little emphasis on how to solve these problems. Similarly, community organizations often see research that is judgmental; they have experienced foundation and government evaluations of their programs as a condition of continued funding.[5]

In many ways, past researchers have "dirtied the nest" and have made it difficult for others to gain credibility in the community. The collaborative research process can overcome the negative view earned by past researchers, by demonstrating that a truly cooperative relationship between researchers and community activists can have positive outcomes for the community. Like any other social relationship, it takes time to win respect from others. In our case, the initial research project helped to establish this trust and respect. The university-community research action relation does have its ups and downs, its spats and celebrations, but the proof of a strong relationship is continued collaboration after six years of working together. This does not represent the only model of community research, but it does represent a powerful model that combines community and academic expertise in building solutions to persistent social problems in urban communities.

[5]New participatory evaluation research models are changing this by involving community organizations themselves in the design and administration of evaluations (Brunner and Guzman 1989; Fawcett 1995; House 1978).

EDITORS' COMMENTS

This case documents the gradual development of a productive working relationship between a university and a community organization in the surrounding neighborhoods. It demonstrates that collaborative research is not an instant or one-time deal. It takes years to develop a productive relationship. Self-interest is also an element in the growth of a good working relationship. The community organization was getting access to quality research that it did not have the capacity to produce by itself. Research completed by a university also provided a political commodity—"legitimate" research done with accepted, rigorous research methods, which the community organization could use to pressure local, state, and federal elected officials on a variety of policy fronts.

The policy research discussed here is somewhat unusual in that it is local in impact, but national in its implications. This is an excellent example of how local research and organizing activity can influence national policy. Particularly as computer-based communications become more accessible to community organizations, the opportunities for local efforts to influence other local efforts in other areas of the country are significant.

The subject of this research is also central to policy in the next century. As our nation's population becomes more diverse, projects that look at ways of sustaining diverse urban neighborhoods will become more and more important in mapping the future of urban neighborhoods. This project has already laid the groundwork for a nine-city study examining what produces stable racial, ethnic, and economic diversity. Funded by the U.S. Department of Housing and Urban Development, this project—involving collaborative research teams in Chicago, Philadelphia, New York, Milwaukee, Memphis, Denver, Houston, Oakland, and Seattle—already has received attention from policy makers in other cities and in Washington, D.C.

Editors' Note: Anyone wanting a copy of the reports published by Loyola and ONE can write to Phil Nyden, Director, Center for Urban Research and Learning, Loyola University Chicago, 820 North Michigan Ave., Chicago, IL 60611, or send e-mail to pnyden@luc.edu.

University-Community Collaboration in Low-Income Housing Projects and Neighborhood Revitalization in Louisville, Kentucky

John Gilderbloom, R. L. Mullins, Jr., Russ N. Sims, Mark T. Wright, and La Tondra R. Jones

Just a few years go, Louisville's historic Russell neighborhood would probably have ranked as one of America's more impoverished inner-city communities. In this 100-year-old African American neighborhood, consisting of 10,000 residents, over half of the households live below the poverty line, one fifth are without jobs, and average household income is $7,600 a year (U.S. Department of Commerce 1990). Liquor stores, pawnshops, and funeral homes are the leading commercial businesses; prostitution and drugs are chronic problems. Today millions of dollars in public and private funds are being invested in Russell as part of an Enterprise Community initiative. Government, higher education, business, and community have come together in a partnership to revitalize this neighborhood.

The Beginning

Surveys of Louisville's citizens over the past several years have shown that housing affordability is one of the most important issues confronting the city. The mayor made affordable housing and neighborhood revitalization one of the top three priorities of his administration. The neighborhood began organizing itself for improvement in the late 1980s and early 1990s. The city of Louisville played a major role in bringing new investment to the area, but these efforts were limited by fiscal realities. A few nonprofit organizations started serving limited clientele in the neighborhood, but they too were restricted by limited resources, varied agendas, and minimal organizing skills. Small contractors started rehabilitating one or two houses at a time. Something was still missing. More players and more intensive organization efforts were needed to help residents further.

The impetus for university involvement began in an academic setting when funding of the U.S. Department of Education's Urban Community Service Program was announced at the University of Louisville in January 1992. Faculty proposed numerous grant ideas as possible projects: improving high school graduation rates, technology transfer, analysis of census data to track neighborhood trends, waterfront development, job training, city planning, and waste disposal. During a six-month period between January and July 1992, over 200 hours of meetings were held with numerous organizations and individuals to examine how the Urban Community Service Program could help the city. Of particular note was a meeting held with presidents of the seven largest Louisville banks as well as with several notable realtors and architect/engineer firms. Four versions of this grant were circulated to over 100 individuals and organizations, and specific projects were selected. The program that developed out of these meetings was called HANDS (Housing and Neighborhood Development Strategies).

The University of Louisville received a $1.5 million grant from the U.S. Department of Education in 1993 for HANDS. The program also obtained in-kind and local matching funds totaling an additional $750,000. HANDS is a holistic approach to neighborhood revitalization that addresses the physical and human sides of the renewal process. This program provides assistance to residents and neighborhood organizations in the areas of education, job and leadership training, and home ownership. A case management component coordinates family assistance to ensure minimal organizational overlap and maximum effectiveness. An evaluation component is also included. The evaluators have helped identify programs that have not been successful. Those programs were either curtailed or terminated and the resources applied to other more successful programs. HANDS brings the resources of the university to bear on an impoverished community through its faculty, staff, and students. Working with residents of Russell and various community partners, HANDS's goal is twofold: (1) build the capacity of organizations and individuals to revitalize Russell, and (2) leverage limited local funds through grants and other sources to provide capital or access to capital for many ventures in the community.

HANDS was designed to become the broker between the resources of the university and the needs of a community. This moved the University of Louisville closer to the broader urban community in which it is located and helped the university fulfill its urban mission. A community advisory committee was established to assist university evaluation personnel in continuously monitoring the program. The committee included leaders from banking, labor, government, and housing organizations. The committee's efforts have resulted in personnel changes, reevaluation of the goals and objectives of the program, and other modifications. To gain insights from outside the community, a national advisory committee consisting of leading scholars, writers, and businesspeople in community development was also created to evaluate HANDS. Committee members make yearly visits to Louisville, tour the HANDS target areas, review evaluation reports, and meet with members of the HANDS community advisory committee along with the various HANDS resource team leaders.

The Russell Partnership: Attracting Moderate-Income Families Back to the City

What is the Russell Partnership? It is a multitude of programs, services, and activities working in and for the Russell neighborhood. It is the efforts of dozens of churches, the city of Louisville, private developers and small builders, local businesses, a consortium of local universities and secondary schools, and thousands of residents striving for a better life. The cornerstone of the Russell Partnership is attracting moderate-income families to the neighborhood by providing opportunities for home ownership. Home ownership is the anchor for stabilizing and revitalizing the neighborhood. We believe that if the neighborhood can attract family-owned housing, business and other commercial enterprises will also locate in the community.

What have partnership members accomplished? The city of Louisville budgeted $1.1 million in public improvements and $900,000 in rehabilitation programs in 1995 alone. The Urban League's Project REBOUND has pledged to build 90 single-family homes in Russell. They have sold 17 houses already. Another nonprofit organization, the Louisville Central Development Corporation, has sold 10 houses, contracted for 8 more, and is negotiating for construction of another 10 houses. Russell also takes advantage of Louisville's citywide homestead program, which performs repairs for the elderly and the disabled.

This flurry of activity has encouraged others to get involved. Banks are providing below-market financing, community groups have organized nonprofit community development organizations, and churches are building housing for their members. A major revitalization effort is also being planned for the 600-unit Village West apartment complex. It has undergone considerable decay, with 300 units boarded up. The Russell Partnership is also training residents to become housing contractors and to develop small businesses. Funds have been identified for a small-business loan program and business incubator for the Russell area.

HANDS has helped sustain and build the momentum of the city's initial investments in Russell. The university works as a partner with local government, business, the nonprofit sector, and other institutions of secondary and higher education to address systemic problems of the Russell neighborhood. The university has played a key role in building consensus and acting as a bridge among various organizations that did not communicate well in the past. The university's Community Design Team is providing services that span the gap between developers, nonprofits, corporations, government agencies, and neighborhood organizations. The team's services include creating master development plans and associated databases on neighborhood conditions; preparing conceptual development proposals for housing, recreation, parks, and other aspects of physical development; developing negotiation strategies for nonprofits with limited experience and resources; and advising developers on barrier-free designs. After reviewing the initial development plan for a small part of the neighborhood, the Russell Neighborhood Advisory Committee asked the team to prepare a master development plan for the entire neighborhood. The team is interdisciplinary, bringing together individuals with diverse backgrounds in sociology, architecture, engineering, urban planning, law, and security design. The design team's purpose is to help neighborhood leaders implement their own vision of Russell's future.

Results of the Partnership's Efforts

The Russell "rebirth" has received a great deal of praise as a model of partnership. President Clinton, in his remarks to the U.S. Conference of Mayors, pointed to the Russell neighborhood as an outstanding example of how such situations can be turned around. Other impoverished neighborhoods in Louisville and across the nation are trying to adopt and replicate the successful Russell Partnership. What are some of the positive outcomes?

- The crime rate in Russell has fallen in the neighborhoods undergoing revitalization and new home construction.

- Russell is recycling the existing infrastructure of roads, sewage, utilities, and buildings to slow down imprudent development in the undeveloped outer metropolitan areas.

- New houses are being built. Many nonprofit and for-profit developers are rehabilitating houses. One nonprofit is planning to renovate 45 abandoned housing units comprising a mixture of single-family and multifamily units. By turning abandoned houses into family-owned homes, inner-city renewal promotes the use of mass transportation and reduced energy consumption. It is also increasing the tax base, providing funds to improve the quality and level of services to the neighborhood.

- Small businesses, the economic engine of America, are blossoming.

- The first new urban park in years will be constructed and traffic patterns changed to make the neighborhood more inviting to current and potential residents.

These are the measurable items. Other small success stories are, perhaps, even more important. A 57-year-young grandmother is now the proud owner of her *first* house. Numerous people without high school diplomas have achieved their GEDs and are now going to college. An African American woman shared her wisdom and instilled pride in a new generation of children. The University of Louisville, after seeing the preliminary results of these efforts, formed the Center for Sustainable Urban Neighborhoods (CSUN) under the direction of the Vice President of Research. The Center has thus far provided research assistance and educational training for several local and national endeavors. Included in this group is the assistance provided for the successful application in 1994 by the city of Louisville for Enterprise Community designation. The U.S. Department of Education has given a tentative award of $1.6 million over a three-year period to CSUN. A local match of roughly $600,000 has been raised, bringing the total grant to $2.2 million. This program is an outreach-oriented partnership among businesses, government, community groups, junior colleges, the University of Louisville, and other universities. The vision is to build upon the HANDS program and help revitalize the West End Enterprise Community by investing in its people and their future. The program components include human development, planning, home ownership, economic development, crime prevention, and entrepreneurship.

Conclusion

This project demonstrates that urban universities with planning programs can provide tremendous creative and technical resources. As a professor of city and regional planning at the University of California at Berkeley has stated, "there is not much justification for continuing to stand on the academic sidelines. America needs its best brains, its most fertile imaginations, in its urban planning profession. And its planning schools need to focus their efforts on feasible solutions" (Hall 1989). The University of Louisville is a leader in working on solutions for affordable housing and revitalizing inner-city neighborhoods.

The Louisville project is a hands-on project that is producing results. These can be counted in the number of houses built or rehabbed and the number of new homeowners. This is not abstract research; work on this project is directly involved in getting real people to move into real housing. John Gilderbloom is Associate Professor of Economic and Urban Policy at the University of Louisville. He is Director of the Housing and Neighborhood Development Strategies program and Chair of the Center for Sustainable Urban Neighborhoods at the university's Urban Studies Institute. The co-authors of this article have all been involved in HANDS from either the university or community side. The involvement of a university—including its faculty, graduate students, and undergraduates—in research and service related to such a project adds to the mix of learning experiences available within the university. Graduate students, in particular, have been involved in many facets of this project. This is also a project that is serving the university's self-interest. It is in the institution's best interests to stabilize neighborhoods in its city. Not only does this produce a more pleasant environment in the city, but kudos to the university increase its credibility and strengthen its influence in the city.

More than most of the collaborations described in this book, local government has been closely involved in the process in Louisville. Most social change–oriented projects include their share of politics, but the participation of top university officials and city of Louisville officials means that this project has been played on a more public political playing field. HANDS has been able to use this to its advantage, as demonstrated by the ability to get President Clinton's attention. Of course, the potential downside of this visibility is increased scrutiny of their activities. Although recent media reports of the project have been very positive, an earlier report did level some criticisms that the project was more PR than substance.

Finally, as with other projects, activities are highly interdisciplinary. When issues are defined in the community and not within an academic discipline, a greater range of disciplines is brought to the table: sociology, architecture, engineering, urban planning, law, and security design. This, of course, complements the variety of leaders in the project, including elected officials, university professors, university administrators, community activists, economic development corporation leaders, bankers, and a variety of nonprofit organizations.

Collaborative, Policy-Related Research in the Area of Fair Housing and Community Development

JOHN LUKEHART, Leadership Council for Metropolitan Open Communities

Race, class, and segregation—defining issues in our society and region to which solutions are critical if we are to remain viable—have frequently been central factors in much of the work in community development. The Leadership Council for Metropolitan Open Communities, a nationally recognized Chicago-based fair housing organization and a participant, producer, and user of much applied research, is itself an outgrowth of a community organizing drive in the mid-1960s. This drive—the Chicago Freedom Movement—directly linked local civil rights efforts with a national movement. Martin Luther King and the Southern Christian Leadership Conference accepted an invitation from local civil rights activists to come to Chicago and undertake a campaign that would focus attention on the inequalities and social problems of racial discrimination and segregation in a northern setting.

In 1966, at the end of a tumultuous spring and summer marked by confrontation (including marches for open housing that were met by violence, well-attended rallies, and pickets at real estate offices that refused to serve Blacks), religious leaders convened a working summit attended by leading civic, business, and political representatives to address civil rights demands. The Leadership Council was founded at this time as the ongoing group charged with the task of promoting open housing and "ending the slums."

Establishing a New Researcher-Activist Network

By 1986, while there had been modest progress for middle- and upper-income Blacks in terms of access to housing and related opportunities, segregation was still the order of the day in Chicago, with a level of segregation for Blacks at 92 (which refers to the percentage of the population that would have to move to another neighborhood to create an even distribution of racial groups throughout the city). Looking for ways of using policy research to further determine where the policy successes had been and where we still needed to know more about the segregation process, the Leadership Council cooperated in a metropolitan-areawide collaborative research project involving 12 university-based researchers and the various members of the Chicago Area Fair Housing Alliance (CAFHA)—a consortium of private and public fair housing groups and representatives from racially diverse municipalities primarily in Chicago suburbs.

Gary Orfield, a member of the Leadership Council's board of directors and then a professor at the University of Chicago,[1] worked with CAFHA and the Leadership Council in coordinating a set of research projects. This work, described by Orfield as the "largest interdisciplinary effort to understand the contemporary fair housing situation ever undertaken" (1987), came to represent a new level of cooperation and interaction between researchers and activists in planning and conducting studies to document experience and practices. Not only did the Leadership Council's and Orfield's efforts bring researchers and community organizations to the same table—many for the first time—but they also brought together researchers, many of whom had never worked together even though they had similar research interests.

The point of the research was to document progress made in fair housing work, evaluate ongoing fair housing programs, and identify factors related to the persistence of segregation in some areas. The goal was to further the development of fair housing as an integral part of healthy communities. While the goal was social change, the research followed traditional, rigorous research protocols. Through a series of meetings in which researchers and fair housing advocates discussed a broad range of issues and research needs, seven projects were identified. Subsequently, two other related research studies were linked to the effort. With these proposed research projects as the basis, an application was prepared under the auspices of CAFHA and submitted to the U.S. Department of Housing and Urban Development, through the sponsorship of the city of Evanston and village of Park Forest—two racially diverse communities that qualified to receive fair housing action grants. The grant was successful not only because these communities had a positive track record in promoting racial diversity and could demonstrate the need to better understand pro-diversity policy development, but also because the project had collected a very impressive set of participants—researchers with impressive research experience and community representatives with considerable practical knowledge in this area. Subgroups of researchers and activists were organized around each of the nine research topics. These smaller research teams defined the research issue as well as the methodologies to be used. The larger collaborative group also served as a sounding board for these smaller project-based teams. In each case, as Orfield had noted, data were "independently analyzed" by trained researchers.

It was understood that researchers would have the final say on matters related to methodology. Research teams did not use one set methodology. Census data, structured interviews, and open-ended interviews were used by different teams in this process. Some projects were best described as oral histories, while others were participatory evaluation research projects. Still others examined census data in conjunction with mortgage lending data available from the federal government. Methodologies were selected to get the best-quality data given the available resources. The topics of the projects included reports focusing on the following: experiences of clients using the counseling services of the fair housing center; experiences of African American families who had made nontraditional moves to predominantly white communities; patterns of mortgage lending as related to the racial composition of different neighborhoods; a compilation and analysis of test results from studies of various Chicago area housing markets; a valuational

[1]Gary Orfield is now a professor at the Kennedy School of Public Policy at Harvard University.

inventory of fair housing groups in the Chicago area; post census (1980) estimates of the racial/ethnic composition of various communities, using birth and death data; patterns of racial change in select Chicago suburbs; trends in home prices in select Chicago area neighborhoods, as related to race; and market failure and federal policy as related to low-income housing.

Once completed, draft reports were circulated to all participants and presented at a major conference held at the University of Chicago. Fair housing, civil rights, government, and community leaders attended this gathering. This was done to gather input from activist-participants, the researchers, and other individuals interested in this policy question. Also, holding such an event at a prestigious institution did contribute to the legitimacy of the research in the eyes of the policy makers attending the event.

Following the conference, studies were finalized and presented at a press conference. We recognized that the media are important players in policy debate. Just publishing research does not ensure that it gets into the public eye and is "consumed" by government officials who might act on the recommendations of the researchers. The collaborative project resulted in ongoing relationships between the researchers and fair housing advocates involved in this process. From the researchers' point of view, they found the environment one in which community leaders appreciated their work and were able to take it and apply it in day-to-day policy efforts. The link to practitioners added an "afterlife" to the research—it did not just sit on a shelf in a library; rather it was taken and used in the community. As Orfield observed, "this project developed at the intersection between the interests of researchers desiring to explore important new questions of race and housing and of fair housing

practitioners hoping for evidence that could help them plan the next generation of the battle against forced desegregation" (1987). Similarly, from the practitioners' point of view, they now had access to an approachable group of researchers who could help them gather information critical to ongoing policy work. Many members of this network created in the mid-1980s either have continued to do research work with each other or have occasionally contacted each other about specific research and policy questions as they have arisen. The fact that the Leadership Council and CAFHA are formal organizations has helped to facilitate this ongoing communication.

One of the successes of the project was the usefulness of the various recommendations coming out of the collection of projects, including identification of a need for more regional approaches to fair housing advocacy; increased funding for local efforts; increased attention to the growing Latino population; expanded public awareness of fair housing laws and individual rights; improved client counseling and escorting services; more systematic assessments of levels of discrimination; and more marketing of housing opportunities for minority renters and home buyers. Additionally, the research was cost effective. It was completed on a budget of $75,000, an expenditure that leveraged significant in-kind and brain-equity investments from other participants. Involvement in such a project was attractive to researchers because of their interest in completing research that would have a real impact on policy; thus they tended to put in much of their own time on the project. By normal standards, this project was "worth" more than $200,000 in the time put in by researchers, community leaders, and students.

The principal shortcoming of the work was the unevenness of follow-through by participating fair housing organizations, individually and collectively. Some of the findings did inform program development for particular groups, but some of the results that had particularly powerful public policy implications—for instance, those related to lending—were not used to the fullest extent possible to prod the industry or regulators or Congress.

Follow-Up Projects

Our research experience had two significant results. First, the model of researcher-activist collaboration and its success in this project led to the initial funding for the Policy Research Action Group (PRAG), described in Chapter 2. It was knowledge of this model of funding smaller collaborative projects that led to the decision of the John D. and Catherine T. MacArthur Foundation, and the Joyce Foundation, to provide initial funding to a broader citywide policy research collaborative.

Second, the establishment of closer relationships between researchers and advocates in the fair housing, pro-diversity community areas produced an informal "think tank" that ultimately became more formalized with the help of the Policy Research Action Group. In 1993 and 1994, PRAG sponsored two citywide roundtables on the issues of racial, ethnic, and economic diversity in urban and suburban communities. The purpose of these gatherings was to gain more of an understanding of what we knew about successful diversity and what additional information we needed. Rather than see these as one-time sessions where we would just talk with each other, there was a real sense that we needed to get something done. After the 1994 roundtable, which 60 people attended, we focused on the need to look at diverse *urban* neighborhoods.

It was recognized that much research had been done on suburban diversity—typically, minorities moving into predominantly white, middle-class suburbs. However, there was not much research done on diverse neighborhoods within cities. With the increased diversity of older American cities and projections for more than 50 percent of the American population to be "minority" by the year 2050, there was strong interest in understanding better how the few multiethnic, multiracial urban communities that existed across the country were faring. Were there lessons from these communities that we could learn in stabilizing other diverse city neighborhoods and helping to create more stable diversity in our nation's cities?

Through contacts that the Leadership Council had with the U.S. Department of Housing and Urban Development, PRAG submitted and received funding for a study of what produces stable racially and ethnically diverse communities in U.S. cities. We are currently looking at 14 stable, diverse neighborhoods in nine cities. Although the work is being coordinated from Chicago, in each of the cities, we have recruited collaborative teams of researchers and community activists to complete the research project. We have set up an e-mail network to allow the researchers and community leaders in all the cities to regularly communicate with each other. Thus, our local work set the foundation for this national study that will link grassroots policy research in nine cities. A national conference was held in June 1996 to discuss the research findings.

So, we set out on another adventure in collaborative research, in which we learn from one another, make discoveries, and confirm or challenge assumptions in the process. We anticipate results that can be used to help solve problems. Collaborative, applied research—which breaks down barriers between the "subjects" and the "objects" of study—is a valuable and productive methodology.

This case study represents a fascinating evolution of ideas and relationships, demonstrating how collaborations can grow and increase researcher and community activist capacities in addressing significant policy issues. John Lukehart is Vice President of the Leadership Council for Metropolitan Open Communities, an organization that serves as a fair housing advocate in the Chicago metropolitan area. Since this report was written, researchers of the diverse cities project were asked by the Fannie Mae Foundation—the foundation of the national mortgage banking entity—to present this research to the annual meeting of researchers, government officials, and community leaders gathered in Washington, D.C. This represents the ability of a grassroots-based, collaborative research action project to influence decision makers at the national level. Within Chicago, the project has also attracted the interest of the mayor's office, which is cosponsoring a policy breakfast with PRAG to present research findings.

The ability to produce lasting collaborative university-community networks is also illustrated well by this project. With stable, creative community or metropolitan-areawide organization to back up the projects and facilitate continued communication between researchers and advocates, the networks have been sustained, and even expanded, over the past 10 years. Also, by defining research issues from a community perspective, research becomes interdisciplinary—unlike most projects developed from within the academy. The researchers involved in the original project organized by Gary Orfield came from different fields: economics, sociology, geography, history, and political science. The success of the collaboration was related not only to the complementary nature of the university and community sides, but also to the interdependence of the disciplines at the research table.

The Fair Lending Coalition: Organizing Access to Capital in Milwaukee

GREGORY D. SQUIRES, University of Wisconsin–Milwaukee, and DAN WILLETT, Fair Lending Coalition

"A pit bull for fair lending: Fair Lending Project uses attack dog tactics to change lending trends." That is how a weekly business newspaper in Milwaukee characterized the Fair Lending Coalition[1] in a 1992 front page headline (Cooper 1992). The article described how a combination of aggressive community organizing and university-based research led to the success of this multiracial, inner-city coalition, which to date has negotiated 10 community reinvestment agreements totaling over $110 million in commitments for new loans in previously redlined neighborhoods. Founded in 1991, the Coalition has relied on both its own credibility as a diverse organization and its ability to work with other institutions throughout the metropolitan area to increase access to capital (property and equipment needed to develop profitable businesses) for residents of the inner city and racial minorities throughout the metropolitan area. Key among the support from other institutions has been assistance from faculty and graduate student researchers at the University of Wisconsin-Milwaukee.

The Fair Lending Coalition consists of representatives from local churches, labor unions, civil rights organizations, and community-based groups. Its board is approximately one-third African American, one-third Hispanic, and one-third White. It has received strong support from the mayor of Milwaukee, local foundations, and other philanthropic organizations. The media have often provided favorable support. The University of Wisconsin-Milwaukee has provided essential information through various research activities. With the support of diverse local actors, the Coalition's primary tools have been two federal statutes enacted in response to a national community reinvestment movement. Collaboration, on several fronts, has led to concrete changes in the availability of credit in Milwaukee.

The Birth and Growth of the Fair Lending Coalition

When the Atlanta *Journal/Constitution* reported in 1989 that Blacks were rejected twice as often as Whites in their mortgage loan applications, it ignited a nationwide debate on redlining that had been simmering for years and continues today (Dedman 1989). Among all the cities in this report, Milwaukee had the highest ratio of Black-to-White rejection rates—four to one— and controversies over mortgage lending in that city became particularly heated. With pres-

[1]The organization changed its name from "Project" to "Coalition" in 1993.

sure from a broad range of sectors, the Democratic mayor of Milwaukee and the Republican governor of Wisconsin assembled a Fair Lending Action Committee (FLAC) consisting of lenders, regulators, civil rights groups, researchers, and others to develop recommendations for closing Milwaukee's racial gap.

After two years of discussion and a report proposing several procedural reforms, there was little evidence of actual implementation of these reforms or changes in lending practices. Frustration grew within Milwaukee's minority community. Greg Squires, a University of Wisconsin-Milwaukee faculty member and a member of FLAC, along with one of his graduate students (who was also a community organizer), discussed this seeming inactivity on several occasions. They concluded that the missing link in Milwaukee's reinvestment effort was an independent organization that had the capacity to utilize the recently enacted federal legislation to "encourage" community reinvestment.

The two key statutes are the Home Mortgage Disclosure Act (HMDA) of 1975 and the Community Reinvestment Act (CRA) of 1977. From its inception, HMDA required federally chartered depository institutions to publicly disclose the number and dollar amounts of their mortgage loans by census tract in all metropolitan areas. In 1990 nondepository mortgage banking enterprises were added to the institutions required to submit reports. Reporting requirements were expanded to include the race, gender, and income of applicants. Lenders were also required to report how many applications were approved or denied along these same variables.

CRA places a continuing and affirmative obligation on federally regulated depository institutions to be responsive to the credit needs of their service areas, including low- and moderate-income communities. Lenders must maintain and publicly disclose a file containing the loan products they offer, the street boundaries of their service areas, copies of CRA evaluations by their federal financial regulatory agency, and any public comments they receive on their CRA performance. Regulators are required to take into consideration a lender's CRA record in evaluating applications for most significant changes in their business operations, including planned acquisitions or mergers, changes in deposit insurance, opening of new branches, and related business transactions. Third parties, including community-based organizations, can file challenges to such applications if they believe the institution has not met its CRA obligations. Regulators can deny such applications, approve them, or delay consideration until the issues under challenge are resolved. Here is where CRA provides leverage for those third parties. Even a short delay in consideration of an application can be costly to a financial institution. At this point lenders are often prepared to negotiate.

In 1991, representatives of several community groups and the university drafted a proposal that would fund both research and organizing capacity around lending issues. This group would also file challenges to bank practices, as allowed under the CRA. A local union provided the first small grant, and a local nonprofit organization provided the office space. The city of Milwaukee and the Milwaukee Foundation then provided funds to hire an executive director, Dan Willett, a veteran community organizer.

Collaboration Between the Fair Lending Coalition and the University

The Fair Lending Coalition has pursued a fairly straightforward strategy. Each year university faculty and staff prepare a set of tables on the most current HMDA reports. These data present information on the number and dollar volume of mortgage loans approved for each of the approximately 200 banking institutions operating in the metropolitan area. Of central interest to the Coalition is the amount of money invested in census tracts that are economically distressed and/or characterized by high proportions of racial minorities. This information is broken down by income and reported separately for African Americans, Hispanics, and non-Hispanic Whites. Application rejection rates are also reported for each racial group by income level.

When lenders file applications with their regulatory agencies, Coalition staff perform a cursory review of their lending record. When an applicant reports lending activity substantially below industrywide averages, additional information is sought. Comparisons are made with other institutions who are lending money in these low-income or minority neighborhoods to counter criticism that low levels of lending may be accounted for by the association between these particular demographic characteristics and bad credit risks. Clearly, racial and economic lending disparities can be accounted for in part by economic considerations of safe and sound lending. But if other lending institutions are serving these communities, it raises the suspicion of discrimination and failure to meet CRA obligations. Since individual loan files are not available to the general public, specific incidents of unlawful discrimination are difficult to prove on the basis of HMDA data. However, when there are substantial differences between the record of a particular institution and the industry average, a visit is made to the lender.

While visiting the institution, the Coalition representative takes information from the CRA files, asks the lender for copies of their underwriting guidelines (which they do not have to make public but they occasionally pro-

vide), identifies locations of other branches, and solicits other information. Lenders have generally been quite cooperative in responding to these informational requests. At this point Coalition and university staff examine the quantitative and qualitative evidence to decide whether a challenge is warranted. The information is then presented to the board for a final decision. If the decision is to go forward, Coalition and university staff prepare the challenge—generally a 5- to 10-page statement identifying deficiencies in the institution's lending record.

Ten challenges have resulted in successful negotiation of reinvestment agreements. Each has been a five-year program with commitment for new loans totaling over $110 million in mortgages and small-business loans. Besides the additional loan commitments, lenders have provided other resources as a result of the negotiated agreements: creation or expansion of basic or lifeline banking services for low-income residents (for example, free or low-cost checking accounts for cashing government checks); implementation of affirmative action programs to increase the number of minority employees; expansion of their contracting for goods and services with minority-owned firms; and opening of new branches in the central city.

While aggressive organizing and intensive research are two critical elements in these reinvestment agreements, other actors are also essential. In addition to providing financial support, the mayor has openly criticized local lenders for the failure to meet their responsibilities under the law and has praised the work of the Coalition. Good relationships have been developed with the local media, which provided substantial and positive coverage of Coalition activities. And volunteers who are drawn from all parts of the city have effectively negotiated and monitored the agreements.

A Win-Win Situation

Several individuals and groups, and indeed the city generally, have benefited from these activities. Five graduate students have been involved in varying capacities, resulting in one master's thesis, two other master's theses in progress, and a Ph.D. dissertation. One of the M.A. students wrote a chapter for a book on community reinvestment (Glabere 1992), and another coauthored an academic journal article (Squires and O'Connor 1993). In the process, these students have received training and the opportunity to apply their skills in various quantitative and qualitative research activities. Research tasks include processing and analyzing the large HMDA data set, examining CRA files and other documents to preliminarily assess compliance with federal fair lending rules, and interviewing loan officers. Two faculty members have been able to expand their research on community reinvestment through their involvement with the Coalition, in part due to grants that have provided them additional time to pursue their research interests.

Local lenders have benefited from the additional business found in areas they previously had not adequately served. No doubt, their involvement with the Coalition also aided them in the CRA examinations conducted by their respective regulatory agencies. The city of Milwaukee also gained from the additional branch banks and loan dollars that have been and will continue to be made available in economically distressed areas. Disparities in mortgage loan rejection rates have not abated, but this may be a reflection, at least in part, of the increasing number of racial minorities applying for loans. Among those applying for mortgage loans other than financing loans, the percentage of African American applicants increased form 5.7 percent to 7.0 percent.

Obviously, these changes cannot be attributed solely to the Coalition. During these years lenders launched a number of programs on their own and in collaboration with others to reach these markets. Lenders and several community organizations began mortgage counseling programs for first-time home buyers. And the Milwaukee efforts both reflect and reinforce a nationwide community reinvestment movement that has resulted in over $60 billion in new loan commitments in approximately 100 cities across the nation since the CRA was enacted (National Community Reinvestment Coalition 1995). The Fair Lending Coalition has proven to be a vital part of Milwaukee's reinvestment effort.

Coalition and Collaboration: Keys to Success

If there is a single key to the achievements of the Fair Lending Coalition and its productive relationship with the university, it is the collaborative nature of the operation. The credibility of the Coalition begins with the broadly representative nature of its board and supporting volunteers. This credibility is enhanced by the research services of the university. Basically, the Fair Lending Coalition has the facts. The collaborative nature of the operation is also evident in the Coalition's external relations. City government, the local media, private foundations, and other institutions and individuals have played vital roles.

There is also an interactive dimension to these internal and external characteristics. Outside groups support the Coalition because of the representative nature of its board and the factual base of its operation. The Coalition, in turn, is doing work that serves the interests of these other organizations and individuals. The Fair Lending Coalition is a many-legged stool. Remove one of the legs and the entire structure becomes less stable. At the same time, each leg is strengthened by its association with the whole. Research, in the absence of effective organizing, would become little more than an academic exercise. And the organizing, without a strong research foundation, would be far less effective. Obviously, financial support from public and private sources facilitates the entire operation, which in turn makes at least a small contribution to the health and stability of the community in which all these actors live.

As Saul Alinsky said, there are no permanent friends and no permanent enemies. Some lenders who previously fought reinvestment activities are now among the strongest supporters. However, with a change in administration, the city might not be as supportive. Foundation priorities change. Newspaper editorial perspectives evolve. But it appears that the success of reinvestment efforts in Milwaukee and other urban communities does depend on the creation of effective coalitions and collaborative efforts. Clearly, universities have a role to play. Achieving fair access to capital is unlikely to occur in any other way.

EDITORS' COMMENTS

This coalition is an example of the dovetailing of local community political capacities with university research capacity in helping to enforce existing federal legislation. Gregory Squires is Professor of Sociology at the University of Wisconsin-Milwaukee and consultant to the Fair Lending Coalition in Milwaukee. Dan Willett is Business Agent and Founding Executive Director of the Fair Lending Coalition. It is not unusual for laws to be passed and not have any effect because there is no watchdogging or enforcement connected to that legislation. What the Coalition has done is to use the information-gathering skills and resources of the university to provide information that can then be used to monitor bank loan practices.

Investment in housing and business is the lifeblood of any community. Institutional discrimination against a particular community in this demonstrated pattern on the part of banks of not giving loans to certain areas of the city (redlining) is particularly insidious. While they may have a sense that they have been discriminated against, individuals have a hard time documenting this pattern. Without a regular and systematic way of collecting and monitoring information on bank practices, discrimination cannot be stopped. Many community organizations throughout the nation have used the CRA as a tool to pressure banks to invest in struggling communities.

This Coalition is also of interest since it has pulled together community organizations, the university, *and* city government. While the authors recognize that the cordial relationship with Milwaukee's mayor may not always be there, the Coalition's ability to get things done has made them a social force with which elected officials must work if they are to maintain political credibility. This underscores the interaction of research and action. Research is not done in a political vacuum. The university's support for this work was affirmed when the coauthors received a Community Partnership Award from the University of Wisconsin-Milwaukee for their work using research to improve the quality of life in Milwaukee's neighborhoods.

Changing Neighborhoods and Research for Diversity in Cleveland

JANET L. SMITH, Cleveland State University,
and BOBBIE REICHTELL, Broadway Area Housing Coalition

This case study presents research completed to address the tensions and issues arising from racial change in Broadway, a large Cleveland community area southeast of downtown. The project was a collaborative effort between Janet Smith, a student in the Ph.D. program of Urban Studies at Cleveland State University, and Bobbie Reichtell, a Housing Development Specialist for the Broadway Area Housing Coalition since 1984. The research, which was conducted as part of an independent study, resulted in a set of recommendations and strategies for the Broadway Area Housing Coalition.

While the research product is significant in this case, the process of collaboration was more consequential to the project because of its effect on the direction and scope of the research. Most notable is the synergy that resulted from two people with different backgrounds, training, and experience coming together to develop a realistic grassroots-oriented strategy to promote stable integration in a racially changing neighborhood. Following is a summary of the research process, highlighting the benefits and insights gained from a collaborative research approach, as well as some preliminary observations on the effect the project has had on the community.

Background

Despite progress made in the area of fair housing, change in the racial composition of a neighborhood still sparks concern among residents and community leaders. In the minds of many, racial change inevitably leads to disinvestment and declining housing values, especially when white, middle-class families move out. For people living in older urban areas, this impression often comes from the firsthand experience of watching once-thriving neighborhoods deteriorate, sometimes quickly, sometimes more slowly. It is these lingering impressions of change that challenge efforts to sustain integration when it occurs, and to promote diversity as a community asset rather than a liability.

In historically segregated Cleveland, evidence of negative reactions to racial change is found in many neighborhoods that quickly resegregated after a few African American families bought homes there in the 1950s and 1960s. This pattern continued in the 1970s as families left to avoid court-ordered busing intended to integrate public schools. Today, many of Cleveland's neighborhoods maintain either a "black" or "white" identity, with very few truly stably integrated.

These conditions and memories are very real to residents in Broadway, a community area comprising North and South Broadway with about 30,000 residents. Until recently, Broadway had been a predominantly Polish enclave. Like many older Cleveland neighborhoods, it has changed over the years. The impact of this change is mixed. Local as well as larger economic trends have forced industrial facilities in the neighborhood either to close or relocate. As jobs moved out, so did many residents, reducing Broadway's population by one third since 1970. Simultaneously, the racial and ethnic composition has diversified, with a small yet growing minority population primarily settling in a few North Broadway neighborhoods. The most noticeable change has occurred in St. Hyacinth, where African Americans made up 12 percent of the population in 1990.

Since 1980, the Broadway Area Housing Coalition (BAHC) has been working to reduce the negative effects of change in the community by rehabilitating existing housing, building new homes, and offering housing-related services to residents. BAHC evolved from a citizens group that worked to stop lender redlining in Broadway. Today, the Broadway Area Housing Coalition is an established nonprofit community development corporation with paid staff and a $400,000 operating budget. It has produced 456 housing units for rent, lease-purchase, or conventional sale.

In 15 years, BAHC has grown to play a large role in shaping the physical transformation of the Broadway area. However, as an agent of change, the organization has also contributed to changing the racial and ethnic composition of North Broadway and the St. Hyacinth neighborhood in particular. While not intentional, housing units available through its lease-purchase and rental rehabilitation programs are primarily concentrated in North Broadway due to the availability of lower-cost homes. These programs are open to all eligible home seekers, creating opportunities for residents in Broadway as well as other low-income families seeking better housing and living conditions. Consequently, a growing minority population has moved into BAHC homes in North Broadway. This places the organization in an interesting position when considering strategies to promote positive images of diversity. On the one hand, BAHC is responsible to its constituents, most of whom are white. On the other hand, as the organization plays a hand in changing the composition of the neighborhood, it also challenges the status quo.

Conditions in the St. Hyacinth neighborhood are both good and bad when compared to the literature that describes stages of neighborhood change (Downs 1981; Goetze 1979; U.S. Department of Housing and Urban Development 1975). On the one hand, the neighborhood is clearly showing signs of physical decline. More than half of the housing units, many of which are in disrepair, are renter occupied, and housing values are nearly half the city median. Furthermore, a high rate of poverty and the loss of institutional support amplify a belief that racial change will negatively affect the neighborhood.

On the other hand, median housing value, median rent, and vacancy rate remained constant between 1980 and 1990, suggesting that while market conditions are poor, they are not changing rapidly. Furthermore, many families with the resources to move out have decided to stay in St. Hyacinth because they like and still believe in the neighborhood. BAHC has also worked with residents to produce a comprehensive physical redevelopment plan that will increase middle-income housing opportunities, improve recreation space, and expand commercial activity. These circumstances suggest promising, although not completely favorable, conditions for some sort of effort by BAHC to address the neighborhood racial change. However, members of BAHC were not quite sure what could be accomplished nor how promising any attempt might be.

The Research Process

The collaboration and initial idea for a research project for BAHC began quite by accident. Janet Smith met Bobbie Reichtell while collecting data from several Cleveland agencies included in a national study of the Community Development Block Grant Program. After Smith completed an interview with Reichtell, they discussed some of the concerns and tensions among long-time residents in St. Hyacinth stemming from an increase in African American residents. Reichtell was interested in doing something to keep the neighborhood from losing ground as BAHC worked to improve its physical conditions, and she was considering hiring an organizer to help residents work through some issues.

At the time, Smith suggested looking at *A Fragile Movement* (Saltman 1990) for some ideas about issues BAHC might need to address and strategies that might be useful. They also discussed the benefits of looking at what others in the Cleveland area were doing to promote stable, racially integrated neighborhoods. While no formal research project was discussed at that time, both knew something was in the works. They agreed that it would be beneficial to learn more about what a nonprofit group might do to promote stable racial change and diversity, and made plans to interview several local fair housing and pro-integration experts in the Cleveland area. At that point, an informal research agenda was set, and Smith and Reichtell agreed to use each other as research partners.

Soon after, Smith proposed using this research experience to fulfill an independent study she was completing on recent legal and policy concerns surrounding efforts to promote stable racial integration. For her, the research presented an opportunity to examine real efforts of local fair housing actors who were trying to promote and maintain stable integrated neighborhoods, and to consider how these actions could be translated to fit in the work of community development corporations. While these are not contradictory activities, BAHC was more than capable of implementing physical redevelopment activities, but was not necessarily positioned to offer pro-integrative programming. The research also offered a chance for hands-on investigation of the concepts and theories of neighborhood change, verifying what did and did not comply with real-world experience.

In turn, Smith's interest reinforced Reichtell's commitment to do something and to take on the seemingly unwieldy task of addressing racial change in St. Hyacinth. While Reichtell was personally committed to dealing with racism, the issues facing the neighborhood, coupled with Cleveland's history of racial division, were not necessarily encouraging. Smith's willingness to work with her depended on personal commitment to identifying possible strategies that Reichtell might find useful in St. Hyacinth. Reichtell also viewed Smith as a good resource for background information (journal articles, books, and so on) and documentation that would support her appeal to BAHC board members and outside funders to hire an organizer to work on race-related issues in St. Hyacinth.

A formal proposal was prepared and submitted for approval by the BAHC board, identifying the scope of research, a time line for completion, and a brief description of the report contents—an assessment of the community conditions, an overview of various means to address racial change, and recommendations for the Broadway area. While this could have been a perfunctory step in the research process, it actually was an important gesture for several reasons. First, it elevated the status of the research from class project to real work (although unpaid) for a real client. Second, by having an outsider from a university look at the neighborhood and suggest that something could be done, it impressed upon board members that this was more than a personal interest of one of BAHC's employees. In part, this may have resulted from a presumption that Smith's analysis was purely objective. However, her position was biased by her own interests and belief that diversity should be a positive aspect of any community. Third, it opened up a dialogue among board members, many of whom had felt all along that BAHC should initiate some action, and encouraged them to learn about their options.

The research began with interviews of local experts on housing-related approaches to stable integration. Both Shaker Heights and Cleveland Heights have active municipal-level programs to promote diversity and enforce fair housing laws. In addition, the Metropolitan Area Strategy Group, a collection of professionals, public officials, and concerned citizens, meets regularly to evaluate progress in fair housing at a regional and national level. These unstructured interviews provided a great deal of insight on how organizations have worked to promote integration since the Fair Housing Act of 1968. They also revealed the frustrations of this movement and the limits of legal actions to prevent discrimination, and provided information about recent efforts to promote diversity through formal training as well as less formal community meetings.

These agencies provided a wealth of information and experience. However, there was a sense from these groups that racial change was still perceived as a negative event in the community. The strategies employed were generally formal, top-down programs aimed at reducing discrimination against non-Whites and encouraging Whites leery of diversity to stay in racially changing neighborhoods. Although useful, these strategies did not necessarily promote a positive view of integration. Both Smith and Reichtell agreed that while some problems in the St. Hyacinth neighborhood were considered "race-related," they did not necessarily warrant a strict "fair housing" response. Rather, conditions suggested a need to open up communication among new and old residents to strengthen the community, as well as confront fears among older residents who had not long ago moved from other Cleveland neighborhoods that had changed. The question then was what role could BAHC play in facilitating this process?

At this point the research expanded to learn more about the concept of community building and helping residents to collaborate in order to create and work toward a positive vision of the St. Hyacinth neighborhood and Broadway. Rather than focus on racial changes explicitly, Smith and Reichtell were interested in grassroots strategies that could build relationships among new and old residents, regardless of their race, ethnic heritage, or economic status. Much insight came from projects Reichtell was familiar with in the Cleveland area. In particular, the Community Initiatives Project sponsored by the Cleveland Meditation Center provided evidence that an organization could facilitate a collaborative, community-building process in a diverse neighborhood among residents who previously had not worked together. Although this particular project initially was not intended to promote diversity, the group of residents and community leaders made this its mission after completing its first year of collaboration.

What these interviews made clear was the need to specifically facilitate a community-building process that could allow dialogue and collaboration among St. Hyacinth residents. As the facilitating organization, BAHC would need to shift its emphasis toward a process orientation aimed at achieving a desired end state. In this case, the end or vision was to be decided by the residents of St. Hyacinth, both old and new, giving the community ownership of whatever plans were made. While it was not uncommon for BAHC to involve residents when developing a physical plan for Broadway, this was slightly different from the "bricks and mortar" practice of community development they usually employed.

This notion of community development is clearly found in academic literature, particularly efforts that are identified as self-help, which Christenson and Robinson (1980) describe as "more process oriented than task oriented." Similarly, Warren's (1971) scheme to describe the range of community development approaches considers the degree of inclusiveness in the process to be a distinguishing feature between a grassroots, "by-the-people" approach to community development and a more top-down planning tactic. Clearly, neither a completely inclusive nor completely exclusive model is ideal. However, a process orientation is better able to engage members of the community in determining the intent, scope, and expected outcomes, which should also strengthen the capacity of the community to work together on other issues in the future.

In writing the final report, this and other literature was essential in melding the data collected from interviews into a proposed community-building process that could be facilitated by the organization. While the report to the board was not constructed as an academic paper, the literature sustained several ideas found in the community, giving credibility to the final recommendations and support for the strategies proposed.

The primary recommendation to BAHC was to develop a process to facilitate community building, employing various activities that would eventually produce a collaborative relationship among residents in St. Hyacinth. Additional housing-related recommendations were also included (for example, marketing strategies, establishing a housing information office, and expanding minority ownership) to address fair housing-related aspects of racial change. As with much of the data collection, the recommendations and strategies were developed collaboratively. Clearly, this can destroy the presumed objectivity and credibility of recommendations from an outsider. While Smith took full responsibility for the report's contents, the collaboration with Reichtell was not hidden from the board. In this case, collaboration allowed an outsider to produce a more grounded and finely tuned report for the organization, and it expanded the organization's ownership of the report because it was produced from within as well as outside the organization. The board accepted the report and approved seeking funds to hire an organizer to work in St. Hyacinth.

Insights and Outcomes

Smith and Reichtell did not deliberately set out to have a collaborative process. Yet, because they had a mutual interest in learning firsthand about possible options for BAHC in St. Hyacinth, the research quickly evolved into a collaborative project. Upon reflection, there were outcomes, both planned and fortuitous, that made this approach to the research beneficial for both parties. Some benefits of this collaboration for the overall research process are as follows:

- Wider range of ideas explored and sources examined beyond that which an academic or nonprofit staff person might discover alone

- Added insight gained from another person with different experiences and perspectives to ask questions and clarify points that might otherwise seem obvious and, therefore, taken for granted

- Educational benefits of the experience, particularly looking at academic literature (both theoretical and empirical research) from the perspective of someone working in the community

- Greater assurance that the research product will be of direct use to the organization since a member was involved in its development and completion

- Greater commitment to implementation and willingness to stick with the project as a result of working with, rather than for, the recipient of the research

For both Smith and Reichtell, this research project continues to provide firsthand experience of the frustrations and joys of trying to facilitate a collaborative process that helps residents to decide the future of their community. While some of the recommendations have only recently been implemented, a preliminary evaluation of the results are mixed. BAHC included the report in a grant proposal to a local foundation, and they received funding for an organizer, who has been facilitating the community-building process by working with the residents and the existing neighborhood council. Some of the community-building strategies have proven unsuccessful, while others have been effective. For example, the organizer has helped start several block clubs, which in turn has strengthened residents' relationships and increased their collaborative capacity.

This capacity was evidenced in a racial incident involving teenagers who firebombed the home of an African American family moving into the neighborhood. While no one was hurt and the home sustained minimal damage, this was neither the message the new family wanted to receive, nor the image the block wanted to convey. Residents quickly responded by putting up money for a reward for the criminals, who were turned in after less than 48 hours. In addition, residents circulated a statement regarding their commitment to a peaceful, open neighborhood, which many neighbors signed. The statement was given to the family as well as published in the weekly neighborhood paper. Soon after, the mayor of Cleveland issued a commendation to the residents, and the family stayed in the home once it was repaired. Although a negative event, the sense is that if it had happened prior to the work of the organizer, it most likely could have taken a very different turn.

As a final research note, the project has proven good fodder for developing a dissertation topic for Smith. Her initial intent was to evaluate the implementation of the research for the organization. However, after reexamining the theories on neighborhood change, her plan is to produce a critical analysis of how these theories have shaped and limited our understanding of neighborhood change and urban space.

EDITORS' COMMENTS

This case is of particular interest because it does not involve two organizations negotiating a research relationship and does not involve an established university faculty member as the primary researcher. The story of the development of a personal relationship connected to a research relationship is an important one to understand. In writing conclusions to our research articles and discussing our methodologies, we generally do not discuss the down-to-earth, personal process through which many of our research relationships evolve. Collaborative research is no exception; in fact, the personal side to research relationships is even more important in collaborative work.

This case illustrates that one graduate student can initiate a collaborative research project. Collaboration does not mean an elaborate process, involving only professors. In many ways, those who have not yet been socialized into the "accepted" ways of doing research are more likely to come up with innovative ways of doing research. Janet Smith's and Bobbie Reichtell's story is one of such an innovative approach to research collaboration. It is also a story that is not over. As Smith's research continues and the collaboration develops, more information will be produced and exchanged.

The substance of the research hits at the heart of policies related to establishing stably diverse neighborhoods. The fears of racial change and its assumed consequences are real in the sense that people act on those fears—real or not. Working on how to counter those fears and demonstrate that diversity does not mean declining property values, increased crime, and deterioration of a community's social fabric is critical work as our country becomes more diverse in the 21st century and cities work to sustain the vitality of their neighborhoods.

Part II

Whose Environment, Whose Problem? Collaborative Research Is Changing the Environmental Movement

In the United States, interest in the environment began about 100 years ago with the effort to conserve natural resources and preserve wilderness. Turn-of-the-century environmental movements were concerned with protecting the "natural world" from degradation caused by industrialization and urbanization. The resurgence of environmentalism in the 1960s and 1970s can be traced to the publication of Rachel Carson's book *Silent Spring* (1962). This meticulously documented study warned the American public about latent dangers in the excessive use of pesticides, and it sparked a ground swell of support for increased regulation of all forms of pollution. Thus Carson's book is a remarkable example of the use of scientific research in the service of an environmental cause.

By the 1980s, however, environmentalism was being transformed by grassroots movements concerned with people's living and working environments rather than a distant wilderness or planetary ecosystem. Robert Gottlieb documents this change in his book *Forcing the Spring* (1993), a social history of American environmentalism. He quotes Dana Alston, an organizer of the first national People of Color Environmental Leadership Summit in 1992. Addressing the summit delegates, including leaders of the Sierra Club, Wilderness Society, and other environmental organizations, Alston declared, "For us the issues of the environment do not stand alone by themselves. They are not narrowly defined. Our vision of the environment is woven into an overall framework of social, racial, and economic justice. . . . The environment, for us, is where we live, where we work, and where we play" (Gottlieb 1993, 5).

The case studies we have assembled in this part on the environment reflect this change in the environmental movement and show how collaborative research on environmental issues—cooperation between academic researchers and local environmental organizations—is affecting social change. As with the other parts of this book, it should be clear that there is no single model for collaborative research, only a shared commitment that academics and community activists have equal power in defining research problems and using findings to address social issues relevant to local communities.

Dismantling Environmental Racism in the Policy Arena: The Role of Collaborative Social Research

ROBERT D. BULLARD, Clark Atlanta University

Environmentalists have played a key role in shaping the nation's regulations and laws governing natural resources, wildlife, and industrial pollution. Although environmental concern cuts across class lines, activism in national organizations has been largely confined to Whites who have above-average incomes and education. Over the past decade, however, environmental justice advocates—a loose alliance of grassroots leaders, social justice activists, lawyers, and a few academicians—have redefined environmental protection as a basic human right. In so doing, they have begun to diversify the agenda of the environmental movement. Most importantly, they have redefined environmentalism to include concern for the "environments" where we live, work, and play, as well as the natural world (Alston 1990).

Today, grassroots environmental justice groups represent the fastest growing segment of the environmental movement (Lee 1992; Bullard 1994). Leaders from West Harlem to West Dallas to East Los Angeles have provided the major impetus for government to begin addressing ecological and health inequities. They have also challenged unfair industry and government practices, including unequal enforcement of environmental, civil rights, and public health laws; discriminatory land use, facility siting, and cleanup strategies;

exclusionary practices that limit participation of people of color on decision-making boards, committees, panels, task forces, and professional staff of governmental agencies charged with protecting public health and the environment; and faulty assumptions in calculating health risks (Bryant and Mohai 1992). Collaborative research between academics and community organizations on environmental issues has played an important role in the emergence of environmental justice activism.

Research on Environmental Racism in Houston

Environmental struggles by people of color have gained the support of a broad cross section of environmental, civil rights, labor, public health, and legal organizations (Lavelle and Coyle 1993). This was not always the case. A decade ago, "environmental racism" and "environmental injustice" had not yet registered on the conceptual radar screens of mainstream environmental groups and civil rights organizations. I know. I was in Houston in 1979 and worked with a group of African American residents who were engaged in a bitter fight to keep a garbage dump out of their suburban middle-income neighborhood (Bullard 1983).

In this early Houston landfill struggle, residents were unable to enlist the support of a single national environmental or civil rights organization. Consequently, the residents formed their own group—Northeast Community Action Group (NECAG)—and hired their own attorney, Linda McKeever Bullard (my wife), to challenge the landfill siting. My wife filed a class action lawsuit to block the facility from being built. The 1979 lawsuit, *Bean v. Southwestern Waste Management*, was the first of its kind to challenge the siting of a waste facility under the civil rights law. My graduate students (at Texas Southern University) and I, motivated by the lawsuit, began a study in 1979 to determine the history of facility siting in Houston. A clear pattern of disparate treatment emerged out of the Houston waste data, a pattern consistent with other forms of racial discrimination reported in *Invisible Houston: The Black Experience in Boom and Bust* (Bullard 1987). We found that, from the early 1920s to 1978, *all* city-owned landfills (five sites) and most city-owned incinerators (six out of eight facilities) were located in African American neighborhoods. This was clearly unequal treatment since African Americans made up only one fourth of the city's population. When the city turned over waste disposal to private industry in 1978, the private disposal company basically followed the pattern established by the city government. Three of the four privately owned landfills used to dispose of Houston's household garbage were situated in African American neighborhoods.

The actions of the city government and the private disposal company amounted to environmental racism. *Environmental racism refers to any policy, practice, or directive that differentially affects (whether intended or unintended) individuals, groups, or communities based on race.* Environmental racism combines with public policies and industry practices to provide benefits for Whites while shifting costs to people of color (Bullard 1993, 98).

Although NECAG and their attorney were not successful in blocking the landfill, the group did change the state permit requirements for waste facilities, pressured the Houston city council to adopt a resolution banning city-owned trucks from dumping at the landfill, and convinced the city council to adopt an ordinance restricting the location of waste facilities (a form of zoning in a city that does not have zoning). Moreover, not a single municipal solid waste facility has been built in a community of color in Houston since that 1979 lawsuit. Our finding that racial discrimination did influence waste facility siting was central to NECAG's argument and thus pivotal to policy changes that occurred at the local level.

Birth of a Movement and the Role of Research in Documenting Environmental Injustice

It is important to note that the Houston protests, the lawsuit, and our research occurred three years before the events that transpired in Warren County, North Carolina—a rural and mostly African American county—which drew national attention to environmental injustice. Oil laced with the highly toxic PCB (polychlorinated biphenyl) was illegally dumped along the roadways in 14 North Carolina counties in 1978. The roadways were cleaned up in 1982. A disposal site was needed for the PCB-tainted soil, and Warren County was selected (Geiser and Waneck 1983). Because Warren County was poor and mostly black, the powers that be expected no opposition.

In 1982, over 500 people were arrested for protesting "Hunt's Dump," named after then Governor James Hunt. Those arrested included District of Columbia delegate Walter Fauntroy, the chairman of the Congressional Black Caucus; the Reverend Benjamin F. Chavis, Jr., of United Church of Christ's Commission for Racial Justice; and the Reverend Joseph Lowery of the Southern Christian Leadership Conference. The protesters failed to block the PCB landfill. Nevertheless, they brought national attention to siting inequities and galvanized African American church leaders, civil rights organizers, and grassroots activists around environmental justice issues. In short, the protesters in Warren County put environmental racism on the map.

The demonstrations prompted Delegate Fauntroy to request a U.S. General Accounting Office (1983) investigation of hazardous waste facility siting in EPA's Region IV—eight states in the South (Alabama, Florida, Georgia, Kentucky, Mississippi, North Carolina, South Carolina, and Tennessee). While Blacks constitute only about one fifth of the population in EPA's Region IV, the 1983 GAO report found that three of the four off-site hazardous waste landfills in the region were located in predominately African American communities. In 1995, both of the off-site commercial hazardous waste landfills in the region are located in predominately African American communities.

The events in Warren County prompted the Commission for Racial Justice, led by Dr. Benjamin F. Chavis, Jr., to undertake its landmark study of the relationship between hazardous waste facilities and race in the United States (United Church of Christ Commission for Racial Justice 1987). This widely quoted study found (1) that three out of five African Americans live in communities with abandoned toxic sites; (2) that 60 percent of African Americans (15 million) live in communities with one or more waste sites; and (3) that three of the five largest commercial hazardous waste landfills, accounting for 40 percent of the nation's total hazardous waste landfill capacity in 1987, are located in predominately African American or Latino communities.

Following our Houston research and coinciding with the Commission's study, I began to document the environmental justice struggles in rural, urban, and suburban African American communities in the South, which culminated in the publication of *Dumping in Dixie: Race, Class and Environmental Quality* (Bullard 1990). Sociology students at historically black colleges and universities conducted interviews for the project. We examined disputes over a municipal landfill in Houston, a lead smelter in West Dallas (Texas), a hazardous waste incinerator in Alsen (Louisiana), a hazardous waste landfill in Emelle (Alabama), and a chemical plant in Institute (West Virginia). *Dumping in Dixie* shattered the myth that people of color are not concerned with environmental issues. We found that all of these local struggles were led by low-income, middle-income, and working-class African Americans from the affected communities.

Influencing Environmental Policy

The momentum of the environmental justice movement and the growing body of research documenting environmental injustice put pressure on the EPA, under former EPA administrator William Reilly, to address equity issues. At the prodding of environmental justice leaders and environmental sociologists, Reilly set up an internal Environmental Equity Work Group, met with an ad hoc group of environmental justice leaders on a quarterly basis, issued a 1992 report entitled *Environmental Equity: Reducing Risks for All Communities* (U.S. EPA 1992), and then created an Office of Environmental Equity and initiated a number of environmental justice projects in the 10 regions.

Environmental justice activists continued to apply pressure as the incoming Clinton administration took shape. Dr. Ben Chavis and I were appointed to the Clinton transition team in the Environmental and Natural Resources Cluster (EPA, Department of Interior, Department of Agriculture, and Department of Energy). In our work with the transition team, we transmitted to the administration a major document, "Environmental Justice Transition Paper," that emerged out of the environmental justice network of activists and researchers. (Ferris 1994). The administration implemented three major Transition Paper recommendations: (1) a national meeting to address environmental health concerns, (2) a presidential order on environmental justice, and (3) the establishment of a committee to advise the federal EPA on environmental justice issues. On February 10–12, 1994, a national "Health Research and Needs to Ensure Environmental Justice" symposium was held in Arlington, Virginia. It was sponsored by the EPA, National Institute for Environmental Health Sciences, Agency for Toxic Substances and Disease Registry, National Institutes of Health, National Institute for Occupational Health, Centers for Disease Control and Prevention, and Department of Energy.

A 20-member symposium planning committee was formed that included an equal number of government officials and representatives from nongovernmental organizations. Representatives included grassroots environmental justice activists, community organizers, research scientists, academicians, and government officials. Four sociologists served on the symposium planning committee.

On February 11, 1994, during the second day of the national health symposium, President Clinton signed the Environmental Justice Executive Order (#12898). This order reinforces, with respect to environmental issues, the Civil Rights Act of 1964—which prohibits discriminatory practices in programs receiving federal funds. The executive order also focuses the spotlight back on the National Environmental Policy Act (NEPA), a 25-year-old law that set policy goals for the protection, maintenance, and enhancement of the environment. NEPA's goal is "to ensure for all Americans a safe, healthful, productive, and aesthetically and culturally pleasing environment." NEPA requires federal agencies to detail the potential effects of proposed federal actions on human health.

The executive order calls for improved methodologies for assessing and mitigating the health effects from multiple and cumulative exposure to hazardous waste, collection of data on low-income and minority populations who may be disproportionately at risk, and assessing effects on subsistence fishers and wildlife consumers. It also encourages participation of the affected populations in environmental health assessment—including scoping and monitoring, data gathering and analysis, mitigation, and the development of alternatives.

In March 1994, Carol Browner, head of the EPA under President Clinton, appointed a 25-member National Environmental Justice Advisory Council (NEJAC). The NEJAC members created four subcommittees: enforcement, waste and facility siting, public participation and accountability, and health and research. I chair the committee on health and research. Environmental justice advocates and our collaborative research is changing national policy, giving the victims of environmental injustice greater legal recourse. But environmental injustice persists.

Dumping on "Invisible" Communities

In the real world, all communities are not created equal. If a community happens to be poor, rural, and African American, it is more likely to suffer environmental burdens than other communities. In 1995, for example, the Nuclear Regulatory Commission had under review a proposal from Louisiana Energy Services (LES) to build the nation's first privately owned uranium enrichment plant in the middle of two African American communities, Forest Grove and Center Springs. A national search was undertaken by LES to find the "best" site for a plant that would produce 17 percent of the nation's enriched uranium.

Local residents organized themselves into a group called CANT (Citizens Against Nuclear Trash) and hired lawyers from the Sierra Club Legal Defense Fund. I was asked to examine the environmental justice implications of the LES facility siting proposal. I found a clear pattern of racial discrimination in the site selection process. African Americans make up 13 percent of the U.S. population, 20 percent of the southern states' population, 31 percent of Louisiana's population, 35 percent of Louisiana's northern parishes, and 46 percent of Claiborne Parish, the region targeted for the uranium plant. An evaluation of the actual sites that were considered in the "Intermediate" and "Fine" screening stages of the site selection process reveals a disturbing pattern of discrimination against African Americans.

The proportion of the population that is black for a one-mile radius around all of the 78 possible sites examined (in 16 parishes) averages 28 percent. When LES completed its initial site cuts and reduced the list to 37 (in 9 parishes), the average population of African Americans in the population rose to 37 percent. When LES further limited its focus to 6 sites in Claiborne Parish, the average proportion of blacks in the population rose again, to 65 percent. Finally, 97 percent of the population in the one-mile radius surrounding the final site selected, "LaSage," is black.

The plant would be located just one-quarter mile from Center Springs (founded in 1910) and one-quarter mile from Forest Grove (founded in the 1860s just after slavery). The facility is proposed for a Louisiana parish that has per capita earnings of only $5,800 per year (45 percent of the national average) and where over 58 percent of the African American population lives below the poverty line. LES officials did not recognize the two unincorporated African American communities in the selection process since they did not appear on their maps. The two communities were rendered "invisible" since they were not even mentioned in the Nuclear Regulatory Commission Draft Environmental Impact Statement (DEIS).

Only after intense public pressure did the Nuclear Regulatory Commission (NRC) attempt to address environmental justice issues as required under the National Environmental Policy Act and called for under Environmental Justice Executive Order 12898. NEPA requires that government agencies consider the environmental impacts and weigh the costs and benefits of proposed actions. These include public health as well as environmental effects, and the consideration of socioeconomic inequalities.

In the Final Environmental Impact Statement (FEIS), the NRC devoted less than a page to addressing the environmental justice issues in the siting of the proposed uranium enrichment plant. Overall, the FEIS and environmental report are inadequate in the following respects: they inaccurately assess the costs and benefits of the proposed plant; they fail to consider the inequitable distribution of costs and benefits of the proposed plant to Whites and African Americans; they fail to consider the fact that the siting of the plant in a community of color follows a national pattern in which institutionally biased decision making leads to the siting of hazardous facilities in communities of color, and results in the inequitable distribution of costs and benefits to those communities.

Among the distributive costs not analyzed in the relationship to Forest Grove and Center Springs are the disproportionate burden of health and safety, property values, fire and accidents, noise, traffic, radioactive dust in the air and water, and dislocation by a road closure that connects the two communities. The NRC had an excellent opportunity to do the right thing but blew it. Even EPA Region IV went on record indicating that the FEIS and environmental report were inadequate and recommended that the NRC conduct a supplemental environmental justice analysis.

Conclusion

Institutional research and environmental decision making have failed to address the "justice" question of who gets help and who does not, who can afford help and who cannot, why some contaminated communities get studied while others get left off the research agenda, why industry is allowed to poison some communities and not others, why some contaminated communities get cleaned up while others do not, and why some communities are protected and others are not. No community, rich or poor, urban or suburban, black or white, should become a "sacrifice zone." The goal of the environmental justice movement is to ensure equal treatment for all Americans. The lessons from the civil rights struggles over housing, employment, education, and public accommodations over the past four decades suggest that environmental justice needs a legislative foundation. It is not enough to demonstrate the existence of unjust conditions; the practices that caused the conditions must be eliminated. As I have shown in this case study, collaborative social research linked to action is an integral part of this movement to change environmental policy.

predominately African American neighborhoods, even though Blacks make up only one fourth of the city's population. Subsequent grass-roots struggles in other parts of the country and supporting research on patterns of environmental injustice culminated in the establishment of an Office of Environmental Equity under former EPA administrator William Reilly and more recently resulted in an Environmental Justice Executive Order, signed by President Clinton. This body of collaborative research, which Bullard reviews, has shifted national policy toward greater concern for environmental justice, and it has changed the scope of research on environmental problems, as can be seen in the focus of our next case study.

Lead Analysis in an Urban Environment: Building a Cooperative, Community-Driven Research Program in Chemistry

ALANAH FITCH, Loyola University Chicago

This case study describes chronologically the development of a collaborative research program in the area of soil lead analysis in which the community decided on the samples to be taken and analyzed by college students in my chemistry lab at Loyola University Chicago. It began with a pilot study of the lead content of soil in a public park adjacent to a middle school in Chicago's West Town neighborhood. This project required the development of local expertise in lead analysis, which in turn led to the complete reconfiguration of the required chemistry majors' instrumental methods class at Loyola, which subsequently led to soil sampling near an urban incinerator, which resulted in the development of a National Science Foundation proposal to more systematically develop and integrate this collaborative research between Loyola University and the surrounding community. What we found, and how community groups have shaped the research agenda and used the results in public policy debates, are two important aspects of this case study.

Rudy Lozano Middle School Soil Lead Mapping

In an unguarded moment I, a chemist, expressed an interest in promoting science education for minority students in the Chicago public school system by involving them in a "real" research project. At the prompting of the Policy Research Action Group (PRAG) at Loyola University Chicago, a working group was convened in spring 1993 to discuss the possibility of empowering inner-city children by giving them real science experience on samples that had implications for community health and environmental politics. The working group consisted of several Loyola faculty members (chemistry, sociology, and natural sciences), public health officials (University of Illinois School of Public Health), an environmental law clinic, and community action groups (Centro Sin Fronteras and Lead Elimination Action Drive, LEAD). The working group needed to consider the age of the participating students (possible health and safety considerations involved), the location where the samples would be drawn (access problems), and the possible impact of the research results. These were not straightforward issues to resolve. The scientists, for example, envisioned water sampling as the safest specimens for children to obtain and the easiest to chemically analyze. The community groups objected to water sampling on the grounds that the limited political capital in the lead public health arena should be expended on the greatest problems, and the greatest problems exist in aging urban homes contaminated with lead-based paint. Focusing on water-derived lead would divert attention from inner-city areas where lead poisoning problems are concentrated to suburban areas with greater political clout but less need.

The final decision was made to sample soils in Pulaski Field House park near the pilot school, the Rudy Lozano Magnet Middle School. This school was chosen because members of the Centro Sin Fronteras community action group were closely tied to the school board and could facilitate implementation of the program. PRAG awarded a $5,000 grant to initiate the school science program. The implementation of the program was placed in the hands of Centro Sin Fronteras, with Loyola's chemistry department providing a site for field trips and data analysis. Approximately 23 fifth grade students, primarily Hispanic of Mexican descent, participated in an after-school science club facilitated by local teachers Jose Santiago and Braulio Gonzalez. Dora Gomez of Centro Sin Fronteras developed the program curriculum.

Analyzing the soil samples for lead content turned out to be more difficult to implement than originally envisioned. Lead analysis was outside my area of expertise, and it took time to develop and refine an analytic process that would generate reliable results. Consequently, the soil samples collected by the fifth graders early in the spring were not analyzed until midsummer. The time lag was a source of disappointment to the school community, and it reflects some of the difficulty in applying a highly technical research system on a volunteer basis.

When the sampling was complete, we compared the data generated in our lab to the results of samples sent to a commercial lab, thereby verifying the validity of our results. We found that the soil in the park does indeed have higher lead levels (± 300 ppm) than desired by the Environmental Protection Agency (± 50 ppm). It is quite likely that the amount of lead present derives from the close proximity of the park to Interstate 94. Two meetings were held in the summer of 1994 and early fall 1995 to discuss possible actions that the community might wish to take based on the research results. Keith Harley of the Chicago Legal Clinic offered to provide services to the community should they decide to pursue the matter. No decision was made to pursue the matter, as the total threat to the community did not, to members of Centro Sin Fronteras, warrant the effort necessary to remove it. With respect to science education, two members of the original fifth grade group interned in the Loyola chemistry lab during the summer of 1995. And this turned out to be just the beginning.

Austin Soil Lead Content Near a Chicago Municipal Solid Waste Incinerator

One positive outcome of the soil analysis project was the complete reorganization of Loyola's undergraduate chemistry course. Having invested a great deal of time in validating our lead analysis techniques, we decided to bring this collaborative, real-world experience to Loyola undergraduates on an ongoing basis. Undergraduate chemistry majors take a senior/junior-level chemistry class entitled Instrumental Methods of Analysis. This class is often characterized by a random sequence of events: exercises on various instruments in which the chemistry, as well as the instrument, changes from lab to lab. The students may be left with the sense of having completed the three-day tour of Europe. Our goal, based on the initial soil analysis for lead, was to provide Loyola students with a problem of real consequence. Once convinced of the importance of this work, we hoped that students would come to exercise their own critical skills in discovering the importance of good record keeping in obtaining reliable results.

Keith Harley of the Chicago Legal Clinic mentioned our willingness to join with a community in soil sampling to the Center for Neighborhood Technology, a group devoted to exploring recycling options within Chicago. Chicago operates a municipal solid waste incinerator in Austin, an older neighborhood that was once the bastion of industry and is currently ranked among the poorest, unstable neighborhoods. Homeowners in that area have been trying to shut down the incinerator, in part because of perceived health risks. The government estimates that the incinerator emits 5.7 lbs/hour of lead, and the Austin Community Council wanted to determine whether that resulted in elevated lead levels in the soil of the surrounding area. In fall 1994, the Instrumental Chemistry class went to three homes in the Austin community and sampled soils as per the instructions of the Chicago Department of Health. This field trip acquainted the students with the homeowners (elderly women who inherited these homes from their turn-of-the-century immigrant fathers) and their concerns, and provided a real-life concern to the chemistry performed by these undergraduate students. One of the homeowners was quite vocal about her concerns for her granddaughter, and one student chose to sample specifically where the granddaughter liked to dig.

At this point we were well equipped to handle soil samples, but it still took time to train our students in lead analysis techniques. Again, from the community's perspective, the results were long in coming. We found that the soil samples gathered near the incinerator had lead content similar to the Pulaski Field House park, with elevated lead levels near the homes. The community subsequently used this information to draw media attention to the perceived health risks of the incinerator. The undergraduate chemistry students, however, came to a different conclusion. They felt that the low amounts of lead were statistically unreliable in the rear yards and even more unreliable as exact figures near the home, but that the pattern of higher lead near the home was consistent with literature values for lead-painted homes (Solomon and Hartford 1976). The students were split as to whether to attribute this high lead level to the nearby incinerator or to paint on these approximately 70-year-old homes. The amount of lead in the backyard was consistent with mean values for industrial urban areas (Kutz 1983).

One student volunteered to sample housing stock of a similar age in the Rogers Park area (no nearby incinerator). The student did so, and a graduate student analyzed the samples. This data was transmitted to the homeowners by Bill Iyring of the Center for Neighborhood Technology. A second student has since designed a soil sampling strategy that directly addresses the role of the incinerator as a health threat by taking into account the prevailing wind patterns around the incinerator in conjunction with physics models of wind patterns and Gaussian plume spreading (Harrop 1994). These soils will be sampled by the fall 1995 Instrumental Analysis Class.

Source of Lead Near the Municipal Solid Waste Incinerator: Dilemmas in Collaborative Research

Even if a soil sampling pattern around the incinerator finds high lead levels, we cannot conclude that the lead around homes in the Austin neighborhood comes from the incinerator. The incinerator deposits lead along the wind plume, which does not predominately move in the direction of the homes we sampled. In order to definitively determine the source of lead, we need a method of finger-printing that lead. After a great deal of library research, we have determined that lead isotopes will allow us to determine whether the lead from the two different locations (house edge and middle of yard) derive from the same source (Russell and Farqhuar 1966). If the isotope pattern is different between locations, then it is probable that the incinerator is not the only, or even the most important, source of the lead. A uniform, weather-generated incinerator plume can be expected to deposit lead evenly throughout the area. If the isotope ratios differ, it is likely that the source of lead near the home differs from the airborne source of lead in the yard, which would be consistent with a lead paint source.

Based on this reasoning, we again are moving into a technological unknown and acquiring an instrument, ICP-MS (inductively coupled plasma emission spectrometer coupled to a mass spectrometer), donated by Waste Management Corporation. This instrument can sensitively analyze for the quantity of lead as well as the mass ratios of the various lead isotopes. We hope to have this instrument available for use in the fall 1995 class. With the help of the Lead Industry Association, we have obtained authentic ore samples from various lead mines having different isotopic ratios. They will be used to validate the method. Validation will probably again delay the implementation of the method long beyond the political schedule of the Austin community.

The Future of Collaborative Lead Research

Based on these efforts, an interdisciplinary (sociology, chemistry, and physical anthropology) and collaborative (Rogers Park public schools and Loyola University) National Science Foundation proposal was developed. This proposal seeks to justify the expense of maintaining these instruments for community-driven research by coupling the lead analysis activities with more traditional disciplinary research and to foster the growth of minority college-bound science students. We are revisiting our original goal of soil mapping driven by elementary school children in the neighboring Rogers Park schools (also largely Hispanic with other minorities), but we are now in a position to deliver results in a more timely way and with a wider array of instrumentation. We wish to have a full-time person (postdoctoral) involved in this project in order to eliminate the large time delays experienced in returning results to the community. Our goal is to generate a complete map of lead in a single community—soil, house dust, paints, bone—and type it by source via isotopic measurements.

It is clear that the data generated by our collaborative research venture may be used for political purposes. We, the chemists, would not draw some of the conclusions drawn by the community about the data; however, we are comfortable in providing the data to the community and allowing them to draw their own inferences. We think that the difference of opinion as to the meaning of the data suggests a need for more science education in the community.

Conclusion

What started as a service project based on integrating a Jesuit (Loyola University) emphasis on ethics into the chemistry curriculum has developed into a major research program—research that is informed by community goals. However, our collaborative relationship is sometimes strained by the problem of delivering results in a timely way. Furthermore, the end use of the data has important political implications that create a dynamic tension between the chemistry end of the research and the community end of the research. We are able to provide data that is used in ways beyond our control, and this suggests the need for greater science education in the community than we have yet provided. Despite these difficulties, the project has been successful in that significant results have been provided to a variety of communities, and just as importantly, undergraduate students at Loyola have invested themselves in chemistry problems that require critical thinking to solve and which will be used by the community in a political context, thus requiring a level of ethical preparation lacking in prior chemistry course work.

EDITORS' COMMENTS

In our second environment case, Alanah Fitch, Professor of Chemistry at Loyola University Chicago, collaborated with a number of community organizations to develop a science education program that targeted minority students in the Chicago public school system. The idea was to teach children science by helping them learn about the risk of lead poisoning in their neighborhood environment. Fitch shows how community concerns (studying lead in the soil rather than lead in the water) reoriented the scientific agenda of the academic researchers involved in the project, and ultimately, the program resulted in a complete revision of the undergraduate chemistry curriculum at Loyola. Thus the collaborative effort generated data useful to several community organizations working on lead poisoning issues, but it also changed the focus of academic research and training in a university science program.

This case also highlights the tension inherent in collaborative research. Community organizations want results they can use immediately and for political gain. Academic researchers tend to work more slowly, often depend on "the enemy" (for example, industry) for research funds, and are pressured by norms of scientific objectivity that make them uncomfortable with the politics of collaborative research on environmental issues. The initial project led to a second study (also community driven) that examined the relationship between a municipal waste incinerator and elevated lead levels in the surrounding neighborhood. The study was not conclusive (a frustration for community health advocates) but the project was an occasion for educating Loyola chemistry students about the tension between "good science" and environmental politics.

Janitors and Dry Cleaners: Constructing a Collaborative Model for Environmental Research

Robert Gottlieb, University of California at Los Angeles

In the academy, the study of the environment has largely been confined to separate disciplines within the physical or natural sciences, often ignoring the social, political, and economic patterns associated with environmental questions. As a result, many urban and industrial environmental issues are narrowly addressed as technical problems, divorced from the social contexts in which they are experienced. This disciplinary model is ill prepared to address the evolution of the urban and industrial environments of contemporary society, which requires a more complex analysis of the intersection of social, economic, cultural, and environmental issues.

Furthermore, it is industry and government rather than communities or workers that tend to be the clients for traditional academic research. These relationships, in turn, reinforce the dominant framing of environmental research as technical subject matter, somehow distinct from people's everyday experience. The absence of community or workplace perspectives in developing research programs on environmental issues establishes insurmountable distances between those who create environmental problems, those who analyze the problems, and those who experience the adverse effects of environmental problems.

This distance between analyst and those affected by environmental problems is also found in the social sciences, where much research focuses on the environmental policy process itself rather than policy stakeholders and the issues they raise. A new model of collaborative research based on a new type of university-community relationship is needed to overcome this divide in environmental research.

Efforts to construct a collaborative model for social research are under way in a number of different forums, although most such programs are located outside the university (Gottlieb 1994; Nyden and Wiewel 1992). The difficulties in establishing a collaborative research model on environmental issues can be traced in part to how environmental questions—and associated social movements and public policies—have been framed and defined, both historically and in contemporary settings. The environmental movement and environmental policy systems have all too often been narrowly associated with efforts to effectively manage or protect the natural environment as something *separate* from urban and industrial settings and processes. There is, however, a powerful tradition of environmental advocacy related to everyday life in industrial communities and among urban dwellers (Dowie 1995; Gottlieb 1993). Such an approach contrasts a mainstream tradition of environmentalism, which today can be understood as advocacy and watchdogging of the elaborate environmental policy process established primarily during the past 25 years, and an alternative environmentalism embedded in local communities and addressing issues of everyday life. This latter movement is associated today with the new advocacy of environmental justice (addressing issues of equity and discrimination along race, class, and gender lines) (Hofrichter 1993) and pollution prevention and toxics use reduction (raising the possibilities of new forms of urban and industrial design of products, processes, land uses, and infrastructure) (Gottlieb 1995).

Both environmental justice and pollution prevention movements have the most direct potential to influence a collaborative model for environmental research. Those influences are just now beginning to be felt within environmental studies and environmental policy programs at a handful of universities around the country where some research has incorporated community concerns. One particular program of community-based research has evolved through an interdisciplinary teaching and research center established at the University of California at Los Angeles. This program, the Pollution Prevention Education and Research Center (PPERC), addresses a broad range of issues associated with industrial production processes and the use of material resources. It has defined its mission as follows: "To conserve resources and reduce or eliminate the use of toxic substances through an interdisciplinary program of education, research and outreach grounded in a philosophy of prevention rather than control" (PPERC 1994).

One of the distinctive aspects of PPERC has been its broad approach to pollution prevention. Rather than conceiving of pollution prevention as merely a technical problem, PPERC's approach addresses the social and cultural dynamics that can serve both as barriers to and opportunities for pollution prevention. At the same time, PPERC projects have linked, through their methodology, research focus, and client relationships, issues of environmental risk and justice, pollution prevention, industrial restructuring, and economic development. The collaborative relationship between environmental researchers and community actors is a fundamental feature of this research. Two such projects are described here.

Example 1: Toxic Cleaning Products Used in Janitorial Service Work

This project involves a series of case studies that seek to document the hazardous elements in cleaning products used by janitorial service employees in commercial establishments, and it provides opportunities for employee input and access to information about these products and less hazardous alternatives. The case studies seek in part to analyze how employee input regarding the use of hazardous products and possible alternatives can result in a more inclusive form of risk analysis and a more effective pollution prevention-based product or process.

Many janitorial cleaning products contain chemicals that are classified as hazardous or toxic, although occupational exposures to such chemicals are poorly regulated and the risks to janitors have not been well characterized. To protect janitorial workers, OSHA regulations require explicit information on the dangers, and they require training on safety equipment where hazardous and toxic products are used (Hazard Communication Standard 1983). However, employers and contractors in the janitorial services industry can't always guarantee that products and safety equipment will be used appropriately, for a number of reasons. The highly competitive bidding situation in the janitorial service industry may not leave employers with sufficient resources for good training and supervision. Language barriers may prevent adequate communication of hazards and handling procedures. Extreme pressures on janitors to clean very quickly may cause them to disregard safety equipment, fearing that it may slow them down. Moreover, monitoring working conditions can be very difficult, since janitorial cleaning is done at so many different locations, whether public, commercial, industrial, or retail buildings, and by many different janitorial service companies (Gardener 1994).

As a result, janitors can be exposed to significant risks in the workplace, aggravated by prolonged and frequent exposures to many different hazardous chemicals. In communities such as Los Angeles, risk and hazard issues are compounded by the fact that the janitorial workforce is made up largely of immigrants. OSHA-mandated "material data safety sheets," often the only source of information about cleaning product hazards, are almost never translated, and the information provided is often obscure and sometimes incomprehensibly presented (Kolp et al. 1993).

One goal of the project then is to determine how janitors perceive the risks from the toxic and hazardous chemicals in cleaning products, and how they act as a result. This is important to know since it affects how janitors will use cleaning products and safety equipment.

Many factors besides information on product hazards influence how workers view risks from the products, and people do not respond equally to the same risk. These factors include a person's economic situation and cultural background, beliefs about control over one's life and environment, and previous experiences with cleaning products.

In pursuing such research it is crucial to develop a framework that allows the janitors themselves to become research participants as well as the subjects of research. This collaborative research model includes identifying the appropriate forums (focus groups, structured interviews, after-hours settings) for gathering information about how risks are perceived and experienced, as well as constructing a stakeholder/participatory model for evaluating products (including "greener" products introduced as alternatives by companies wishing to reduce potential hazards and liabilities). In one of the more striking preliminary findings of the project, companies that introduced greener products without workforce (stakeholder) input discovered significant resistance from janitors who were still required to perform the same tasks within the same time frame; that is, product changes were attempted without process changes in the way the tasks were performed. Such janitor resistance was in turn identified as a barrier to pollution prevention. This outcome contrasted significantly with another case study that established a stakeholder process at the outset, and the janitors themselves became part of the evaluation process of identifying risks; selecting an alternative product; reviewing how tasks could best be performed; and then comparing the performance, risks experienced, and costs involved (City of Santa Monica 1994).

Ultimately, this project seeks to develop a set of evaluation tools for decreasing environmental and occupational risks from cleaning products. Such a pollution prevention tool kit needs to include a set of guidelines for evaluating and selecting various cleaning products; recommendations for training in how to use products and communicate product risks; and guidelines on methods for obtaining janitor feedback on cleaning procedures and cleaning product performance and risk. Without a participatory framework, this tool kit could not be successfully developed.

Example 2: Greener Garment Care— From Dry Cleaning to Wet Cleaning

This project involves a detailed analysis of the issues associated with the use of perchloroethylene in the dry-cleaning industry and the opportunities and barriers for switching to a nontoxic cleaning process. The project includes an analysis of the structure of the dry-cleaning industry, a comprehensive survey of dry cleaners in the Los Angeles and Chicago regions about their choice of cleaning technologies, and an examination of the potential for community-industry collaboration in developing incentives for less toxic production choices. The project in Los Angeles is specifically exploring the potential for input and participation by Korean community groups (70 percent of the dry cleaners in Los Angeles are Korean owned) in developing demonstration projects based on this model, while also addressing the Korean dry cleaners' deep-seated mistrust of government regulation of chemical use in the industry (Hill 1995).

In the past three decades, dry-cleaning operations in the United States have increasingly relied on the use of perchloroethylene (perc) as their preferred solvent, establishing dry cleaning as the single largest market for perc. Perc, however, has come to be regulated by federal and state agencies as a hazardous air pollutant. Such regulations have assumed the absence of alternative, non-perc-based cleaning technologies (U.S. EPA 1991). However, recent evaluations of a new approach to dry cleaning—substituting water for chemicals in the cleaning process, or "wet cleaning"—suggest a possible pollution prevention framework for eliminating the use of perc. Yet significant resistance to this approach remains within the dry-cleaning industry itself. In urban centers such as Los Angeles and Chicago, industry resistance to environmental regulation and acceptance of a pollution prevention alternative is influenced by the presence of a single dominant ethnic group (recently arrived Korean immigrants) within the industry. The ethnic dimension to this industrywide resistance means that technological feasibility is not enough to encourage the adoption of pollution prevention practices. Other social and cultural issues are at work that complicate the transition to cleaner alternatives.

This project thus seeks to address two related issues: the feasibility of a pollution prevention outcome in the dry-cleaning industry, and the ethnic and community issues associated with it. The project initially undertook a comprehensive review of the environmental, economic, and industry-specific issues related to perc use in dry cleaning; it was a classic pollution prevention research question. At the same time, the project also seeks to evaluate the viability of the wet-cleaning process as an alternative technology at the Los Angeles demonstration site. But this classic pollution prevention research question—is there a viable alternative technology—cannot be answered in isolation from the analysis of the community and ethnic group dynamics associated with dry-cleaning industry attitudes. Thus an analysis of the policy instruments and financial and technical resources that can be linked to specific community-based strategies is necessary if potential pollution prevention outcomes are to succeed.

The key to this approach is the collaborative, participatory nature of the research process. Understanding the dynamics of the dry-cleaning industry and the interplay of regulator and regulated community is crucial to the question of whether an alternative pollution prevention approach is accepted and ultimately prevails. In this instance, the research process is aided by the participation of Korean community groups, including the Korean Youth and Community Center, both in exploring community dynamics and identifying appropriate policy instruments capable of accomplishing a pollution prevention outcome. The interest of the Korean community groups has been heightened in part due to the possible choice of a wet-cleaning shop as a viable investment opportunity for Korean liquor store owners whose establishments were destroyed during the civil unrest in Los Angeles in 1992.

Conclusion

Each of the University of California at Los Angeles projects described here requires a degree of collaboration in order to accomplish the kind of research proposed. The "Toxic Cleaning Products" project, for example, is contingent upon the active participation of the janitors in identifying risks and evaluating alternative products, and ultimately in establishing an inclusive stakeholder model in pollution prevention decision making. The dry-cleaning study, though structured around evaluations of industry structure, chemical use, and technological alternatives, similarly requires an understanding of the social and cultural context in which the industry has evolved, including chemical use, choice of technology, and response to government regulation. Involvement of both the Korean community groups and the Korean dry-cleaning trade association has been essential to the research process itself. Community-based collaborative research not only represents a new approach for university researchers working on environmental issues, it signals a reexamination of the research process itself.

EDITORS' COMMENTS

Whereas Case Study 7 approaches the lead problem from a single discipline—chemistry—this case study argues for the importance of interdisciplinary work and the value of the "bias" introduced by community perspectives. In this case, Robert Gottlieb, Professor of Urban Studies in the School of Public Policy and Social Research at the University of California at Los Angeles, discusses the collaborative research activities of the Pollution Prevention Education and Research Center at the university. Gottlieb starts from the premise that research on environmental issues must distance itself from industry and government and instead be allied with community interests. He shows how the involvement of "subjects" (janitors and dry cleaners) in the research process changes the research outcome and leads to a more inclusive form of risk analysis and more effective pollution prevention products to be used in industry.

Gottlieb makes a strong case for interdisciplinary, community-based research on environmental problems, arguing that the "science" of environmental problems must also be contextualized by social scientific insights. If the environment is where we live, work, and play, Gottlieb argues, then research agendas ought to grow out of the concerns of local communities. People for whom the issues matter need to be involved in defining environmental problems and participating in solution-oriented research.

Local Knowledge and Collaborative Environmental Action Research

Devon Pena, Colorado College, and
Joe Gallegos, Farmer and Activist

Knowledge is power, and where there is power there is resistance. Foucault's maxim certainly holds for the contested terrain of environmental politics. Between 1988 and 1992, the authors of this case study participated in a local community campaign against Battle Mountain Gold (BMG), a transnational mining corporation with operations in North and South America and the Pacific Basin. BMG operates a strip mine and cyanide leach vat processing mill in the Rito Seco watershed about three miles outside of San Luis, the oldest town in Colorado (see Pena and Gallegos 1993).

One of the most difficult aspects of our struggle against BMG involved efforts to document and legitimize local knowledge in the face of the enormous "discursive power" wielded by corporate attorneys and experts in public policy-making settings. This case study discusses some of the difficulties we encountered in seeking to document, legitimize, and use local knowledge in two institutional sites involving conflicts over the environmental impacts of development. We also discuss the need to actively challenge "expert" knowledge in the political context of environmental impact assessment. Finally, we discuss some ethical and political issues posed by collaborative environmental action research involving cooperation between university-based schol-

ars and grassroots activists. In our case, the collaborative research project involved simultaneously documenting and using local knowledge to challenge "expert" claims.

Local Knowledge and the Cult of Scientific Expertise

An enduring problem in the politics of environmental impact assessment is how to involve the local citizenry. Even when the local community is united and well organized against an environmental polluter, documenting and utilizing local knowledge presents numerous challenges. The way political and legal institutions acknowledge and legitimize different kinds of truth claims in public discourse is the source of the most salient difficulty. As one social critic notes,

> The formation of an academic "expert" legitimizes the [exclusion] . . . of those who have taught themselves—by experience—or who otherwise insist upon an equality of reciprocity in anything called the production of social/cultural knowledge. (Cohen 1993, 23)

Historically, the environmental impact assessment process favors the analysis by scientific and legal experts and devalues the perspectives and knowledge of local citizens. We call this the "cult of expertise," and it creates a situation in which privileged positions (that is, government and corporate experts) go unchallenged in determining the outcome of public debate on the merits of environmental protection (Levidow 1992). The result is a loss of opportunities for democratic participation by citizens in the important decisions that affect local communities threatened by environmentally harmful developments. The privileging of expertise can have a corrosive effect on participatory democracy and undermine local efforts to exercise control over regional environmental planning.

During the BMG struggle, our approach incorporated local citizens into research activities documenting scientific opposition to the proposed gold mine and processing mill. We began with a fundamental assumption: Local citizens have accurate and detailed knowledge of the local environment, and this knowledge can be explained and utilized in scientific and legal discourse (Shiva 1988; Pena 1992). Interviewing local residents, we found that their knowledge of the local watershed and ecosystem was extensive, sophisticated, and in the end more accurate than that of the so-called experts. By using ethnographic techniques, we collected information on the hydrology, ecology, and climate of the watershed. We documented the natural and cultural history of the watershed through this research. This local knowledge was useful for a variety of assessment hearings and in preparing legal testimony by local residents opposed to the BMG project. We also used it in education and media campaigns.

In every context in which we presented this local knowledge, the conclusions drawn by residents opposed to the mining project turned out to be accurate. For example, during the Mined Land Reclamation Board (MLRB) permit hearings, local residents testified that BMG's reclamation plan would fail because trees and grasses cannot grow without irrigation water in the arid conditions of the San Luis Valley. Ranchers also objected that grasses had to be actively protected from overgrazing by wildlife or livestock, and they provided numerous examples of the limits to grassland reclamation in the harsh environment of the area (with average annual precipitation of eight inches, a mean growing season of four months, an average elevation of 8,000 feet above sea level, and winter temperatures that regularly dip below freezing). These empirical observations, built on a vast reservoir of multigenerational familiarity with the ecology, geology, and climate of the locality, turned out to be quite accurate: All the trees in reclaimed areas have died; areas reclaimed with dry land grasses have been overgrazed or were never successfully established as indicated by their hummocky (sparse and isolated) growth patterns. The reclamation plots are a major source of erosional runoff that is choking streams and poses a threat to the operation of the area's ancient gravity-based irrigation ditch systems (*acequias*). Local testimonials also attested to the damage the *acequias* would receive given the flaws of BMG's reclamation plans. Again, local knowledge proved more accurate than that of the mining corporation's hires: scientific experts who, it must be noted, lacked knowledge of the unique environmental and cultural qualities of the locality.

However, limits were placed on the use of this local knowledge in the context of the water court proceedings associated with the BMG mine (Pena and Gallegos 1993; Pena 1996). The court was not willing to consider or recognize the use of local residents as expert witnesses; this was a status granted only to scientists and lawyers. The judge at one point privately remarked: "This would have been more interesting if the opponents [to BMG] had more money to hire better experts" (Pena 1996). This poses the obvious dilemma of a need to reform the legal concept of "expertise" which, as currently construed, denies local citizens much of a voice in court. But this further poses the dilemma of who is to take the role of legitimizing agents in the construction of public policy discourse. Although the legacy we inherit as academic scholars is not adequate for the task of empowering local knowledge against "scientific" claims, academic researchers must actively challenge the status of "expert" knowledge and convince judges that science can be grasped by "nonexperts." But this is not enough. Judges must be persuaded that local knowledge is also valid and reliable. Yet, scarce case material exists to construct the legal precedents that will legitimize the knowledge claims generated through oral history, ethnography, and other field research methods that fall outside the bounds of traditional hard sciences, whose claims are all too readily accepted by the courts.

Fortunately, some recent developments open the door to the use of ethnographic evidence with the potential to legitimize the "expert" status of local knowledge:

> Lawyers and judges who, until recently, rejected oral historical testimony have come to believe that it constitutes necessary evidence in certain types of cases. One of the biggest advances in this regard has been a liberalization of the types of evidence that are admissible in the courtroom. . . . The two issues which have been most problematic in the use of oral history in land-related litigation are *materiality* or relevance and the legal *reliability* of evidence. (Briggs 1987, 254; also see McLaughlin 1977; Teitelbaum 1983)

While the admissibility of local knowledge of the environment was readily attained in the MLRB hearings, it was much more difficult to obtain this result in the trial case dealing with BMG's application to transfer agricultural water to industrial uses. Colorado water law, based as it is on the doctrine of prior appropriation, treats water as a commodity that can be severed from the land (for further discussion see Pena and Rivera 1996). The judge in this case did not have to consider environmental factors, including the impact of transferring water from farming to mining or the degradation of the quality of *acequia* water rights by an inadequate reclamation plan that had been previously approved by the MLRB. The ethnographic evidence focused on issues related to water quality and the protection of historic water rights in a unique cultural ecological context; these facts were deemed immaterial to the case.

Given the limits of Colorado water law—its exclusion of environmental and cultural values from legal discourse—we must work to reform the doctrine of prior appropriation so that ecological and cultural knowledge is admissible on the strict grounds of materiality and rules of evidence. This is an explicitly political project that social scientists must embrace if collaborative research in this area is to yield solid progress in the empowerment of local people on environmental issues. As one land grant scholar and activist notes,

> The rejection of oral history is not a theoretical and methodological question alone, however, but one that has profound political implications. Oral history is people's history. . . . Oral testimony provides derailed evidence regarding the use of common lands and the nature of customary law. In many cases, it is not only the best evidence on these points, it is the only evidence. . . . *oral history is power*. It is a resource controlled by the community and most accessible to local residents, and it plays a critical role in the community's self-definition. Oral history

can also be a powerful tool that residents can use in defending their land and way of life. To claim that oral history is unreliable, that it does not deserve a central role in research and litigation, is more than an intellectual posture. Rather, it robs local communities of one of their most important weapons . . . [and] a crucial means of resisting the destruction caused by land loss [and degradation]. (Briggs 1987, 258–260)

The discursive authority of science in the context of legal proceedings must be challenged, but this can only be done if we legitimize local knowledge as an authority on matters related to environmental protection and cultural survival. After all, how can the critique of authority be assembled unless it is based on an alternative "people's science" —the material and empirical comprehension of the natural and cultural world through local, place-centered knowledge? As Paul Feyerabend has noted,

> The *theoretical* authority of science is much smaller than it is supposed to be. Its *social* authority, on the other hand, has by now become so overpowering that *political interference* is necessary to restore a balanced development. (Feyerabend 1978, 216; also see Ormiston and Sassower 1989)

Ethical and Political Issues in Collaborative Research

While the legitimation of local knowledge encounters numerous legal obstacles, the process of collaborative research is confronted by a number of ethical and political problems of its own. First and foremost is the "ownership" of the documented local knowledge. Academic researchers must not claim local knowledge as their own. Social researchers, in particular, have a responsibility not to publish results unless the community agrees to the distribution of the research findings. Moreover,

scholars should publish research findings as members of participatory teams involving local residents. If ethnographic and oral history materials are the people's history, then academicians must not appropriate this knowledge by claiming exclusive authorship of published works resulting from collaborative research projects. This would constitute a violation of the ethics of collaborative research and would also undermine future cooperation between researchers and communities. The scholarly appropriation of local knowledge is intellectual imperialism at its worst.

Another important issue is related to the conceptualization of research agendas and research designs. Scholarly researchers have a tendency to follow *etic* (expert-based) values in determining research questions and methods. They do so with faith in the conventional norms of canon-building and the modern-assessment view of authority (Ormiston and Sassower 1989, 98). Collaborative research must be governed by *emic* values, that is, the truth claims and procedures for gathering knowldege that are generated by the community of local participants. Emic methods are a necessary strategy for collaborative research since local people are involved not as "informants" or "subjects" but as co-investigators who define the research question and develop methods for generating evidence. In the context of environmental action research, collaboration must be based on recognition of local knowledge as the fundamental basis for building an understanding of ecosystems and watersheds. The procedures must also build autonomy—the transference of research skills from the scholar to local participants.

Communities formed for the purpose of analyzing and solving a problem are riddled with ambiguity and contradiction. The existing divisions of class, race, gender, and other socially constructed differences can generate conflict and dissent within the collaborative community. The social researcher must be aware of these divisions because they pose political difficulties that can undermine collaborative work. One of the problems we encountered involved claims made by a local who was personally opposed to the presence of academic researchers in the community. This individual played the role of the self-anointed "gatekeeper" and made numerous attempts to alienate locals from the academic researcher. Our response was to present the researcher as a consultant and not a leader, which was in fact the nature of the collaborative relationship. The gatekeeper alleged that the researcher was manipulating locals and imposing his own agenda on the community. The collaborative research team responded by declaring that local people were perfectly capable of deciding for themselves whom to work with and establishing the conditions of the relationship on their own terms.

Another problem involved tensions rooted in the tendency of the researcher to "exoticize" the locality and the tendency of the local participants to romanticize their own culture and environment. These tendencies must be avoided if local knowledge is to obtain power in the context of legal and technical discourse. While the researcher viewed the locality as an "endangered rural culture," the locals thought of their community as exceptional, and many of them lamented the loss of "better days gone by." This tension came to the surface when the researcher pointed to the loss of land ethics in the local community. It was a blow to the community's own self-identity as stewards of the environment. Discussions focused on how some locals were themselves engaging in environmentally destructive practices, for example, overgrazing, wildlife poaching, and excessive tree cutting.

The collaborative team arrived at a new consensus. We came to recognize that social change can undermine traditional land ethics and that this was a serious political problem that had to be confronted. If we were to make claims on behalf of local knowledge as ecologically sustainable, then we could not allow our opponents and critics to use the examples of overgrazing and poaching to undermine the credibility of the research. It was necessary to acknowledge that culture is not static and that the intrusion of the capitalist market in the region is an erosive force that produces conflict and change within the community. Moreover, it was necessary to document not just the examples of stewardship and sustainable use of the commons; we also had to document the struggle between "land stewards" and "pasture poachers" (see Pena 1994 for further discussion).

The presence of an outsider, such as a scholarly researcher, can result in the identification of contradictions that may escape the notice of locals. These contradictions, rooted in the political and economic life of the community, can undermine the collaborative relationship if locals feel threatened or betrayed by the researcher. However, this new knowledge can also empower the community by pointing to problems that might destroy the credibility of local knowledge. An outsider is perhaps in the best position to reject romanticism and indicate the pitfalls of the place-centered identity politics generated by locals. This, of course, means that unequal power relationships can emerge from collaborative projects, but there is no certain way of dealing with these pitfalls.

Our struggle against BMG forged a strong relationship between an academic researcher and the local community. The relationship continues to unfold and has resulted in a number of other research projects to document the environmental and cultural history of the area. These projects are oriented toward social action. The current research efforts focus on new problems posed by timbering operations in the watershed and the struggle to restore the common lands of the community (see Pena 1996). We are at a point when the research findings are being integrated into a variety of local educational and media campaigns. For example, the local community has organized a foundation to restore the common lands. La Sierra Foundation of San Luis publishes a weekly newspaper, *La Sierra*, which includes a series on the "Myths of Industrial Forestry." The series is based on local knowledge and recent research by conservation biologists. It thus represents a unity of local and scientific knowledge in the service of public education. Much of the research we conducted during the BMG campaign has also been integrated into reports and public meetings dealing with the development of a watershed management plan for the commons.

Collaborative research is an empowering endeavor, but it must confront a variety of legal, ethical, and political challenges that can undermine the legitimacy and credibility of local knowledge. Our work to build collaborative research communities must recognize that the process involves political projects that can challenge the "cult of expertise" while cultivating the autonomy of the community to conduct its own research. Until regulatory agencies and the courts embrace local knowledge as legitimate, academic scholars will be needed to empower local communities and present evidence in these settings. Beyond our direct participation in collaborative research, academic scholars must launch a direct challenge to the strict construction of authority in legal and scientific discourse. This, inevitably, will require efforts to reform the laws governing environmental impact assessment. But it will also require that social researchers establish strong alliances with natural scientists eager to work at undermining their own privileged position as experts. Collaborative social action research, and particularly environmental action research, must not just involve cooperation between academicians and local community groups; it must necessarily involve collaboration between social and natural scientists, lawyers, and other professionals willing to abdicate their authority in the interests of the empowerment of local knowledge against the narrative power of technical and scientific rationality.

EDITORS' COMMENTS

Devon Pena, Executive Director of La Sierra Foundation of San Luis and Professor of Sociology at Colorado College, and Joe Gallegos, a rural Colorado farmer and activist on environmental justice and sustainable agriculture, are coauthors of this case study, which seeks to legitimate local knowledge in environmental struggles. The authors argue that in conflicts over environmental impact assessments, the legal system gives undue credit to the "expert" scientific knowledge produced by development interests and government officials at the expense of local knowledge (cultural and environmental expertise based on the lived experience of locals). They show in their own research how local environmental knowledge is often more accurate than knowledge produced by the science of outside experts.

Pena and Gallegos make a strong case that collaborative environmental action research ought to challenge the hegemony of official science in legal and policy conflicts over development in rural areas where local knowledge is accurate and viable. They also discuss some of the difficulties of collaborative research and warn that participants must guard against unequal power relations in defining problems, conducting research, and disseminating results. Like Gottlieb, Pena and Gallegos show the importance of local knowledge in environmental action research.

Creating New Partnerships for the Urban Environment

KEITH HARLEY, Chicago Legal Clinic

This case study is actually about three cases in which academic-community research partnerships were formed to address urban environmental issues. In each case, the Policy Research Action Group played a key role in enabling the formation of meaningful research partnerships between community-based organizations in southeast Chicago and Chicago-based academic institutions.

Case 1: Protecting Nonprofits from Unknowingly Acquiring Contaminated Property

In 1989, the Chicago Legal Clinic initiated a community-based environmental law program to provide education and advocacy services to community organizations confronting urban environmental problems. Almost immediately, there was demand for a type of environmental service not anticipated by the Clinic's staff or board. Nonprofit community development organizations sought legal services to address environmental contamination of property they acquired or planned to acquire.

In some situations, clients sought advice before purchase. For example, in one case, a nonprofit development organization sought to acquire several city-owned parcels to build

affordable, single-family housing for the purpose of stabilizing a residential community near several old industrial sites. A Clinic attorney advised both budgeting for and obtaining an environmental assessment of the parcels. As a result, two parcels were rejected based on "subsurface anomalies." Other parcels were substituted. The potentially ruinous costs of excavating the "anomalies"—underground storage tanks—and remediating any contaminated soil were avoided.

Other situations, in which the Clinic became involved after the transaction was already initiated, were much more difficult to resolve. For example, a nonprofit agreed to accept the donation of an abandoned warehouse in the middle of the commercial district of a Chicago neighborhood. Before completing of the transaction, the nonprofit asked the Clinic for an opinion on the environmental aspects. This request led to an environmental assessment which, in turn, revealed environmental problems that would cost approximately $500,000 to resolve. The nonprofit refused to proceed with the transaction; litigation ensued through which the nonprofit's obligation to complete the transaction was avoided.

A fundamental conclusion emerged from these and other similar situations: An ounce of knowledge about the environmental aspects of

real estate transactions is worth a pound of subsequent litigation. A simple responsive action was planned. The Clinic decided to develop and distribute a plain-language guide to environmental issues in acquiring real estate, specifically tailored for nonprofits operating in and around Chicago. The Clinic developed an outline around four recurrent questions: (1) what are common environmental problems in the acquisition of property; (2) what are the important environmental laws; (3) what are the interests of key actors in the acquisition process; and (4) what steps can be taken to protect a nonprofit organization?

The problem in converting this good idea into a good product will be readily understood by any legal services attorney. The problem was finding time, especially to perform the research necessary to produce a factually and legally well-grounded manual. This research famine was particularly evident in scientific, engineering, and health information about problems such as asbestos and lead, where legal literature was also not helpful.

It was at this point that the Clinic received a request for proposals from the Policy Research Action Group, which was offering student researchers for community-generated projects. Through this process, Brian Banks, a Ph.D. candidate at the University of Illinois Chicago, was assigned to work as a researcher at the Clinic. On the one hand, Brian's internship was tightly structured. He was given the proposed table of contents of the manual at the beginning of the project and directed to focus research on certain sections. On the other hand, once the structure of his research was clearly defined, Brian was given great freedom in terms of how he completed his research. Providing Brian with this freedom proved to be very helpful; the final product reflects both his ingenuity and his own sense of how the

manual could be most helpful to community-based organizations.

The Clinic produced the 60-page manual, entitled *Not-For-Profits Beware!—The Property You Acquire May Be a Toxic Trap*, in 1992. The manual was first presented at a conference hosted by a local umbrella organization for nonprofit community development groups. Distribution of the first printing of 200 copies was targeted to development organizations identified mostly through the Clinic's foundation partners. Once these were distributed, the demand for the manual—not just from Chicago, but throughout the nation—was enormous. The Clinic received more than 800 unsolicited requests for the manual in just over one year, mostly because of word-of-mouth recommendations. It is difficult for the Clinic to keep the manual in stock. Today, the Clinic plans to update and reprint the manual, again using student researchers.

Case 2: Creating a Community Environmental Resource Center

At one time, the region that forms a crescent around the southwestern tip of Lake Michigan was a priceless ecological jewel, home to wetlands and dunes, part of the great Mississippi flyway, with lakes, natural harbors, and rivers existing in complex balance with the Great Lakes to the north and the plains to the south. This was the Calumet Basin. In the 1880s, in an attempt to assert dominance over the economy of the Midwest, the city of Chicago incorporated the Calumet region that stood within Illinois borders. The city filled wetlands and aggressively recruited heavy industry and manufacturing. Small neighborhoods followed, with the homes of workers backing onto the fences of factories and the edges of waste dumps. By the turn of the century,

industrial development spilled into Indiana. Towns like Gary were created for, and became synonymous with, the breakneck growth of American industrial capitalism.

There was a price. Every engineering marvel—the creation of canals linking Lake Michigan to the Illinois River and the Mississippi, the carving out of Lake Calumet, the development of the Indiana and Calumet Harbors—erased forever some aspect of the region's delicate ecosystem. Seemingly endless supplies of clean water and open land gave rise to indiscriminate dumping of industrial and municipal wastes. And perhaps most ominously, there were never effective borders between blue-collar neighborhoods and areas of intense industrial activity; to live in the Calumet Basin was to breathe toxic emissions, drink polluted water, and live on top of industrial waste heaps.

In the next 20 years, the landscape of the Calumet Basin will again fundamentally change. The recession of the early 1980s closed many of the steel mills and related industries, impoverishing neighborhoods. Abandoned sites once housing thriving operations are now toxic waste dumps, stifling redevelopment projects. Active industries that still operate in areas of high population density must balance the urgent need for sound environmental practices with economic survival. Evidence is now emerging that contaminated sediments in waterways and toxic runoff from dumps may threaten Lake Michigan.

In 1992, three organizations, the Chicago Legal Clinic, Chicago State University, and the Center for Neighborhood Technology, joined in a partnership to design a system-based response to address environmental issues in the Calumet region. From the perspective of these three organizations, the environmental crisis in the Calumet Basin reveals some basic flaws in the decision-making process. Effective citizen participation in environmental decision making and planning depends on ready access to public records and experts who can help interpret oftentimes esoteric data and processes. In turn, even if citizens are on an equal footing with government agencies and private corporations by being well informed, constructive dialogue cannot occur without a neutral meeting place. Finally, there must be a forum for well-grounded, long-term planning by local neighborhoods trying to participate in forming their own destinies.

In response, the three partners designed the Calumet Environmental Resource Center (CERC). CERC's mission was to provide residents of the Calumet Basin with the resources they need to participate effectively and proactively in environmental decisions that affect the region's neighborhoods, ecosystems, and economy. As its first undertaking, CERC was designed to assemble the full range of environmental resources relating to the Calumet Basin, and make these resources easily accessible in a single site at Chicago State University.

In 1992, CERC received a $5,000 research grant from the Policy Research Action Group. These funds, in turn, were used to hire Chicago State University student researchers who lived in the Calumet region to assemble environmental resources, and to purchase materials. A similar grant from the Environmental Defense Fund led to hiring several law student researchers from the Environmental and Energy Law Program at Chicago-Kent College of Law.

These student researchers ultimately acquired, organized, and made publicly available a collection of more than 1,600 resources. Chicago State University now maintains the CERC. The university provides administrative support through its Neighborhood Assis-

tance Center, a large room in its library that houses the repository, a meeting facility, and an adjoining computer center where citizens can access on-line services. Recently, the university hired a full-time staff person for CERC.

Case 3: Enabling Public Participation in Brownfield Redevelopment

What should be the highest environmental priority for southeast Chicago? When the group People for Community Recovery (PCR) developed an environmental agenda for southeast Chicago in summer 1993, their first item was "clean up contaminated sites." From the perspective of PCR and many of the groups that contributed to the development of the agenda, the prevalence of abandoned, contaminated sites throughout southeast Chicago threatens residents' health, safety, and welfare; jeopardizes the remaining wetlands and wildlife in the region; and discourages local economic redevelopment.

The first recipient of PCR's agenda was Region V of the U.S. Environmental Protection Agency, which was embarking on a geographic initiative for southeast Chicago. Today, there are signs that Region V and its state and local counterparts are accepting the challenge to address the havoc caused by former industrial and waste disposal sites on the southeast side.

Drawing from a list of sites proposed by PCR, Region V is determining whether some sites should be eligible for federal "Superfund" money to pay for cleanup. Twelve local sites are now receiving expanded site inspections through Region V. Although at one time these sites were not considered a high priority, Region V is taking the unusual step of reconsidering the U.S. EPA's initial determinations

in light of a 1990 revision in the national ranking scheme by which sites are prioritized.

Several less serious sites, which are not eligible for Superfund priority, are also receiving renewed attention. A federal grant will enable the Illinois Environmental Protection Agency to perform site studies, a prerequisite to cleanup. The Illinois State Water Survey continues its work to characterize the nature and effect of groundwater contamination in the region. Sites like the former Wisconsin Steel property are being remediated by private companies under the Illinois voluntary cleanup program. And the city of Chicago is convening an innovative "brownfields" task force to help devise practical reforms for improving the cleanup and redevelopment of contaminated properties.

At one time, the challenge for people committed to cleaning up contaminated sites in southeast Chicago was simply to get the attention of federal, state, and local environmental officials. The new challenge, no less daunting, will be to participate in the often drudging process of site characterization, cleanup, and redevelopment, on a site-by-site basis, to ensure the efforts undertaken will in fact enrich the neighborhoods and ecosystems of southeast Chicago.

Using a $3,300 research grant from the Policy Research Action Group, the Chicago Legal Clinic is working in partnership with the Environmental and Energy Law Program of Chicago-Kent College of Law to acquire and distribute information for many brownfield sites in southeast Chicago. The research model is as follows:

- **Document acquisition** Using the Freedom of Information Act, primary documents in the possession of the federal, state, and local environmental protection agencies are being acquired. A cooperative agreement with Region V of the U.S. EPA has been developed for the expedited release of its expanded site inspections.

- **Document review** Documents are being reviewed to determine site history, the nature and extent of contamination, remediation efforts, and responsible parties and enforcement agencies. Wherever possible, private parties engaged in remediation efforts are encouraged to release and/or develop materials for the general public.

- **Create summary sheets** Fact sheets providing essential information in an accessible, uniform format will be created; a uniform format for making primary documents available will be created.

- **Distribute resources** Fact sheets will be distributed to community organizations in affected neighborhoods, with invitations to review primary documents at CERC, and to have in-person seminars.

The expected completion date for this project is September 30, 1995. Since the inception of the project, the policy implications of this effort have been underscored by the city of Chicago's multi-stakeholder brownfields forum (the Chicago Legal Clinic and many southeast Chicago organizations are participants).

Conclusion

Environmental policy making is focusing more and more on urban settings like southeast Chicago. This offers remarkable opportunities for local residents to participate not only in solving neighborhood environmental problems, but also to redefine public participation generally. These opportunities will be lost unless these communities have ready access to environmental information and to technical and advocacy services. Academic-community research partnerships like those described here can be successful in enabling meaningful community involvement in urban environmental issues.

EDITORS' COMMENTS

Keith Harley is the Director of the Environmental Law Program at the Chicago Legal Clinic and the author of Case Study 10. Harley's research on the legal aspects of certain environmental problems in the Chicago area was facilitated by the Policy Research Action Group (PRAG). With a series of small grants from PRAG, Harley was able to research legal issues that help nonprofit organizations to protect themselves from unknowingly acquiring contaminated property. The information assembled by the Clinic has been enormously beneficial to nonprofit organizations—more than 800 of which solicited copies of the report. In another instance, Harley's work with community organizations on the southeast side of Chicago and Chicago State University helped establish the Calumet Environmental Resource Center, which is housed in Chicago State's library.

One of the lessons from these projects is that collaborative research is a rich training ground for students at the graduate and undergraduate level. Students involved in action research learn more than methodology; they also develop commitments to social research agendas that are concretely beneficial to community organizations. In other words, training students in the real-world setting of collaborative research can change their vocational aspirations. Our next and final case in the environment section beautifully illustrates this point.

Social Science and Environmental Activism: A Personal Account[1]

PHIL BROWN, Brown University

In August 1995 I spoke at a memorial service for Irv Zola, a major figure in medical sociology, who died in December 1994. As I said then, I learned from him, starting in graduate school in 1975 and continuing until he died, that sociology and social justice were linked, and that you could fashion a life in which you served both academic and political goals. Even more so, I learned that you couldn't get one really right unless the other was included. Irv Zola put enormous effort into disability rights activism and disability scholarship. He was one of the most significant leaders of the disability rights movement: leading organizations, fighting legal battles, challenging universities and professional associations on accessibility. At the same time, he was the most forceful developer of a new scholarship on disability, publishing in mainstream and less-than-mainstream journals, and starting a new hybrid journal, *Disabilities Studies Quarterly*.

A Background in the Politics of Mental Health

I begin with this, since this model appealed to me, based on my background. I entered graduate school after being intensely involved in civil

rights, antiwar, and related political movements since high school. In college I helped form Psychologists for a Democratic Society, one of the so-called "postgrad SDS" groups. We organized against the elements of psychology theory and research that supported war, poverty, sexism, and racism. We opposed psychosurgery and electroshock, and fought for the rights of mental patients, who in the 1960s had fewer rights than imprisoned felons. Like others, we held events and demonstrations at professional meetings, a major activity in those days. Still in college, I joined a new group that put out a magazine called *The Radical Therapist*, pursuing similar goals to Psychologists for a Democratic Society but with a more nationwide presence and supported by a growing national movement critical of mainstream psychotherapy as well as the more institutional abuses. Our masthead read, "Therapy means change, not adjustment." Increasingly we worked with mental patients rights groups that were spreading all over the country, and we found ourselves on the picket lines a lot. By the time I applied to the Brandeis sociology program in 1974 I was convinced that I would conduct research and write about these issues that I was taking to the street. From my dissertation all through my early years in the professorate, I studied and wrote about these same political psychology issues, with special emphasis on

[1]This case study is based on a presentation at the American Sociological Association, August 22, 1995.

patients' rights. I also wrote for very political publications, kept active on the front lines, and hoped that my academic work would have some impact on the real world. I felt I got it right when I was asked to speak to audiences that covered the gamut: patients' rights organizations, as well as a meeting of the New England mental health commissioners.

Why this background? To show that it was a completely logical step into studying toxic waste activism while supporting the activist groups. There were so many similarities between patients' rights and toxic activism. Let me mention a few: Patients were so often more accurate observers of the institutional psychiatry scene than were mental health professionals and social scientists. And, of course, the same was true of victims of environmental crises, who typically were the first to observe toxic disasters and environmental health effects. In both cases, the lay experience of illness differed from the professional one, as did the causal arguments. Both types of citizens faced considerable resistance from the governmental and scientific worlds, and both were stigmatized for their suffering. Both had a number of conditions and symptoms that were vague and hard to concretely identify. Both were often deemed untrustworthy narrators of their lives. Both worked hard to set up alternative services and groups to better deal with their problems. Both challenged the supremacy of unbridled technology, and both poked holes in the notion of value-free science. Finally, both led to important social movements that shaped much of the public discourse and action on their problem areas.

Activist Scholarship in Environmental Areas

My first excursion into environmental activism occurred when I began to study the childhood leukemia cluster in Woburn, Massachusetts.

That led to several articles (Brown 1992; Brown and Masterson-Allen 1994) and to my book, *No Safe Place: Toxic Waste, Leukemia, and Community Action* (Brown and Mikkelson 1990). I was convinced that the citizen's group in Woburn correctly viewed the problem and its source, and that they were being stonewalled by the responsible corporations and several layers of government. Interviewing families whose children were sick, a number of whom died, gave me an emotional understanding and investment as well. I viewed myself as a person who was both a scholar and an agent of political action. I believe the Woburn litigant families felt similarly, for two reasons: I was introduced to them by their lawyer as a trustworthy researcher who wanted to tell their story, and I interviewed them in tandem with my coauthor, a psychiatrist who had already interviewed them for psychiatric health effects and whom they trusted. It was not hard to realize that I would become a member of FACE, the Woburn activist group, and to take up their side in arguments with state Department of Public Health officials, in discussions with the National Academy of Sciences environmental epidemiology working group, and in many conferences and other venues. As late as 1995 I continued doing this, working with activists and epidemiologists to counter a recent Department of Public Health report that argued against an association between the Woburn pollutants and reproductive and childhood disorders.

Woburn was especially interesting because citizen activists worked alongside scholars in conducting a major health survey to detect the relationship of toxics and disease and death. Although my entry into studying Woburn came after the Harvard/FACE health study, that community-university collaborative approach drove much of my interest in the situation. Precisely because popular epidemiology and related citizen activism is a synthesis of action and research, the sociologist's task must also be to bridge that action/research combination. By this I mean that we are "translating" a form of citizen science through our form of citizen scholarship.

A related concern is to develop a research agenda that more broadly supports and advances toxic activism. In this light, my work on popular epidemiology has helped, I hope, to challenge the official epidemiology paradigm, so as to help citizens' groups. I view my work on the history and politics of the toxic waste movement as a way to help academics better understand that movement and participate in it. More broadly, I see the part played by myself and my environmental sociology colleagues as helping the larger public understand the importance of this phenomenon. I have extended my interests to the issues of gender, class, and race, which are significant both for academic and activist understanding of the toxic waste movement. (See Brown 1995; Brown and Ferguson 1995; Brown, Ciambrone, and Hunter, forthcoming.)

Another arena of environmental activism is in lending professional and organizing skills to activists in places that I am not studying myself. I have been helping people in Hanford, Washington, as well. This began with supervising a dissertation on the lay efforts to uncover the health effects of decades of Hanford radiation. It continued with my participation in a conference there last fall, and now involves my helping the Hanford Health Information Network design a research instrument to collect data for a large archive of people's health problems in the tri-state area affected by Hanford. I have also been involved with citizens in the New Bedford, Massachusetts, harbor cleanup, suggesting ways that they can integrate cleanup efforts with economic development. Similarly, I have been contacted by concerned individuals in Massachusetts and Rhode Island to help figure out how to investigate suspected toxic exposures in their neighborhoods, and I have been able to help them get to the right sources for this.

I also use the campus learning environment as a place to spread the word about environmental activism. I have developed an environmental sociology course that is centered around environmental health effects and environmental justice, and have introduced these topics into several other courses as well. I have developed several lecture series for which I have brought Lois Gibbs, Devra Davis, David Ozonoff, Beverly Paigen, Richard Clapp, and others to my campus to speak.

The media provide many opportunites to support toxic activism. In one case, I participated with community activists in a Massachusetts public TV program designed to get interactive involvement from public school teachers on environmental health. And at the urging of my university's news bureau, I have written op-ed pieces on Woburn activism.

Finally, I support local and regional toxic activist groups. For example, I lent my support in building the annual conferences of the Massachusetts Campaign to Clean Up Hazardous Waste and in getting concerned citizens to bring their problems to this statewide/regionwide group for help in understanding the source of their problems.

Negotiating the Terrain of Activist Scholarship

A question that underlies activism requires our attention: How do we negotiate the ground between the scholar and activist roles? I am fortunate in not experiencing—at least knowingly—any negative consequences for my mix of scholarship and activism. I realize that others may face more difficult circumstances. Perhaps some safety procedures are necessary. Certainly, our written language in sociology should not sound like leaflets. I don't mean that we write turgid positivist prose, but there is a lot in between. We should also ground our work in existing theories and approaches, of which there are enough to shape and inform these efforts. We are fortunate that environmental sociology has built itself on solid theoretical grounds, and by reinforcing that legacy, we can strengthen our influence and acceptability. By showing that our work is part of a larger field, we protect ourselves more. We should also make sure that we know enough about the scientific issues involved, for two reasons. One, we want to make sure we are taking the most plausibly correct position, and two, we want to avoid looking like untutored amateurs when defending our work in print or in person.

Mentorship is important here. We need to show our students the best models of activist scholarship by ourselves and others, and encourage them to work in that mode. I have supervised a number of M.A. theses and Ph.D. dissertations on environmental health and women's health issues, and I see this as a way to support citizens' groups. Just to mention three dissertations at present: One student is working on community response to an autism cluster in Leominster, Massachusetts, another on health effects and community activism at the Baird and McGuire Superfund site in Holbrook, Massachusetts, and one other is finishing a study of women's experiences with silicon breast implants. In all these cases, the students are taking similar scholar/activist positions to my work in Woburn. We need to always make clear that citizen action research has contributed valuable scientific knowledge to the environmental sciences, and that the action-oriented research of scholars has helped bring this to fruition.

Sociology has once more become integrally associated with social reform. Although some sociologists managed to keep up this connection, the professionalization of sociology made it difficult. Environmental sociology, one of the newest subfields, has been significant in rekindling that social reform connection, in large part because it derived its subject matter from the environmental social movements. Our task of integrating social science and social activism can help retain and rekindle the spirit of human betterment that has long been a part of sociology.

EDITORS' COMMENTS

Phil Brown, a sociologist at Brown University, has worked with community organizations to help them better understand their environmental health problems. Brown's autobiographical comments on his own career path illustrate how mentorship from academics committed to social scientific research and achieving social justice can change the lives of students and the communities in which those students work as collaborative researchers. Brown's starting point in his research on the Woburn leukemia cluster was that the residents of that community knew many important things about their problems that government health officials and academic researchers were unable or unwilling to appreciate. Again, in this case, the affected community was allowed to help define the problem and was thus empowered in the quest for understanding and a resolution to the problem. Brown also discusses how successful collaborative research establishes a basis for conducting other community-based environmental research, as he is now doing in Hanford, Washington. Finally, Brown discusses the politics and epistemology of the sensitive issue of integrating social science and social activism and concludes that doing so will "help retain and rekindle the spirit of human betterment that has long been a part of sociology."

Part III

New Models for Community-Based Research and Learning

The walls of the ivory tower are crumbling, or so the following cases argue. Part of what communities need to address today when they are confronting social problems is the development of a new model for education and research that brings together, on the one hand, the intellectual resources of the academy and, on the other hand, the concreteness of experience and clarity of vision of people in local communities. We can no longer afford to think of education and research as something that happens separately from the everyday lives of people struggling to build working communities. These people need the resources of the academy, and increasingly, academics need to be involved in research that addresses concrete social problems if our disciplines are to maintain a vitality.

The first case study in this part describes SCIENCE 2001, a model for taking science education to the streets. It is a practical way in which a university is working with a community to raise scientific literacy in children and adults who do not know basic scientific facts that affect their everyday lives. Three other case studies—King and Ramasubramanian; Kennedy, Stone, and Colon; as well as Ferman and Shlay—describe models of how universities can weave education and research together as part of the teaching process. Not treating these two functions as separate matters, all the authors look at new integrative models of education and community action.

Madeline Talbott's case study describes a community-based leadership training project run by ACORN, the grassroots housing group. The assumption is that there are talents in all communities—including low-income communities—that need to be identified and developed. Finally, Gallagher and Nahan take on what some say is the most important thing that many of us do in our lives—raise children—but for which we typically receive little training. In a context sensitive to cultural differences in parenting perspectives, Gallagher and Nahan describe a project that is aimed at improving the support system for children in Detroit's inner city.

SCIENCE 2001: A Community-Based Model for Promoting Scientific Literacy

JoBeth D'Agostino, Bryan Wunar, Diane Schiller, and Stephen Freedman,
Loyola University Chicago

The need for educators in the United States to reassess their approach to teaching science is quite clear. In international studies of performance in science and mathematics, American students rank near the bottom, and presently there are few signs of improvement. The latest National Assessment of Educational Progress (NAEP) study found that "despite some small recent gains, the average performance of 17-year-olds in 1986 remains substantially lower than it had been in 1969" (Rutherford and Ahlgren 1990). In assessing the challenge, *Science for All Americans* cites the lack of teacher education, "crushing teaching loads," textbooks that emphasize bits and pieces of information over understanding facts in context, and lack of cooperative learning as some of the reasons for this shortfall in scientific literacy.

The need for improved science instruction methods is especially urgent in the Chicago schools. According to ACT Assessment for the Midwest, the national mean ACT scores for 1989 in the natural sciences was 21.2. In Chicago, by comparison, the mean was 16.2. The elementary schools near Loyola University Chicago's Lakeshore campus feed into three area high schools where the average ACT mean score in the natural sciences was still lower, only 15.1. For students at the elementary level in these communities, the most recent test results available indicate that students perform below the national median grade equivalent (Iowa Tests of Basic Skills 1990). Comparing fifth and seventh grades, national averages were 5.8 for fifth grade and 7.8 for seventh grade. In comparison, the average scores for area public schools were 5.5 and 6.9, respectively.

According to a report by the Carnegie Corporation (1992), the children of America have a great deal of unstructured, unsupervised, and unproductive time, much of which is spent alone. Carnegie's National Education Longitudinal Study surveyed 25,000 eighth graders and found that 27 percent of the respondents regularly spent two or more hours alone at home after school. Respondents from families in the lowest socioeconomic group were more likely to report that they were home alone for more than three hours. The Carnegie report also indicates that children want more contact with adults who care about and respect them, and they want more opportunities to contribute to their communities.

In fall 1991, the SCIENCE 2001 project was created to address the deficiencies in science education that had been documented in the Uptown/Edgewater/Rogers Park communities surrounding the Loyola Lakeshore campus.

SCIENCE 2001 is a partnership between the School of Education and the College of Arts and Sciences of Loyola University Chicago and the surrounding community. The general goals of this project are to enhance scientific literacy and to provide structured educational activities for the community surrounding Loyola University Chicago. Toward this end, four separate populations have been targeted: current elementary teachers in the targeted communities, elementary education majors who would be entering the community in a teaching capacity, families residing in these communities, and established local community organizations.

A number of premises underlie the basic structure of the SCIENCE 2001 project. The research questions for this study were developed to test these assumptions. The specific questions were as follows:

1. How can university resources aid in increasing teachers' confidence and effectiveness in presenting science to their students?

2. Can established organizations in the community act as a conduit for science education by collaborating with institutions of higher education to access the resources available for implementing science literacy programs?

3. Can scientific literacy be enhanced if the larger community of families are reached on a consistent basis?

We set out to test these premises by developing a comprehensive scientific literacy program that targets not only current teachers, but teachers in preparation, families, and community support for science learning. Each of the research questions and the ways we addressed them will be discussed.

Aiding and Preparing Elementary School Teachers

SCIENCE 2001 was initiated to answer the question: *How can university resources aid in increasing teachers' confidence and effectiveness in presenting science to their students?* The SCIENCE 2001 staff discovered that this question needed to be addressed at two distinct levels: in-service teacher staff development and pre-service teacher education. As a result, efforts to develop programming to meet the specific needs of each group were undertaken.

In order to aid in-service teachers in presenting science to their students, the SCIENCE 2001 staff developed a series of thematic science workshops, emphasizing the integration of activity-oriented and technology-based instruction throughout the curriculum. Elementary school teachers from the Chicago public schools and the Chicago archdiocesan schools that serviced students residing in the targeted communities were invited to attend the series of science education workshops. Faculty from the Loyola University Chicago School of Education and Department of Natural Science worked collaboratively to develop age-appropriate activities and materials to be presented to the teachers. These workshops were designed to model successful science teaching methods, teach the basics of scientific inquiry and science process skills, and provide the materials and teacher resources necessary to successfully implement the hands-on strategies in the classroom.

Teachers completed self-report inventories describing how they used the materials and activities from each in-service. Eighty-eight percent of the teachers successfully implemented the activities in their classrooms. These teachers stated that the class time spent doing science increased throughout the period of in-service. Participants reported that their students found the activities interesting and were more willing to perform science-related tasks. The teacher workshops have continued each academic semester since their inception in fall 1991. While new teachers have continually been invited to participate in the SCIENCE 2001 workshops, we maintained a core group of teacher participants throughout the program. These teachers returned to their schools to share the materials and teaching strategies by providing staff development in-services for their colleagues. This model of in-service instruction has enabled SCIENCE 2001 to reach well beyond the number of teachers directly participating in the workshops.

In addition to improving the attitude and effectiveness of in-service teachers, SCIENCE 2001 developed a component to enhance the preparation of pre-service teachers. The emphasis of this component of the program was to provide education majors with a sufficient science knowledge base, effective science teaching methods, and the opportunity to apply the teacher training in a clinical setting. Teacher education majors at both the undergraduate and graduate levels participated in the SCIENCE 2001 project as science education interns. Their duties consisted of attending in-service teacher workshops, working as teacher's aids in elementary school classrooms, and teaching at after-school science clubs.

From their journal entries, implementation reports, lesson plans, and evaluation questionnaires, we concluded that the internship experience was an important supplement in their teacher preparation program. Most students reported that they learned more from their course work after participating in the workshops and clinical experience. All interns indicated that they view science as an essential part of the elementary school curriculum and prefer an activity-oriented method of teaching science. The interns indicated that their level of confidence in performing science-related tasks increased as a result of the internship. All interns responded that they would recommend the internship to fellow education and science majors.

In addition to the internship program and other clinical opportunities for education majors, the SCIENCE 2001 staff has worked to strengthen the undergraduate curriculum for education students. Faculty from the Natural Science Department have continually revised the curriculum for nonscience majors enrolled at Loyola University Chicago. This is a very important aspect of the project since the liberal arts core at Loyola requires three natural science courses. We have worked closely with the Office of Teacher Education to alert them to courses that model an activity- and technology-based approach to science instruction. With the combination of a strong science knowledge base and effective teaching methods, the SCIENCE 2001 project has developed a successful design for preparing the teachers of tomorrow.

Connecting University and Community Resources

In order to address the issue of improving scientific literacy in the community surrounding the Loyola Lakeshore campus, the SCIENCE 2001 staff needed to establish contact with resources beyond the university. In addition, we realized the importance of providing educational opportunities for children in and out of school. With this in mind, we set out to establish working relationships with established organizations within the community.

Our search for community-based youth service agencies led us to Alternatives, Inc. The After School Action Program (A.S.A.P.) sponsored by Alternatives serves as a leader for a network of community-based organizations throughout the Lakeshore community. They provide a means of disseminating information to all of the organizations, as well as a structure for maintaining relationships between the people working for the different organizations. A.S.A.P. had access to the organizations and the children they served, but did not have the resources necessary to provide structured educational interventions. It was this connection that provided SCIENCE 2001 access to the community.

SCIENCE 2001 previously established a series of science clubs at several local elementary schools. Although these programs provided effective science instruction for the children involved, educational intervention outside the schools needed to be addressed. The staff worked closely with A.S.A.P. to establish a network of community-based science clubs. SCIENCE 2001 interns were placed in after-school programs located throughout the Uptown, Edgewater, and Rogers Park communities. They were responsible for presenting hands-on science activities to their science clubs one to two days per week. The SCIENCE 2001 staff placed an emphasis not only on the science concepts and processes being taught, but also on the real-world application of science.

The children participating in the science clubs were primarily enrolled in Chicago public schools and ranged in age from 7 to 14 years old. The science clubs provided the children with structured educational opportunities in nontraditional settings. The after-school programs participating in SCIENCE 2001 programming included federally subsidized housing developments, church organizations, immigrant mutual aid associations, and community outreach agencies. All of the coordinators of these programs indicated a high level of interest in math and science programming following one academic year of participation in the science clubs. The interaction between the interns and the children was identified as a strong point of the program. The college students were looked upon as role models for the young children, who do not have many consistent mentors in their lives. All of the community sites expressed great interest in continuing the science clubs.

This collaboration with the community organizations set the stage for further programming. The SCIENCE 2001 science clubs stimulated interest among other community-based agencies. The SCIENCE 2001 science club sites were maintained and new sites were established within and outside the A.S.A.P. network. A.S.A.P. continued a leadership role in their network sites, overseeing the operation of the sites and recruitment of children and parents. The SCIENCE 2001 staff developed activities and materials emphasizing the real-world application of science and provided training for interns and parent volunteers.

In response to the success of the community-based science clubs, the SCIENCE 2001 staff developed the Loyola Community School. This program has been established to bring children in the Loyola Lakeshore community on campus. Three organizations from the science club network were invited to select middle school students to participate in the Loyola Community School program. The children participate in educational experiences at Loyola that may help them gain the skills necessary to meet their goal of achieving a college education. The program places university students as teachers for small groups of middle school children. The Loyola education majors develop lessons focusing on science, math, computers, and reading and present the activities to the children each session. The Community School consists of courses that meet for three hours every Saturday morning throughout each academic term, and a combination of academic programming and recreational activities for four weeks each summer.

This program has provided mutual benefits for the children in the community as well as the Loyola education students. The children receive structured academic activities that meet their individual needs and are provided the opportunity to build self-esteem and interpersonal skills necessary to succeed in today's world. The undergraduate students gain valuable supervised clinical experience, in which they can directly apply their course work to a teaching situation.

The Loyola Community School project has been very successful. The number of children and Loyola students involved in the program nearly doubled for the second semester of programming. The interest in the project indicates that this connection between institutional resources and the community will serve as a model for future community-based programs.

Family Involvement in Learning

Research makes it clear that the role of parents and families is pivotal to a child's learning and to education reform. The National Education Goals emphasize the importance of developing "partnerships that will increase parental involvement and participation in promoting the social, emotional, and academic growth for children" (1990). The SCIENCE 2001 project established programs to address the question of increasing scientific literacy in the family.

In an attempt to increase scientific literacy in the families residing in the Loyola Lakeshore campus community, the SCIENCE 2001 staff developed the Annual Loyola Family Science Night. This program was an opportunity to bring the families of all the children participating in the SCIENCE 2001 programs together. Families were invited to the Loyola Lakeshore campus to experience the wonders of science. Each year, parents and children who attend participate in hands-on science activities, computer simulations, technology application stations, and a children's literature book hunt. The science activities are developed and facilitated by SCIENCE 2001 staff, teacher participants, undergraduate interns, and the community-based science clubs. The large numbers in attendance have been the measure of success for these events.

While the Family Science Nights have been successful, families need to be reached on a more consistent basis to have a lasting impact. To address the research question of how to increase scientific literacy in the family, the SCIENCE 2001 staff began looking for a means of bringing education into the homes of children and their families. To accomplish this effort, the SCIENCE 2001 staff worked with the Chicago Access Corporation. The result of this collaboration was COUNTDOWN and SCIENCE * POWER, two interactive family television programs. The Chicago Access Corporation enabled us to make mathematics and science instruction available in the homes of cable television viewers with the use of their Hotline 21 television studio.

Each year, SCIENCE 2001 broadcasts SCIENCE * POWER, an interactive cable television program, into the homes of families throughout the city of Chicago. Using the Hotline studio, members of the SCIENCE 2001 team developed activities for presentation in this live television format. An interactive program, SCIENCE * POWER allows children watching at home to call in and participate on the air with the staff. Each show includes a series of hands-on science activities that the children can perform at home using everyday materials. Each week, a challenge question/activity is presented, and the viewers are encouraged to send their results and responses to Loyola. Each child who answers the question receives a children's book focusing on science.

COUNTDOWN, an interactive mathematics television program, was presented by faculty members in the project. Like SCIENCE * POWER, COUNTDOWN is produced live, using the Chicago Access Corporation's Hotline studio. The program, featuring an all-female cast of math educators, broadcast its 100th episode this season. COUNTDOWN presents mathematics concepts and uses language arts activities and children's literature to enhance the math topics.

The Chicago Academy of Sciences endorsed this means of family education, and signed on to participate in the presentation of SCIENCE * POWER. The success of these two projects led to the expansion of this approach to educational programming into the suburbs of Chicago. The Bensenville School District has established COUNTDOWN: Bensenville, with the support of Loyola University Chicago. This program is produced by teachers from the Bensenville School District and is broadcast to viewers in the northwest suburban communities of Chicago. The Skokie District 68 schools are in the process of developing interactive cable television for children in the North Shore communities. We support their efforts in providing educational programming for the students living in these suburban communities.

Conclusion

The SCIENCE 2001 project proved to be a successful model for improving the level of education for students in the community surrounding the Loyola University Lakeshore campus. Many individual efforts have previously been undertaken to increase the degree of science literacy among students in this community, but these were short-term reforms limited by the lack of funding and time constraints. By connecting the resources available to the university, local schools, and community organizations, we are initiating educational change on several levels.

The impact of SCIENCE 2001 on science teaching is a result of the model of in-service training. The in-service model provides staff development opportunities for in-service teachers and plays an integral role in the training of effective pre-service teachers. By combining science content knowledge, the appropriate methods and materials of science teaching, and an immediate opportunity to implement the strategies in a classroom situation, SCIENCE 2001 renders support for quality science education.

Pairing community organizations and the university has produced science education opportunities for elementary school students and university education majors. Such efforts as the Loyola Community School and the establishment of a network of after-school science clubs are products of this collaboration. In each instance, young students are presented with science and its real-world applications outside the traditional school setting, while university students are given a clinical site to practice their teaching skills and develop the confidence necessary for successful science teaching.

SCIENCE 2001 promotes scientific literacy through partnerships that reach the family unit on a consistent basis. The SCIENCE 2001 project draws upon local school and community resources to assist in the presentation of the Annual Family Science Night to engage children and parents in performing science activities. This same approach to science education is brought into the homes of Chicago-area families through the production of interactive cable television programming. It is this ongoing effort to incorporate science into the lives of children and their families that can have a lasting impact.

The SCIENCE 2001 project finds its strength in uniting community and university resources. The project aims to increase scientific literacy among all members of the community and, in the process, provides specific benefits for each participant. This goal is becoming a reality because of this mutual relationship between the university and the community, and SCIENCE 2001 hopes to continue the lasting cycle of educational change.

EDITORS' COMMENTS

This project was initiated by science educators at Loyola University Chicago who were concerned about the national—and specifically local—decline in science literacy among children. In collaboration with public schools in the Edgewater/Uptown/Rogers Park neighborhoods and several local community organizations, these educators started a program called SCIENCE 2001. Their goal was to increase scientific literacy throughout the community by connecting the resources of the university with neighborhood schools and community groups. SCIENCE 2001 truly is a collaborative effort, and its success depended on the ability of different community institutions to work together to address this growing social problem. Together the partners created science education opportunities that previous programs—developed and administered by single agencies—had failed to produce. In-service training by Loyola staff provided local school teachers with critical science education resources that they utilized successfully in their classrooms but that also led to the development of a network of after-school science clubs, an Annual Family Science Night, and science programming for local cable television, thus involving families and community groups in science education. This remarkably successful program provides a collaborative, community-based model for promoting scientific literacy in urban settings.

Research as Praxis: The Role of a University-Based Program in Facilitating Community Change

MEL KING, *Massachusetts Institute of Technology, and*
LAXMI RAMASUBRAMANIAN, *University of Wisconsin–Milwaukee*

This case study presents the links that have developed between the Community Fellows Program housed at the Massachusetts Institute of Technology and community advocates across the United States over a 25-year period as a model of dynamic university-community collaboration. We give examples of successful projects that have evolved as a result of this collaboration. In particular, we discuss several recent initiatives undertaken by the Community Fellows Program that directly and indirectly address issues affecting young people and youth workers. These initiatives have benefited the targeted communities, researchers, and university students who worked on these initiatives, in addition to the university community itself. We argue that the flexible design and structure of the Community Fellows Program have made it possible for the benefits of this program to spread beyond the immediate Boston/Cambridge area where it is located.

Community Fellows Program Philosophy, Structure, and Goals

The Community Fellows Program (CFP) is a one-year non-degree program functioning within the Department of Urban Studies and Planning at MIT. It has a mandate to serve community activists and advocates from the United States and Puerto Rico. This model was developed based on prior experience in the 1960s, when a collaborative link had been established between the Urban League and the Department of Community Psychology at Boston College. That program resulted in the creation of the Community-University Center for Inner City Change. The CFP has been in existence since 1971 and has served more than 200 individuals from many parts of the United States, including Puerto Rico, and from the Dominican Republic.

The program was established on the premise that reflection and research are critical in any social change effort. The CFP offers an opportunity for community activists addressing issues of racial, economic, political, and gender oppression to step back from their work in the field and spend some time on their personal, intellectual, and job skills development. They are simultaneously able to reflect on their work and place it in a larger sociopolitical and economic context. Through this process of reflection and analysis, participants are able to design a program and prepare an implementation plan that effectively addresses issues of concern in their communities. The program is based on the belief that developing individuals is key to developing communities.

Participants in the year-long program learn tangible skills that they can use when they return to their communities. These skills include grant writing, effective communication techniques, and the use of computers for a range of tasks such as word processing, computing, and database management. In addition, participants learn to identify and understand the dynamics inherent in group situations and resolve conflicts that may emerge in their work. Participants also have the opportunity to study other community-based programs and share information about the latest research on issues relevant to their work.

A typical participant in the Community Fellows Program develops a well thought out proposal for a program that addresses an issue affecting her or his home community. The proposal includes the classic elements of any research proposal: a statement of the problem, a study design, a budget, time line, and implementation plan. The participant identifies potential allies and establishes collaborative relationships with other agencies and individuals in the community. While in the program, participants also explore funding opportunities to support the program. Finally, participants visit their home communities every six to eight weeks and are required to present their ideas to their own organization and constituency in order to keep these groups informed and involved.

Support resources in the department and throughout the university are made available to program participants. These include participation in refresher courses to improve basic mathematics and computer skills; the opportunity to sit in on courses at MIT, Harvard, Radcliffe, Wellesley, and Boston University; access

to library resources; assistance in writing; and complete access to sports and leisure opportunities available to any MIT faculty or student.

Participants enter the Community Fellows Program in one of three ways. Some of them come from a city government department or government agency. These participants are nominated and come to MIT with the support of their departments. They remain on their department's payroll and return to their jobs at the end of the program. A second group began participating in the CFP three years ago. They come from programs and organizations supported by the Kellogg Foundation. These organizations use their program funding to support a person attending the CFP. The third group of participants is sponsored by non-government agencies and community groups who send a person to the CFP to design and develop a program on their behalf. The participation of these individuals often depends on a combination of foundation and community support.

Evolution of the Community Fellows Program

When the program began, participants came together to work on different issues of concern to them. In 1988, the director of the CFP visited the Middle East as part of a U.N. commission to look at issues affecting children and young people during the Intifadah. His realization that more children were dying in the United States in a time of "peace" than during the Intifadah in the West Bank and the Gaza Strip demanded some reflection which, combined with his experience as a youth worker for over 40 years, generated some new program objectives.

We began to focus our attention on one substantive area—youth issues. Our recruiting efforts and the feedback we received in the past six years indicate that we have struck a chord. Communities throughout the nation are grappling with a variety of issues such as gun violence, drug abuse, crime, teen pregnancy, and AIDS—issues directly affecting the lives of young people. Bringing individuals working on diverse issues together made it possible for them to understand the complexity of different substantive areas. On the other hand, bringing together participants who are all working on youth issues offers some distinct advantages. There are increased opportunities for networking and learning about innovative and successful programs in other communities. By focusing on youth issues, program fellows are more effective in providing support and feedback to each other because they share a deeper understanding of the substantive issues involved.

Youth Development and New Information Technology— The Current Focus

Since we began to direct the focus of the CFP toward addressing youth issues, we have created an impressive body of knowledge based on real experience from the field. For example, participants have designed programs to reduce recidivism among young adults; created educational curricula to nurture entrepreneurship among elementary and middle school students; and developed preventive approaches to address teen pregnancy, alcoholism, substance abuse, and AIDS. Other participants have developed approaches to foster creativity and leadership among young people. Some participants have begun to look seriously at the support networks that surround young people, particularly the critical role played by adults in the development of a young person.

Through his research, Delroy Calhoun, one of the program participants working to place young people in sustainable employment, discovered that their success or failure depended greatly on whether there was a caring adult mentor on the job site. A study conducted by an informal youth/adult alliance called WeCare also found that caring adults have a significant positive influence on the lives of young people. One of our program participants produced a monograph summarizing these findings (McGee 1995). Calhoun's research emphasizing the importance of caring adults triggered further research. We started an ongoing documentation project titled "What Works With Youth?" It is based on interviews with youth workers around the country and is designed to measure the features of a successful youth program. As part of this project, we conducted a conference in Wingspread,[1] for which we brought together youth workers who had participated in the interviews and others from different parts of the country and shared our preliminary findings. One of the most important outcomes of this conference was the creation of an opportunity for youth workers in the field to come together and hear the struggles and successes of others like themselves. Additionally, it was important for youth workers and program funders to hear articulate young people and adults talk about gaps in service provision.

This conference challenged youth workers to think about new program models for theories while questioning the rationale behind existing programs. Participants recognized

[1]The Wingspread Conference was supported by the S. C. Johnson Foundation, in addition to the foundations supporting the Community Fellows Program. A report of this conference can be found in the Wingspread Journal (Ramasubramanian 1994).

that effective youth work required study and a willingness to change. Finally, they realized that it was important to move the discussion of concepts raised during the conference to their own agencies and communities and strategize on the development of an effective and innovative youth agenda. The concerns expressed by our program participants during the conference demonstrated that youth workers immersed in their day-to-day activities needed support and affirmation. We publish a newsletter, titled "What Works With Youth?" to gather and disseminate successful experiences of youth workers around the country.

Since the mid-1980s, the Community Fellows Program has attempted to facilitate community-based computing. As with other initiatives, the impetus for this project came from program fellows who were working in community-based agencies interested in the potential of computing technologies. One of the first initiatives sponsored by the CFP was Community Bytes, a project supported by Lotus Corporation. This program introduced and provided basic computer training to the directors and staff in four community-based organizations in the Boston area that sought assistance from the CFP.

During the spring and summer of 1991, the CFP at the Massachusetts Institute of Technology, with support from the Boston Redevelopment Authority and the HayMarket Peoples Fund, sponsored the Roxbury City View project in which MIT researchers worked with a selected group of seven students from Jeremiah Burke High School in Boston. The project had three main objectives. First, it was intended to familiarize young people with computer mapping techniques, which would help them visualize their neighborhood and use these techniques to develop solutions to planning problems. Second, the project was intended to provide a mechanism for capacity-building with youth by involving them in the actual research and analysis. Finally, the project was designed to provide youth, youth-serving agencies, organizers, and funding agencies with accurate information about the community's needs.

Our experiences in facilitating the use of computer technology by young people has convinced us that it is one of the substantive areas that needs to be incorporated into the curriculum of the CFP. This is because we believe that information technology will play a critical role in the lives of young people in the coming years. The statistics on information technology acquisition and its use indicate that young people and people of color are more likely to be denied access to computer-based information technologies. We are also aware that young people will be severely handicapped in the new information society, because they will be students, employees, and active participants without the skills and knowledge to cope in that society.

As a way of mapping the terrain and in order to get some perspective on the issue, we recently conducted a conference called the New Technologies Workshop[2] in which several past and present participants in the Community Fellows Program participated. We learned through this conference that there was a big gap between information haves and have-nots. We also learned that in order for local communities to come on-line, they need to have access to more than hardware and software. They need to develop critical thinking

[2]This conference was supported by AT&T, the Benton Foundation, Kellogg Foundation, Ford Foundation, and MIT.

and a world view that appreciates the potential of information technology to address specific community needs.

The workshop has created many spin-offs. First, a number of workshop participants from the Boston area attended a program developed by Mitch Kapor and Caeser McDowel, with support from AT&T. This six-week hands-on course introduced the heads of several community agencies and foundations to new information technologies. Several former community fellows as well as participants in the original Community Bytes project attended. At its most recent meeting, participants discussed follow-up activities and directions to continue the work started through the study groups. Some of the activities planned are listed here.

- Participants agreed that the development of an on-line network would be a useful vehicle to communicate the position of community agencies, particularly those agencies serving people of color, on a variety of issues.

- One of the participants in the workshop highlighted the value of the group supporting the city of Boston's Blue Ribbon School Building Commission in their efforts to get technology into the public schools. The group has agreed to work on this area, and one of the participants who is a member of the Commission has agreed to provide information about the school building plan and other related information, which will be on the World Wide Web.

- One of our elected officials, a former Community Fellow and a study group participant, has recently designed his home page on the World Wide Web and has become one of the two or three individuals in the state legislature to do so. He is communi-cating with others and his constituents through the Web.

- We cosponsored a Technology Summit Summer Institute at MIT[3] in August 1995 in which 60 Boston public school teachers participated. This workshop increased their awareness and made it possible for them to see the benefits of using these technologies to support their classroom work. This workshop introduced information technology concepts to adults working directly with young people.

A second spinoff from the New Technologies Workshop, the Youth Voices Collaborative, has been created and supported by workshop participants. In this program, 22 young people from a variety of community organizations have just completed an eight-week course on new technologies. They created a home page for themselves on the Web and will be developing a youth-run bulletin board to foster and facilitate communication among youth.

Finally, the Community Fellows Program has submitted a major proposal to the Telecommunications and Information Infrastructure Assistance Program of the National Telecommunications and Information Administration. The proposal seeks to address inequities in access to information technologies by developing sustainable community-based information networks in six underserved communities. Participating communities will be brought on-line and equipped with suitable hardware, software, and hands-on training. Participants will develop their analytical skills and use information technologies to assist their day-to-day problem-

[3]This workshop was sponsored by the Community Fellows Program and the Dean's Office at the School of Architecture and Urban Planning at MIT.

solving and decision-making efforts. This project will foster intergenerational learning and facilitate collaborative work. It will network participating communities with each other and MIT, and with past and/or incoming fellows from that community. The project will enable participants to think critically about the promise and potential of information technology while placing the resources of MIT and the Community Fellows Program within their reach.

Conclusion

The Community Fellows Program is constantly evolving to meet the needs of program participants and to respond to the major issues affecting our communities. Under the rubric of youth development, we are addressing a multitude of issues related to education, health, crime prevention, mentoring, leadership development, and community development.

The impact of the Community Fellows Program is evident in the variety of programs and initiatives that are being developed in other parts of the department and the school. First, the research agenda at the Department of Urban Studies and Planning has been influenced considerably by the presence and the success of the Community Fellows Program. Youth development is now seen as a legitimate area that must be addressed by planners. The number of students participating in funded and unfunded research projects with the CFP and in the fellows seminar has increased rapidly in the past five years. For example, one of the student researchers has now moved on to the University of California, Santa Barbara, where she is pursuing a doctorate in sociology. Her master's thesis evolved directly from her participation in the "What Works With Youth?" project.

We also see faculty focusing on youth development issues as part of their planning and public policy courses, discussion groups, and grant proposals. For example, the international equivalent of the CFP, called the Special Program in Urban and Regional Studies, has a session discussing youth development within its seminar series. In addition, one of our senior faculty is organizing a colloquium on advanced technology, low-income communities, and the city. It appears that the department is taking seriously the issue of looking at the nature of advanced technologies and their impacts on communities. In addition, the university students and faculty have been able to take advantage of the experiences and rich knowledge that the fellows bring to the program.

Second, individual researchers have been very successful in linking their research agenda to the program. One of the researchers who worked on the Roxbury City View project was able to develop and market a user-friendly software program called City View/Town View, which allows users to map their urban environments using simple menu-driven commands and attach their own graphical interpretations and data to it. This program has been very successful in helping both young people and older adults visualize and conceptualize their own living environments and use their visualization as a base map to talk about issues in that environment.

Researchers who participated in CFP projects have moved to develop their own research agendas based on their experiences. For example, the decision of one of the authors, a doctoral candidate at the University of Wisconsin-Milwaukee, to look at participatory research concepts and understand the role of new information technologies in community-based decision making resulted from her participation in the fellows seminars as well as the Roxbury City View project,[4] which highlighted the potential benefits of participatory research.

Finally, the CFP has influenced both projects and programs in other parts of the country. In 1992, the Department of Urban Planning at the University of Wisconsin-Milwaukee (UWM), in conjunction with the UWM Teen University Program, offered an Urban Geographic Information Systems (GIS) workshop.[5] The workshop was designed to help the participants understand the power and potential of GIS capabilities within an urban environment. Through the workshop, participants were to become aware of information about their own neighborhoods and communities and learn how to use this to enhance decision

making. The design of the Urban GIS workshop was influenced by the Roxbury City View project. The University of California at Los Angeles has developed a program to work with grassroots activists along the lines of the MIT Community Fellows Program.

The Community Fellows Program has nurtured the development of individuals who participated in the program. Our participants are more aware of the importance of creating policy and ensuring its sustainability. Being at MIT has opened new avenues for personal development for our participants. They have learned the new innovative computing and analysis techniques as well as techniques to understand and resolve conflict. They have begun to look at organizational and institutional issues that affect their programs' success. They have also begun to understand the complexity of doing youth programming that really meets the needs of young people. The fact that former fellows have returned to participate and shape the direction of new projects, such as the New Technologies Workshop, is one indication that they are able to take advantage of the program's resources to serve themselves and their communities.

---

[4]This project demonstrated that involving young people in the data gathering and research efforts increased their awareness and interest in the learning process. It also pointed out that youth in urban communities were aware of urban issues to a greater extent than expected by adults and outsiders. Finally, it showed that young people had the capacity to develop creative solutions to urban problems.

[5]This workshop was funded by Environmental Systems Research Institute in California and by UWM.

EDITOR'S COMMENTS

The Community Fellows Program at Massachusetts Institute of Technology is a long-standing effort by a university to make its research support resources available to community organizations across the country. Mel King is Director of the Community Fellows Program in the Department of Urban Studies and Planning at MIT, and Laxmi Ramasubramanian is a doctoral candidate in the Program in Environment-Behavior Studies in the Department of Architecture at the University of Wisconsin-Milwaukee. The Community Fellows Program is designed to give community leaders working in social change organizations an opportunity to conduct research relevant to their work, time to reflect on the "big picture" of the social issues they are addressing in their communities, a place to share their experiences and research findings with other community activists, and resources to develop new research skills useful to their organizations. This program illustrates how the university can help leaders of community organizations develop research capacities. Moreover, CFP's emerging focus on youth programs and new technologies illustrates the synergistic benefit of conducting research on social issues in a collaborative setting.

Bringing the Community Into the University

MARIE KENNEDY and MICHAEL STONE,
University of Massachusetts, Boston

The College of Public and Community Service (CPCS) at the University of Massachusetts at Boston (UMB) is a predominantly undergraduate college, offering nontraditional adult students a program combining liberal arts and professional education. Collaboration between community and university is at the heart of the CPCS approach to education for careers in public and community service. Believing that both community and individual empowerment are enhanced the more community and college are interwoven, CPCS recruits students from low-income and working-class communities and labor unions; encourages graduates to work with and in the interests of these communities; brings community leaders and rank-and-file union leaders into the college to teach; facilitates student and faculty work on interactive projects with community and labor groups; and rewards faculty research grounded in community issues. Our definition of community-university collaboration includes all of these ways of creating interaction between community and college.

The Center for Community Planning, one of five career centers at CPCS and the center in which we teach, has been in the forefront of developing and utilizing all these methods of promoting collaboration, and the examples we discuss in this chapter are drawn primarily from experiences in our center, which is typical of CPCS.

Community Development

Central to decisions about student recruitment and the design and delivery of the curriculum at the Center for Community Planning is a particular understanding of what community development means. What do we mean by community? And what do we mean by development? When we think about the communities we work with—where we recruit our students, do our field projects, and focus our research—we are talking about particular disenfranchised groups, communities that don't have political power, or that have less economic power or opportunities than other communities in the greater Boston area. By development, we mean more than just bricks and mortar, specific job creation, or legislative reform. We aim to work with people in a way that increases their control over the decisions that affect their lives, developing people's capacity to intervene in their own environments and to bring justice to their lives.

This means working in community development in ways that are in the interests of people who have been left out of effective decision making for one reason or another. This usually stems from economic disenfranchisement, but it may intersect with race, gender, and other factors as well. We work with groups with whom we share a certain basic set of values concerning equity and equality. Our field projects work with groups that are unfunded, underfunded, or cannot easily acquire research and technical assistance without our help.

We work for and with communities whose voices aren't even heard in public arenas and try to empower people in ways that will not hurt other community members; that is, we work toward *community* development, not simply *individual* development. We do not simply hope that individuals themselves will be able to achieve a sense of personal satisfaction, accomplishment, or a better standard of living (goals that most higher education programs hold); rather, we insist that it be done in some shared way that recognizes the collective interest.

Community Planning Students— Access and Transformation

The fact that most of our students are older, from working-class backgrounds, and are diverse racially and ethnically makes it more possible than in a traditional university to confront barriers to community development, such as classism, racism, sexism, homophobia, ageism, and individualism. At CPCS, we have particularly emphasized access to groups that historically have been seriously underrepresented in institutions of higher learning —people with uneven academic backgrounds, women, older people, people of color, and low-income people. We actively recruit such students; we have a policy of open admissions; and we gear our curriculum and select our faculty with an eye to overcoming the sociological and psychological barriers to academic success faced by many of our students.

The institution is not only responsible for recruiting and enrolling people from underserved communities; in order to retain students from these communities, CPCS is committed to designing and delivering educational services

that are culturally sensitive. This means paying attention to both big and small aspects of how the college functions to serve this student population. It means adjusting (and readjusting, given demographic changes in the Boston area) our approach to curriculum design, our styles of teaching, methods of evaluating student work, class scheduling, faculty composition, and the types of student support services and facilities that are provided.

For example, some years ago a group of Native Americans were recruited into the college. One of the authors worked to get tuition waivers, arranged assistance as needed in basic skills development, and located some classes at the Boston Indian Center that were scheduled at times convenient for the students. But, in spite of these and other efforts to promote their success at CPCS, none of the students were doing well academically. Further investigation (individual and group conversations as well as classroom observation) revealed that for this particular group it was not culturally acceptable for the individual to stand out from the group; one was not supposed to excel as an individual, only along with the group as a whole. The solution was obvious, but not one that many institutions of higher learning could implement: evaluate the work of the group as a whole, while giving individual credit. It was relatively smooth sailing from then on.

While we have few admission standards (other than a target student profile), we have exit standards that can be generalized in a description of the type of graduate we aim for—competent, confident, and purposeful. We consider the transformation of individual students, within the context of community responsibility, our biggest success.

Over the course of their time in the college, many students have shown impressive growth in self-confidence. What they have gained is not simply a set of skills that they have developed or improved, but a sense of who they are and a sense of confidence about their capacity to do things. Here, where the students are the same people as those in communities we seek to empower, it is a fundamental measure of our contribution to community development. Our students, through their education here, their exposure to working on projects, and their exposure to students from different racial and ethnic groups, become much more powerful in their own communities.

At CPCS, students can earn academic credit through demonstration of prior learning, which they do with guidance from faculty. Helping students to name and "own" what they already know, and helping them to generalize from specific prior learning to applicability in new situations adds greatly to a sense of confidence. For example, K. C. came into the college with an interest in women's and community issues. She had some volunteer experience but was very insecure about her knowledge and her skills. She felt that no one would take her seriously, and she didn't take herself very seriously. Giving herself credit for what she had learned through her volunteer experience was an important part of her education. A few years later, this woman had established herself as a community housing developer with a strong track record and came back to CPCS to lead a well-attended public forum on housing issues.

Another rather different example of the growth that takes place at CPCS is a woman who, unlike K. C., had been very competent and assertive in her job. She was an aide to a state senator and had been his campaign manager. She was discouraged about the field of planning, having before her as an example the planning that goes on at the State House, and she was thinking of studying something else. As we discussed our approach to planning

and community development, it hit her that while people in the State House were very good at planning a campaign or getting a bill through the legislature, their version of planning failed to involve in the planning process the people whose lives are most affected by those plans. She is now considering a job change and is enthusiastic about her education and future possibilities working in community development.

Many CPCS students have a long history of working in the direct delivery of human services; others are the clients of these same services. Often these students are discouraged about the possibility of doing more than providing "band-aids" (as providers) or utilizing them (as clients), but they lack an alternative vision or way of working. At CPCS they gain awareness of the structural roots of the problems they've been confronting on an individual level and for which they have often blamed the individuals they serve or themselves, if they are clients. Students learn how to work with groups of people to formulate, plan, and implement a significantly different approach. This new awareness, combined with planning, is tremendously empowering. For example, one Community Planning graduate, who had been working (mostly unsuccessfully) on a case-by-case basis to gain mortgages for residents of a redlined area of Boston, later systematically analyzed the situation and worked with others to organize the community as a whole to pressure for (and win) significant concessions from banks and insurance companies.

Delivering the Curriculum in the Community

College education in any subject area for people historically denied access to higher education will contribute to community development in a broad sense. Just the fact that graduates get training and the credentials needed to get jobs with decent wages means that we are helping individuals to improve themselves. But, at CPCS, and especially in the Center for Community Planning, our curriculum—the types of activities and jobs for which we are preparing people—is more directly tied into community development issues.

In our curriculum, we emphasize taking on real and critical community issues. Our hands-on approach to community planning prepares graduates well for graduate studies and ongoing work in public and community service. Typically, graduates of the center are employed at midlevel to senior positions in community-based service agencies, community development corporations, local government, state agencies, and grassroots community organizations. Several are elected public officials on the local and state level, and the mayor of Boston is a graduate of the Center for Community Planning.

Many of our competencies (demonstrating competence in various areas rather than passing courses is the way in which credit is given at CPCS) require that the student be involved with a real problem, with a real group, investigating a real community. Students explore the contrast between official and resident definitions of a community; they document community issues and assess needs; they assist in formulating and clarifying community goals and devising and prioritizing strategies; they work on action plans, feasibility studies, grant proposals, and funding strategies for implementing community, union, and agency priorities; and they design procedures for evaluating the effectiveness of such endeavors. Sometimes this has meant working with other students on projects with faculty-selected community groups, but more commonly, students work individually or with other stu-

dents on projects that they initiate, with groups that they're already involved with or that they seek out because they're interested in the issue.

For example, a student welfare rights group that is still active in the college was the result of a number of students, many of whom were AFDC recipients, working with faculty to oppose threats in the early 1980s to AFDC recipients' right to be full-time students. In building the organization and doing community outreach, students were able to demonstrate a variety of competencies, and they were successful in achieving a number of their specific goals; they even produced an award-winning radio show. A current project of this sort is the Roofless Women's Action Research Mobilization in which recently homeless women have been brought into the college to form the core of a participatory research team reaching out to homeless women across the state. The goal of this project is both to learn more about reasons for women's homelessness and to organize homeless women to have a stronger voice in policy debates about housing and homelessness.

Many students do individual projects related to community or labor issues with which they have experience. Here are several examples:

- J. C. had been a volunteer working with a person with AIDS. From this experience, she decided that she wanted to do something about the inadequacy and insensitivity of services for people with AIDS. She undertook a project to develop a hospice in her community using the Community Planning curriculum and teaching resources to develop the skills to carry out this project, and launched a professional career as an AIDS hospice advocate and consultant.

- R. Y., a refugee from Cambodia and an activist within the Southeast Asian refugee community, identified cultural barriers to utilization of public safety services by Southeast Asians. He demonstrated much of the Community Planning curriculum through his design of cultural sensitivity training, which he delivered to police in several communities as well as to groups of Southeast Asians.

- R. R. is an industrial worker active in her trade union local and regional labor council. Through working on Community Planning competencies for her degree, she made a major contribution to the labor council's strategic planning project, which was aimed at better meeting the needs of rank-and-file union members and increasing the effectiveness of the labor council in addressing economic, social, and political issues.

- D. L. was a leader working to preserve open space in his town, organizing successful ballot initiatives for the town to purchase tracts for preservation and becoming a regional advocate and spokesperson for environmental issues. This experience provided the foundation for his work in Community Planning, which led eventually to a position with the Fish and Wildlife Service.

Field Projects: Teams of Students Working Under Faculty Supervision with Community Organizations

Perhaps the part of the Community Planning program that is most recognizable as community-college collaboration is our Community Planning Apprenticeship program. The center regularly provides students the opportunity to work on part of their degree through participation in field projects serving community organizations in the greater Boston area. Teams of students under faculty supervision work interactively with underfunded, grassroots community, labor, and advocacy organizations serving the interests of low-income communities on issues defined by the community organization. Students acquire and demonstrate technical skills, learn to analyze the political aspects of community planning, and become aware of social values in planning processes while providing research and technical assistance. In addition to the professional assistance, depending on the degree of their involvement, community members acquire participatory planning skills that they can apply in other situations.

Because the center's curriculum focuses on generic planning skills, students have been able to demonstrate competencies through projects addressing a wide variety of issues, such as the language needs of immigrants, affordable housing, media bias against Latinos, public housing tenants' rights, community control of development, youth roles in community development, antiimmigrant attitudes in a rapidly changing neighborhood, public transit and economic development in communities of color, training needs of health care workers, and alternative land use planning, to name just a few.

These projects generally last for two semesters. In the first semester students become familiar with the issue, the community group, and the neighborhood. Along with the community group, they analyze community needs and, based on this assessment, work interactively with community members to formulate development goals. In the second semester the student-community team develops and prioritizes alternative strategies for achieving the goals. Finally, they design implementation plans for high-priority strategies. Of course, this is the ideal scenario. Given the unpredictability of working with underfunded or nonfunded groups, almost anything can happen in practice. However, our experience is that regardless of what happens (including groups with whom we are working disappearing altogether), if a teacher can "roll with the punches," students get a terrific education through these projects.

Along with specific research and planning skills, students and community members grapple with the frustrations and celebrate the achievements of working in a team and being part of a participatory planning process. By working with under- or nonfunded grassroots organizations, students experience the excitement of working at the base, where the most compelling, conflicting, and critical urban problems and solutions begin to emerge. They learn a great deal about organizational forms and development, the strengths and weaknesses of different styles of community leadership, and urban power relations.

A recent project addressing youth issues in a multiracial urban neighborhood illustrates some of the possibilities and problems of Community Planning apprenticeships. Initially, an adult neighborhood watch group requested our project. Because they wanted to focus on youth issues, we expanded the community team to include a youth worker organization and a group of youth consultants that we identified. Through a small grant from Campus Compact, we were able to pay the youth consultants, which gave the important message that they had essential knowledge to contribute.

CPCS students, adults between 30 and 55, initially worked on identifying and candidly discussing their own attitudes toward youth, which provided them the basis to turn over power to the youth consultants. The needs assessment relied heavily on a "youth speakout" that the youth consultants planned and

chaired. The major problems revealed in this speak-out revolved around two interrelated issues: infrequent and poor communication between youth and adults and between officials (especially the police) and residents, both youth and adults; and lack of intergenerational and resident-official sharing of decision-making power amongst those who are most affected by decisions. Goal-setting for neighborhood community development focusing especially on youth was conducted separately with each of the three groups. The process was the same for each group. A visioning question was posed: "Think ahead five years; envision a community that is safe and healthy, especially with regard to youth. What are some of the things that come to mind?" Participants wrote down and then shared, in a round-robin, at least five points each. These comments were recorded, grouped into categories, and then ranked by participants. The results were brought to a joint meeting, where all three groups worked together to devise a common set of community development goals. Finally, students worked to devise and prioritize alternative strategies and developed implementation plans for high-priority strategies.

Our project provided an important forum for youth to make their concerns known to officials and to adults in the neighborhood. Youth consultants learned important skills—how to design, do outreach for, and conduct a major town meeting. As a result of their success, these young people have gone on to produce a weekly call-in cable television program on youth issues and to be featured speakers in a number of citywide public events. The city is attempting to form groups of youth consultants in other neighborhoods. The adults in the neighborhood really heard for the first time some of the issues that young people are concerned about. They found that they had some common problems in, for example, communicating with the police. The neighborhood watch group and the youth worker group formed a stronger working relationship.

Community Planning students learned important planning skills, including insights and knowledge that could only be learned in a real situation. They learned to value less-tangible results of a planning process (for example, empowerment of the youth consultants), and several expressed the view that the project had changed for the better the way they relate to their own teenaged children.

One common problem we faced was that the real world does not unfold on the semester schedule. This is particularly a problem in participatory action research (PAR) projects in which the direction and pace is unpredictable and determined by a community-level process. In practice, this meant that after the goal-setting process, the project ceased to be participatory as students hustled to finish their work (and get their academic credit) by the end of the second semester.

The products of PAR are often intangible. Frequently, students and community members felt they weren't accomplishing anything, especially during the month and a half of weekly meetings with the youth consultants preparing for the youth speak-out. Only afterwards, when the youth consultants favorably compared how we had worked with them to the way most adults worked with them, did the students begin to understand their role in empowering the youth.

It was hard for the student team, as well as adult community members, to keep turning over power to the youth consultants and to strike a good balance between capacity-building and turning over power. It was hard to work with the youth consultants, who, like most teenagers, weren't completely reliable in terms of showing up on time (or at all). Finally, most of the youth consultants had dropped out of the project by the second goal-setting meeting. Following are some possible reasons for this: youth expected instant results from their participation, and that didn't happen; the youth consultants got very busy after the town meeting—they accepted many speaking engagements and the responsibility for a weekly TV program; neither the neighborhood watch nor youth worker group consolidated the relationship that began with the town meeting; the CPCS team had a month and a half semester break and didn't sustain contact with the youth during that period (the assumption being that the neighborhood group would take on this role).

In spite of these drawbacks, the project was a tremendous success for the CPCS students and the community. For CPCS students, analyzing the strengths and weaknesses of the project and their roles in it produced educational benefits at least as important as learning and practicing specific planning skills. The youth consultants have gone on to give voice to other young people in their city; the mayor's office is replicating our planning process throughout the city; the neighborhood group has received funding and political support to implement several of the recommendations developed in the project; and, finally, several community members have become students at CPCS.

Legitimating Community Leadership and Faculty Research

A brief description of two additional forms of college-community collaboration will round out this discussion. A rather unique way in which we contribute to community development is the formal legitimation we provide for the expertise of community leaders and the work of community organizations. We frequently bring in community leaders as adjunct faculty to teach in areas in which they work every day. Sometimes they don't have the credentials that university teachers are "supposed" to have, but what we are saying in hiring them is that we value their expertise. We are saying that the work they do, what they think, is important and credible and that their practical experience is something we need and do not necessarily get from somebody just because they have a doctorate. This stamp of approval on the part of the university often gives community leaders credibility with government and funding agencies and even with their own constituency. And, of course, we gain firsthand insight into critical community issues and state-of-the-art community development practice.

We also credit the importance of what community groups are doing by using local community struggles as case studies in our teaching and by bringing in speakers from local community organizations to our classrooms and forums. It can be quite a shot in the arm for a group to read about their local struggle, to see it being used as a teaching tool for others, and to have community leaders showcased at forums. Just as we have tried to balance our curriculum in terms of theory and practice, we have always emphasized having a full-time faculty that is similarly balanced; we emphasize having teachers with some actual experience in the field. In hiring faculty, we value community planning experience equally with academic credentials. What this means is that we have closer ties with various community groups and issues than is usually true in a university. Our professional practice and research is tied into the immediate work of local community groups. Although we are not directly working for community groups anymore, we all serve on community boards, provide technical assistance and credible advocacy for community groups by being expert witnesses at hearings, do formal research, and produce professional reports as well as books and articles that directly help community groups and promote community development. Often through what we write and speak about we generalize from specific experiences in ways that can be utilized by other community groups facing similar problems; at other times our analysis helps raise a group's consciousness of purpose or of the lessons of history.

College-Community Collaboration Taken as a Whole

None of the methods discussed here for promoting collaboration stands alone. Each one builds on the other, and particular strands are less important than the whole weaving. Each institution of higher learning will utilize different strands and end up with a somewhat differently patterned cloth. But with commitment and creativity, university-community collaboration can be a highly effective educational tool and can strengthen university-community relations, while promoting community development. At CPCS, the major components of our collaboration with the community are agreement on community development as a primary goal of collaboration; the empowerment of our students, who come from low-income communities and continue to serve those communities after graduation; our curriculum, which emphasizes a hands-on approach to critical urban issues; our field projects, focusing on community-defined issues; and our teaching resources, utilizing experts from the communities we serve and emphasizing an activist faculty.

EDITORS' COMMENTS

The Center for Community Planning in the College of Public and
Community Service (CPCS) at the University of Massachusetts at
Boston is similar to the Community Fellows Program at MIT examined in Case Study 13 in that they are both designed to bring the community into the university. But while the MIT program provides a
one-year research fellowship for community advocates, CPCS is an
undergraduate college that combines liberal studies and professional
education, which actively recruits students from low-income and
working-class communities. The ultimate goal of the program is to
facilitate community development by building the intellectual capacities of individuals from local communities, who then return to work in
community development corporations, grassroots organizations,
social service agencies, and the like. The program places students in
community organizations to do research on real social issues; thus,
collaboration between the university and the community is at the
heart of this program. This practical experience turns out to be critical
to the jobs graduates land upon completing the program, as several
examples in this case illustrate. In sum, this program facilitates community development by making college available to people who historically have not had access to higher education and by designing
curricula and fostering research that is community driven.

The Academy Hits the Streets:
Teaching Community-Based Research[1]

BARBARA FERMAN and ANNE B. SHLAY, Temple University

Most social science graduate programs require students to take at least one research methods course. Although these courses vary dramatically across campuses, they typically teach the craft of how to do research separate from the content of the research itself. Actual research may be used to illustrate a method, but research content and its intended audience are not considered to be central to learning how to do research, particularly empirical work. Yet method, topic, and audience are intrinsically connected. The presentation of method as abstract science serves as an ideological device for maintaining conventional beliefs that the production of social science represents value-free, politically neutral activities. At the same time, bringing content, a nonacademic audience, and users of research to the research planning table invites criticism of research bias. Researchers are trained to be agnostic about either who uses or needs their work or even what it is about. As a result, much social science research is either of lim- ited utility (because of its irrelevance to real-world problems) or inaccessible (because of the method of presentation or form of publication—for example, in obscure academic journals).

New models for training students in the art of thinking about and doing research are necessary—models that challenge the segregation of method from content and that invite as well as legitimize alternative research processes. With this goal and as part of a larger campaign to more effectively leverage university resources as tools for social change, a new type of course was introduced at Temple University. This course, Community-Based Research, was designed as an applied research methods practicum for conducting collaborative research with community-based organizations as clients. In this case study, we describe and evaluate the course.

Course Structure and Goals

The central feature of the course is that students undertake a research project that is conducted for a local organization. Research topics do not emanate from either the students in the course or the professors teaching it. Rather, all topics originate from local organizations with the goal of being useful in aiding and informing the activities of the organization.

[1]We thank Irv Acklesberg, Frank Brodhead, Chris Schweitzer, Jonathon Stein, and Richard Weishaupt for being community-based contact people for this course, and students Susie Clampet-Lundquist, Neil Donahue, Richard Gilbertie, Svenja Heinrich, Gerardo Lopez, Mary Maguire, Amy Menzer, Eileen Morgan, Theresa Singleton, and Cameron Voss for pulling it off with good humor and dedication.

The course format is that students attend a weekly seminar and discuss assigned readings in research methods and urban studies. Students conduct the research projects under the supervision of the teaching faculty and the contact person from the local organization—the person in the organization who collaborates with the students and provides them with an understanding of the local context, utility, and need for the research. Linking content to method, the course brings with it a central theoretical orientation known as an "institutional approach" (Shlay 1993). The course is directed toward examining the decision-making processes within and between urban institutions as sources of powerlessness and inequality in cities.

The course had three complementary goals. First, the course was launched as an experiment, as a pilot demonstration in linking Temple University to the community. Students were told of the experimental nature of the course and were therefore aware of the investment people had in it. Second, the course had pedagogical goals. We intended to train students to conduct applied research with actual clients, to develop an appreciation for this type of research experience, and to be exposed to nontraditional researchers as role models. We hoped that students would discover the legitimacy of doing this type of research, get a sense of the joys and pain involved, and appreciate the higher stakes that come with doing this type of research. The basic pedagogy was to introduce students simultaneously to the *application of method* and to the *application of research* with the ultimate goal of exposing them to real-world organizational needs for research. Third, the course was an organizing vehicle—we tried to build a collaborative research community linking Temple University researchers to the surrounding community. The goal was

to demonstrate the capacity for doing rigorous research tied to social change and to provide local organizations with useable and useful research projects.

Course Content

The course readings combined methodological training with substantive exploration of key issues in political economy. The approach to methods was twofold. First, we sought to provide the students with training in basic techniques of research design and data collection. Second, we tried to provide an understanding of the research process that went beyond the conventional academic model—the solitary researcher engaged in pure scientific inquiry that is value free and undertaken solely to further the knowledge base within the discipline. At the same time, we promoted a concept of research that stressed objectivity and rigor but that also recognized the political and ideological contexts in which research is conducted and the multiple uses of this research. This approach was more difficult to implement than typical approaches to teaching research methods but also yielded more for the student researcher.

To introduce students to different models of the research process, readings were chosen that focused on collaboration, conceptualization, and the use of research. The assigned materials illustrated the experiences of the researchers conducting activist-oriented research. Collaboration between academics and community activists, while potentially quite fruitful for all participants, is fraught with tensions. The readings provided an overview of these tensions, an examination of which ones can and cannot be resolved, and how to deal with these tensions.

The readings also focused on the role of ideology, perspectives, and paradigms in informing the research process. For example, there are numerous paradigms of economic development that will lead the researcher in different directions. Similarly, the concept of community can be a highly contested one. Focusing on conceptual issues helped clarify the fact that no matter how rigorous, research is embedded in larger social and political structures and is never value free.

In addition, the readings illustrated the various purposes that research can serve. Supplementing the traditional model of "pure research," the readings contained examples of research that is designed to inform social change, research that is educational both at the individual and societal levels, and research as a tool for individual and community empowerment. The readings in urban political economy also served a dual purpose. First, they provided an overview of the political and policy aspects of economic restructuring and the impact on cities. In so doing, they provided the larger context within which the research projects fell. These readings underscored the need for community activism and for the type of research that the students were conducting. Second, these works were used to supplement and reinforce the methodological component. Students were encouraged to critically evaluate how effectively the authors constructed their arguments. This included an assessment of research methods (historical, case study, synthetic, ethnographic, comparative), data collection techniques, data analysis and usage, and overall presentation.

The course research projects were developed jointly by us and a group of people from community-based organizations.[2] The project topics were initiated by the community. There were three major criteria for including topics in the course. First, each topic had to represent a legitimate research project; a legitimate topic

was not muckraking but one directed at systematically addressing a research question using conventional social science techniques. Second, each topic was evaluated according to the amount of time it would take to research it; topics were included only if we believed that the research could be completed within one semester (although in practice, this was difficult to determine). Third, accompanying each research topic was the requirement that a person within the local organization be the designated contact person for the students and be willing to work with them and to be on-call.

These criteria permitted the inclusion of seven projects. For each project, we did a write-up that included a description of the contemporary issue to be addressed by the research, the organizational client, and the contact person; a description of the organization; a description of the project, the research questions, and the major tasks associated with the research.

We gave these write-ups to students on the first day of class and asked them to determine their first and second choices of topics by week two of the semester. The rapid speed at which students were required to commit to a topic reflected the need to have them begin the research immediately and get into the field so that they would be able to complete their field-work and write their final reports in a reasonable amount of time (in theory, by the end of

[2]The groups included both citywide and locally based organizations. The people represented Tenant Action Group (a citywide tenant advocacy and fair housing organization), Community Legal Services (Philadelphia's legal assistance for low-income people), Regional Housing Legal Services (a regional housing assistance and advocacy organization for low-income people), and the Neighborhood Economic Survival Coalition (a coalition of local organizations formed to increase the flow of capital to communities).

the semester). Ten students split up into five research teams, and each team chose a topic. The topics were economic development and barriers to small business credit, state cutbacks in General Assistance, the operations of Philadelphia's Department of Licenses and Inspections, rental housing subsidies and housing mobility strategies, and the efficacy of employment and training.

To stagger the workload and to provide feedback on the research process during the course of the semester, three discrete assignments were required. The first assignment was to develop a research design for the selected project. The second assignment was a review of the literature associated with the topic. The final assignment was a research report that included the research design, literature review, and the empirical findings associated with the project. Each successive assignment represented a piece of the final report. The goal was to have students engaged in writing and doing research simultaneously so they would not need to put the entire report together all at once. By the end of the semester, five reports were completed.

Conclusion: Learning by Doing

This foray into teaching community-based research yielded many lessons, including how to define collaboration, how students should represent themselves in the research process, and what organizations and students are best suited for collaborative research. Other issues will require equally careful consideration as the process of learning by doing continues, but some observations from our project follow.

Collaboration

The collaboration between the researchers and the community was only a partial one. The research topics were identified by local organizations and the projects were designed with considerable input from them. Yet the final products did not incorporate feedback from these organizations, in part because of time constraints imposed by the end-of-semester deadline. But it is also true that as teachers of research, we remained within the canons of the more traditional model of applied research, in which research is typically conducted *for* someone rather than *with* someone. In addition, no attention (by either teachers or students) was placed on either how the research could or should be used by the organization. Defining the work of collaborative research remains an issue that needs sustained attention.

Representation

A thorny and unresolved problem was determining how students should represent themselves to people in the process of doing this research. We called this "the problem of representation." Do students tell informants that they are conducting research for a graduate seminar, thereby representing themselves as students gathering information for no social and political purpose? Or do they say that they are conducting research for a local organization, one typically with clear and well-known political motives? Either form of representation is accurate. However, the graduate student representation may yield the most information (more data), while the applied community-based researcher representation may limit access to information. The access problem exists even when the data being sought is legally in the public domain. Students were instructed to represent themselves as students because that was their primary role. Each student paid tuition to take this class, and our job was to teach them research methods. The production of research for locally based community organizations was secondary to the course's main mission as a learning experience. Yet this argument, although plausible at the time, only temporarily deals with this issue. The balance between securing access to information and the ethics of how research is represented is at best tenuous.

Screening

As a demonstration project, we were concerned that it work well. The quality of the students and organizations was critical to ensuring success. Therefore, we did not embrace every organization or issue but, rather, screened both students and organizations very carefully. Screening resulted in committed participants and high-quality work, both central to allowing us to continue this type of activity. But the screening process raises two fundamental issues. First, screening itself is elitist. Second, if screening is necessary for success, what happens when the screening criteria are relaxed? Assigning students who are neither motivated nor qualified to work with an organization does not help that organization. Similarly, placing students with a contact person in an organization who does not provide the necessary time, attention, or guidance ends up cheating the student.

Time Constraints

Designing, teaching, and taking this type of course is very labor intensive for faculty and students. This is a hands-on course that requires a lot of preparation prior to the semester as well as constant attention and intervention during the semester. A unanimous complaint from the students was about time, namely, that one semester was not enough

time to do justice to the experience and to complete the required work. Students did not complain about the amount of work they had to do, but rather the amount of time in which they had to do it. Realistically, this type of course should be taught as a two-semester sequence. The first semester would focus on the research process and designing the projects, and the second one would be devoted to fieldwork and writing the research reports. Future efforts will be directed at building this two-semester sequence.

Quality

The quality of the students' work was bolstered by having a client for their work. There was a general consensus among the students that they were more motivated by having a person relying on them for a product than what a grade could ever do.[3] That students would be motivated to do better work because of the structure of this course was a pleasant surprise. But that students, striving to do their very best, were under severe time constraints is a serious lesson that must be taken into account for future course planning. Lessons about the process of collaboration, we expect, will be ongoing.

[3]This attention to quality and not to grades per se was evident in the revisions students did to their reports. Because students turned in their reports at the end of the semester, it was not possible to formally ask students for revisions as part of the class. Therefore, we asked students to voluntarily revise their reports and write an executive summary to accompany each report after the semester was over and the grades had been turned in. All students agreed to do the revisions. One student wrote the executive summary after she had already graduated! Another student, intent on making it his best possible job, had to be told to stop revising his report because it was getting in the way of his other schoolwork.

This case describes the efforts of a social science graduate program at Temple University to develop a research methods course that teaches students how to conduct research incorporating a community perspective in defining the problems, designing the research, and utilizing results. These academics worked with community organizations in the area to identify research problems that were subsequently assigned to students in the methods course, giving students real experience with community-based research. The authors discovered that this approach was indeed more sensitive to community needs and thus more useful for community organizations. They also discovered that the real-world research experience was particularly exciting for students but that the constraints of a semester created undue pressure on completing projects in an arbitrary time frame. The authors argue that because they are abstract, methods courses in the social sciences tend to present research as an activity occurring outside social and political contexts. This case offers an alternative model for graduate education in the social sciences that embraces the community perspective.

The Chicago ACORN Leadership Development Project: A Model for Community-Based Learning

MADELINE TALBOTT, *Chicago Association of Community Organizations for Reform Now (ACORN)*

ACORN (Association of Community Organizations for Reform Now) has been doing successful leadership development for 25 years. As a neighborhood-based, multi-issue, direct action organization of 100,000 dues-paying member families in cities across the country, ACORN is notable for involving low- and moderate-income people in leading their own fights for housing, bank loans and mortgages, improved public schools, jobs and fair wages, and decent living conditions. As a result, working people, senior citizens, and the unemployed have found themselves at the forefront of issue campaigns and the organization itself. This case study describes and critically evaluates ACORN's new leadership development program as a model for community-based learning.

Leadership development occurs through a variety of activities. Newly emerging leaders initially learn by doing—through holding and chairing house meetings, coming to planning meetings to plan the neighborhood meeting or an upcoming citywide event, and by taking roles in meetings, actions, and negotiations. Leaders also develop as they build the organization—they talk to friends and neighbors to encourage them to join the organization, turn out their co-workers and relatives to ACORN events, and participate in fund-raisers. Formal leadership development includes the national week-long "leadership school," which ACORN runs at least once a year; the three day "Spanish-speaking leadership training," which is also annual; and quarterly day-long leadership trainings in each ACORN city, which are usually run by local leaders themselves but sometimes include a national ACORN trainer.

Origins of the Leadership Development Project

In 1994, prompted by the following three factors, the Chicago branch of ACORN began developing a new approach to leadership development. First, the local organization was 11 years old, well recognized for its outstanding community organizing in two very low income African American neighborhoods of Chicago (Englewood on the south side and North Lawndale on the west side), and was discussing expansion. Fully 1,000 of the organization's 8,000 members were living outside of the two targeted neighborhoods, and that trend was growing. As a result of dramatic success in the organization's Reinvestment Campaign (an issue campaign to stop redlining by Chicago banks), families were coming to the organization from all over the city seeking help in getting a mortgage. Most of the families were African American, a significant number were Latino, but they were not concentrated in any one or two neighborhoods. Leaders and organizers felt that the organization had to begin to operate as a citywide organization, rather than as local neighborhood organizations in two communities. If not, the new members would have no way to participate, and the organization would be unable to capitalize on its fastest growing membership base—citywide, "at large" members. But the challenge of organizing and representing a citywide constituency in the nation's third largest city was daunting. Where leaders had learned to feel confident speaking for the thousands of members in Englewood and North Lawndale, they felt the need for more training in order to be able to interact with citywide players on a variety of new issues; thus they began to discuss a program that would help them prepare for that role.

Second, leaders and staff were participating in an internal evaluation conducted by the Woods Fund of Chicago, a local foundation that had funded community organizing for 10 years and was evaluating its performance and making plans for its future. As a recipient of Woods funding for 8 years, ACORN leaders and staff were involved in several of the discussions about the successes of community organizing and areas that needed improvement. Indeed, the evaluation reached the conclusion that, of those organizations funded significantly over the years by Woods, ACORN was the only effective community organization in very low income communities of the city. (ACORN had also received the Community Organizing Award in 1993, given by Woods, Wieboldt, and MacArthur foundations to recognize the best example of community organizing in the city). Discussions throughout the year about the lack of citywide leadership from the low-income community, the lack of visibility of leadership from any

community organizations, and the lack of grassroots leadership especially from the African American community convinced ACORN leaders that there was clearly a vacuum that needed to be filled. Further discussions about the need to develop membership, not just leadership, into active and effective participants in their own organizations led ACORN representatives to initiate internal discussions about a leadership development program that would eventually train thousands of members.

Third, Chicago ACORN had been growing steadily for 11 years by signing up dues-paying family members door to door. In the last two years, its capacity had grown tremendously, thanks to a new emphasis on members acting as volunteer organizers in the areas of membership recruitment and turnout. Between 1992 and 1994, income from dues doubled and turnout at big events tripled, partially as a result of members getting more active in these areas. With more members and more active members, the organization needed a corresponding increase in members' and leaders' ability to initiate, plan, and implement issue campaigns. We had members' involvement in building the organization; now we needed a broader involvement in campaign strategy and issue analysis. The question, then, that the organization was posing internally was, How do we provide leaders and then the members at large with tools to make them more effective community leaders? The Leadership Development Project (LDP) was our answer.

Leadership Development Project Goals

Throughout 1994, Chicago ACORN staff and leaders talked about the kind of leadership program they wanted to develop. Here are the basic components the Chicago ACORN board approved by the end of the year:

1. The training would have a popular education component; that is, the initial trainees would construct a series of trainings for hundreds and eventually thousands of members that would be run by ACORN members and leaders themselves.

2. The initial training series would invite "experts" in order to give the participants a broad view of the subject matter, but rather than give lectures, experts would be asked to conduct exercises and discussions that could eventually be duplicated by the trainees themselves. In fact, after every two-hour "expert" session, LDP participants would spend an hour evaluating the session and discussing how to run a similar session themselves.

3. The methodology for the training series that the LDP developed must be participatory rather than instructor or lecture oriented.

4. The training must bring each topic back down to the communities in which participants live and allow them to see how the topic affects them at home.

5. The training must be action oriented. ACORN members have a rich tradition of using direct action to state their position on issues and argue that position, to win change and commitment, and to get powerful players into good faith bargaining. They did not want to be frustrated with information that overwhelmed them about their problems and powerlessness, but failed to lead to action.

The Use of "Experts"

We decided to involve outside experts in four phases of the yearlong LDP. The substantive issues we explored included looking at an overview of the economy and politics in the country, city, and neighborhood; focusing more closely on specific issues of concern in our communities (housing, schools, and jobs initially); bringing in local power brokers to discuss how the city and our communities work; and offering skill sessions in specific areas that leaders identified an interest in (for example, public speaking, working with media, planning campaigns, politics, research, and computers). We talked to Pat Wright at the Center for Urban and Economic Development at the University of Illinois at Chicago (UIC) to provide some of the specific issue and community information; June Lapidas at Roosevelt University (she had done some work with the Center for Popular Economics previously) to provide some economic background; John Donahue, who was currently directing the Chicago Coalition for the Homeless but had previously worked with a popular education network in Latin America called Servicio de Educacion Popular; Dan Swinney and Nadja Papaillon from the Midwest Center for Labor Research, on plant closings and developing a local "high road" economy; Doug Gills from UIC, on the Chicago Empowerment Zone process; Barack Obama, community organizer, lawyer, and politician, on a power analysis for the city of Chicago; Sheila Radford Hill from UIC, on school to work; Fred Hess from the Chicago Panel on School Policy on failing schools; and many others.

LDP Participants

We spent two months inviting our members and leaders to participate in the program. We developed a fact sheet and application form that we mailed to each member family, and we announced the program at every meeting and event. The requirements for participation that the board approved were willingness to participate in two-to-three-hour sessions one evening every other week for a year, with two weekend retreats, and commitment to recruit and train 25 others once the training was complete. We limited the workshops to 25 participants. Despite the enormous commitment of time required to complete the program, we received 40 applications. The board interviewed the applications and approved 25 participants by the end of February.

The participants were all African American. Nine were board members of Chicago ACORN (elected by their local neighborhood ACORN group). Two were officers of Local 880, Service Employees International Union (AFL-CIO), a sister organization of ACORN's that organizes home care workers and has a statewide membership of 10,000. Ten more were very active members in the organization. Four were not very active; in fact, they were relatively new to any sustained involvement in the organization. Nineteen participants lived on the south side, 12 of those in the Englewood community—a low-income, African American community. Five participants lived on the west side, in the North Lawndale community—another low-income, African American community of one- to four-flat buildings. One participant lived in the suburbs.

LDP Curriculum

The first four sessions were on economics, jobs, and wages. June Lapidas, associate professor at Roosevelt University, had done graduate work with the Center for Popular Economics, and she led three of these—how the economy works; history of the economy since World War II; and the role of banks and finance. Dan Swinney and Nadja Papaillon, director and staff member of the Midwest Center for Labor Research, provided an analysis of the local economy and the tremendous role that organized groups can play in getting policy makers to choose a high-road, high-wage approach to economic development.

LDP participants enjoyed the sessions and attendance was high. Though it quickly became clear that 5 of the trainees were not going to participate, the other 20 were very involved, and began to bring in news articles and books they found that were related to the issues of the economy. Though the style of the presentations to date had been more lecture than discussion and exercise, there was an attempt by all presenters to involve the trainees in the discussions, and June Lapidas made some efforts to develop small group assignments and replicable exercises. Members expressed a sense of excitement about the process; they reported that they were reading the papers more carefully, brought in lots of articles on the minimum wage, plants closing, declining wages, and increasing profits. One member brought in a very conservative attack on the IRS and Federal Reserve. Another bought economics textbooks at a Goodwill store. They were heading in different directions but feeling both interested and challenged.

The Popular Education Model

The most fruitful session by far was a weekend retreat with John Donahue, director of the Chicago Coalition for the Homeless. Donahue spent years working closely with Servicio de Educacion Popular in Latin America, an organization that worked with Liberation Theology. When we first discussed how to conduct the retreat, participants were nervous about the applicability of a training method that worked in Latin America. How would it work with African Americans, they wondered. But the attraction of looking at the relationship of the Bible and the economy overcame other concerns, and the participants decided to give Donahue a try. What resulted was the most popular portion of the Leadership Development Program. The weekend gave participants a chance to get to know each other better, have some fun, and relax. Donahue's methodology, more than the content, was the hit of the weekend. Each of four sessions he conducted followed a similar process:

1. Posing a question, followed by additional questions (for example, What is our world like today? Was it always that way?)
2. Discussion
3. Introduction of concepts by the trainer, including writing key ideas on the board in a chart or diagram
4. Further discussion
5. Summary

It seems simple and straightforward, but Donahue, by spending more time listening than lecturing, and by changing the training to accommodate the input of the participants, convinced the trainees that they could, in fact, become trainers. By Sunday morning, they broke into groups and developed and implemented their own version of the training they had heard the day before. The level of self-confidence and excitement was very high. The trainees were ready to become trainers.

By using a popular education methodology, Donahue had built up the trainees' self-confidence in their own ability to be the trainers. In July, the LDP participants recruited 48 new trainees to spend all day Saturday with them in a training session that they ran themselves. Using Donahue's format and style, but changing the content fairly significantly, the new trainers ran a session on the basics of ACORN, the relationship of the Bible to our work in ACORN, what the economic and political scene is like in the world around us, and a planning session for the Chicago ACORN Jobs and Living Wage campaign—an effort to win

jobs and higher wages from corporations that receive city subsidies. The training was a big success, receiving very positive reviews from all the new trainees. The participants in the Chicago ACORN Leadership Development Program had begun to succeed in one of their goals: developing and conducting a training for many additional members of the organization.

Additional sessions of the LDP program focused on housing (Pat Wright, UIC); empowerment zones (Doug Gills, UIC); school to work (Sheila Radford Hill, UIC); and failing schools (Fred Hess, Chicago Panel on School Policy). Though the presentations were somewhat interactive, the participants decidedly felt that they might have trouble reproducing them as trainers themselves. There was too much information of a technical nature, sometimes about issues that had no clear action proposal. Participants liked the sessions, but started to rebel against the methodology. After their popular education experience, they were impatient with the lecture format.

Conclusion

The Leadership Development Program continues. It is moving away from the expert lecture format toward more discussion sessions with nonexperts. The group is exploring a series of popular education workshops on the economy developed by the Labor Institute. They plan to bring in experts for specific tasks, and to that end, Pat Wright and some graduate students from UIC will present background information on the trainees' communities that they have culled from census reports and other sources.

In October, LDP participants will hold another full-day session for new trainees. They have decided to do some basic training on ACORN, on the economy, and then to break into small groups on living-wage jobs and school improvement. The day will be participatory rather than lecture oriented and will end up with an action plan on the issue of interest. LDP members think they can turn out 70 or more to this training. And they are committed to continuing the trainings until they have each trained 25 new people.

The Leadership Development Program has produced a leadership core that is more committed and more self-confident than ever before. The solidarity developed by the partic- ipants, and their increasing commitment to the struggle, are perhaps more important than any particular content in the training. We are moving toward establishing regular training series that we are committed to running for the membership at large, thus deepening the understanding and commitment of hundreds and eventually thousands of low-income people in Chicago neighborhoods to organize and work for a better community.

EDITORS' COMMENTS

In this case we learn that community leadership development happens from the ground up as well as the top down. Whereas the two previous case studies described bringing the community into the university, in this case, Madeline Talbott, the Director of Chicago's Association of Community Organizations for Reform Now (ACORN) describes bringing university expertise to the community, at the community's invitation. Chicago ACORN's model of leadership development—patterned consciously after Liberation Theology's reflection/action dynamic—illustrates the ability of community organization to develop themselves. The Leadership Development Project (LDP) participants utilized academic "experts" to help them develop models for helping themselves. The LDP has produced a leadership core that is more committed, self-confident, and well equipped to continue their struggle for fair housing, better schools, and more jobs.

Cross-Cultural Parenting on Detroit's Eastside: Establishing Community-Based Parenting in Multicultural Neighborhoods

BARBARA GEORGE GALLAGHER and NEVA NAHAN,
Wayne State University

This is a case study of one aspect of a collaboration between a group of academic partners from Wayne State University in Detroit, Michigan, and a multicultural neighborhood on the city's eastside. The collaboration's multifaceted initiative employed an interdisciplinary approach to address the issue of youth crime and safety. One of the university partners utilized a community-based model to achieve the goal of a self-sustaining community parenting education movement.

A bottom-up, grassroots approach was used to establish community-based parenting education that would be defined and run by residents to address shared parenting concerns and issues. A university-funded community parent organizer (CPO) facilitated, trained, and assisted neighborhood leadership on parenting issues related to violence in and outside the home that were identified by the community. In this model, the role of the university was conceptualized as a facilitator of community-developed parenting education programs. This differs from the traditional direct service delivery approach, typically a top-down model, centered on an expert-client relationship.

The community-based parenting education model resulted in a shared vision and commitment at the neighborhood level because it was community-driven and the emphasis was on the process of facilitating program development. The model demonstrates that when decisions about the kinds of parenting programs to be provided are part of the process among community residents, and when these residents are invested in the initiation of program activities, they are more likely to provide continuing support. Including community residents in all aspects of the efforts gives them a sense of ownership. An interactive engagement process was created in which the community was an equal partner, and the emphasis was on the transfer of skills to community residents to foster individual, group, and community self-sufficiency after the life of the collaboration. Applied anthropological approaches, such as participant observation, informal interviews, and active listening in order to understand how community residents perceived parenting, helped the CPO gain trust from the community and facilitated the development of community-driven programs and culturally and linguistically appropriate curricula for the community-based parenting education initiative.

University Partners and Neighborhood Selection Process

The Urban Safety Program (USP), a community education and capacity-building effort focusing on reducing violence at the neighborhood level, was created in 1992. The U.S. Department of Education's Urban Community Service Program (Title XI) provided funding to start the program at the Center for Urban Studies at Wayne State University. The USP formed a collaborative group of interdisciplinary university partners from the College of Urban, Labor and Metropolitan Affairs.[1] Staff and faculty from across the university came together for the project. Participating units include Center for Peace and Conflict Studies, Geography and Urban Planning, Urban Families Program, Survey & Evaluation Services, and the Urban Linkage Program.

The USP collaborative group formed a neighborhood selection committee to identify a community-based organization as a partner in the collaboration. The committee notified 300 community-based organizations in Detroit of the application process, and 45 responded. Of those, 13 completed the application process. To be considered, applicants were required to submit detailed organizational and program documentation, such as a mission statement, committees, bylaws, 50l(c)(3) status, service area demographics, major crime problems, youth and anticrime programs, housing reha-

bilitation/renovation efforts, and so on. In addition to these criteria, a history of community action in a low-income, ethnically diverse neighborhood was a key element. The committee visited the sites of the top three candidates and chose the Emmanuel Community Center as the USP's first neighborhood partner for collaborative activities.

Emmanuel Community Center and Neighborhood Description

The Emmanuel Community Center (ECC), funded by the Episcopal diocese through its affiliation with the Emmanuel Episcopal Church, maintains a staff of seven (one executive director, one senior volunteer funded by the Urban League, and five VISTA volunteers). The community center, referred to by some as "Emmanuel," is an emerging community-based organization located in the center of the neighborhood. Residents of the neighborhood report that almost every night gunshots can be heard. Over the past seven years, the staff at ECC has diligently maintained a presence in the community, working to help residents identify the strengths of the neighborhood and to build on these to make the community a safer place to live.

ECC's executive director and her staff had prepared a "wish list" of potential activities and efforts centered around six community task forces: housing, beautification, business development, youth programs, intercultural relations, and crime prevention. The selection committee felt that Emmanuel's task forces would interact well with the university partners. In addition, ECC also had a working relationship with two local elementary schools, a significant youth and crime problem, and a staff willing to become a partner with the USP collaborative group.

---

[1]The terms *collaborative group* and *partners* are used here according to the definition in Mattessich and Monsey (1992).

Sharp contrasts exist in this neighborhood: Residents on the eastside are primarily African American (78 percent), while people living on the westside are a mix of white (51 percent) and African American (45 percent), with a small percentage of Latino and Asian residents. There is a large population of Chaldeans (Catholics from Iraq), who probably make up the majority of the white population in the community. (Chaldeans are not categorized separately from whites for census purposes.)[2] The eastside is characterized by empty lots, debris, and dilapidated houses, although sections of the westside have similar features. As one heads north, the pattern of urban blight diverges into whole blocks of single, well-maintained houses and several small apartment buildings. Along the main north-south thoroughfare there is a scattering of small businesses and convenience stores, the majority owned by more affluent Chaldeans living outside of the neighborhood.[3] A bustling retail area exists in the Chaldean community centered around the Chaldean Sacred Heart Church. Ethnic restaurants, stores, and bakeries, a pharmacy, a video store, beauty shops, barber shops, and various legal and social service agencies line both sides of the street. Socioeconomic indicators of employment, education, crime, and poverty levels are significantly worse in this neighborhood than in the rest of the city of Detroit.[4]

Urban Safety Program Collaborative Group Initiative

Over the past three years, the USP collaborative group developed and implemented an intervention plan to build ECC's capacity and empower the neighborhood through an array of activities. Conflict resolution training and peer mediation was offered to the elementary school students, teachers and community leaders, and the youth in the ECC summer programs. Parenting education, family conflict resolution training, and babysitter certification were offered in the schools and the ECC. USP also provided ECC with strategic planning, technical assistance, monetary and staff support, and a Crime Prevention Through Environmental Design plan for the neighborhood. Student interns and graduate research assistants with experience and interest in dispute resolution, parenting education, and social work were placed on-site at ECC and with the Chaldean Federation of America.

Most of the collaborative group components were incorporated into Emmanuel's preexisting programs. While parenting education was not a preexisting program, it was on ECC's wish list. They wanted cross-cultural family education, but they were unsure about the appropriate form it should take within their community. One of the collaborative group members, the Urban Families Program (UFP), funded by the Detroit Health Department's Bureau of Substance Abuse, provided a community parent organizer (CPO) on-site at ECC to facilitate the development of community-based parenting education. The

[2]Whites constitute 22 percent of the population in the city of Detroit (1990 census). Chaldeans, a religious and linguistic minority from Iraq, speak Arabic and Chaldean—a modern version of the ancient language Aramaic. Over 60,000 Chaldeans live in the three-county Detroit metropolitan area (data from the Chaldean Federation of America).

[3]The affluent Chaldeans have cornered an economic market in which they dominate, similar to the Koreans on the West Coast. In the Detroit metropolitan area, Chaldeans own over 2,000 convenience stores, supermarkets, and other businesses.

[4]In Detroit, 26 percent of the families are on public assistance compared to 40 percent in the Emmanuel neighborhood. Twenty-nine percent of the families in Detroit live below the poverty level, compared to 51 percent in the Emmanuel area (1990 census).

CPO had a diverse and relevant background and took a contextual approach to community issues.[5]

Theory Into Practice

After an initial few weeks of learning about the community and meeting staff and residents, the CPO and the executive director of the ECC began discussions on the best way to approach the community on developing parenting education initiatives. They agreed that work would focus on four progressive areas:

- **Needs assessment** It was recognized that the CPO would need to learn about the community and how its residents would perceive parenting education. Identifying parenting issues through discussions with community leaders and residents was a way of understanding the meaning of parenting to two distinct cultural groups, African Americans and Chaldeans.

- **Community/parent education** Providing initial programming and resources to the community on parenting was used as a mechanism to explore the possibilities of introducing parenting education in this setting. Programs would be a way to present and model parenting workshops and identify local residents who could assume leadership roles in the future.

- **Training** The transfer of skills was a key element in the community capacity-building process. Residents who could be trained as community parent facilitators

[5]The CPO's education and work experience were in the fields of parenting education, early childhood education, and special education, and most recently as a program evaluator for the Detroit Health Department's parenting education program. She is writing her Ph.D. dissertation in anthropology.

were identified. Nurturing staff, volunteers, and community residents who could eventually assume leadership roles was seen as key for community self-sufficiency after the life of the grant.

- **Community action plan** It was agreed that a work plan for the future be developed so that the community could follow it once funding for the CPO was gone.

The CPO spent time working on the following objectives: learning the cultural norms and values in the neighborhood; learning how the ECC, schools, and other local organizations operated; understanding how parenting education might be accepted as an issue in the neighborhood; identifying common community parenting topics and interests; and understanding the meaning of parenting so the recruitment strategies and curriculum would be culturally and linguistically appropriate. Imbedded within each of these steps was the recognition that materials would need to address the ethnic diversity within the community. Specifically, curriculum and materials had to be culturally and linguistically appropriate to both African American and Chaldean families.

Approaches and Strategies

The CPO took a grassroots, bottom-up approach as opposed to imposing a predetermined direct service model on the community. This involved putting considerable time and effort into "getting to know the lay of the land." This is believed to be critical in community-based program development and capacity building, especially when an outsider is involved in community problem solving.

The other collaborative group members implemented programs using traditional service delivery approaches. For example, the Center for Peace and Conflict Studies had trained facilitators and a curriculum on dispute resolution and peer mediation training to be delivered in the schools. Geography and Urban Planning used two graduate classes to work on Crime Prevention Through Environmental Design, which meant that certain academic obligations, restrictions, and deadlines had to be met and took priority over community needs. These two projects were not designed to elicit community-generated activity. Rather, they provided services without an emphasis on how the topics might continue to be addressed once programming ceased.

The following applied anthropology approaches were used to achieve the program objectives in this case: participate in and observe various community activities; conduct informal interviews with ECC staff, other agencies, residents, teachers, clergy, and others; listen to ECC staff and parents to understand how they discussed and approached parenting.

These objectives and approaches helped to develop rapport, credibility, and trust within the community. In the USP evaluation interviews, staff commented on how easy it was to talk with the CPO and how she opened their eyes to ways that parenting could work at ECC. The executive director said,

> And so a trust relationship really had to start early for us. It was just fortunate that we had that kind of click and that it worked without us struggling and trying to make it work. It wasn't hard to communicate and [the community parent organizer] was just real open.

Parenting was a part of the ECC mission; it was recognized by the organization as a way to get to the children of the community and move toward a change:

There was an agenda there in terms of how to reach out to families and children early on.

> We knew we wanted to deal with the whole family, not just the children. We knew there was a need there, but we didn't really have the staff.

This collaboration between the CPO, the ECC, and the community allowed the programming to be shaped in a way that was appropriate for the context, both in the setting at ECC and in the community. This was important in finding the right fit between content and form. The actual shape and content of programming grew out of discussions at the ECC, as well as with community residents. The executive director said,

> We talked an awful lot about what I thought, what [the community parent organizer] thought, where the community was. We also always involved community parents to give us feedback. It was not her idea, my idea, it was all of us coming together to talk about what was realistic.

ECC staff reported that the community parent organizer helped provide resources and information about the options available to the center. This included talking with community residents about their views on parenting. During the summer of 1993, the CPO, ECC staff, and student interns and volunteers conducted a door-to-door needs assessment dialogue with residents on selected blocks in the community. This provided a basis for understanding how parents might perceive parenting education efforts. The CPO found that residents were generally not intrigued when asked "are you interested in parenting education," but that they were receptive to "learning new ways to help keep your children safe." This distinction between interest in parenting versus an interest in activities that would help their children shaped how workshops and events were presented and provided a basis for planning workshop content. Through the experiences at ECC, three phases of the model have been identified.

Phase I—Direct Service as a Way to Build Awareness and Identify Leaders

Building awareness within the community that parenting is an important issue to address and that effective parenting is a skill that can be learned was the initial phase. Direct service had to be implemented immediately due to the grant requirements; however, parenting education was initially provided as a mechanism to explore the possibilities for parenting in this setting. All activities were planned, developed, and implemented jointly; the CPO made it a practice not to operate without having a staff member and/or a community resident involved at each level. This method facilitated community ownership of the programming and skill development, and it allowed the CPO to gain important information about the community in order to assess their parenting needs, issues, and concerns.

During this phase a series of Craft and Talk Workshops were started; the crafts were seen as a way to engage participants with language differences while facilitating a discussion among parents about safety for their children. Babysitter training was implemented to teach teens the responsibilities of safe babysitting, age-appropriate activities, and child management skills. It was also seen as a way to introduce teens to the realities, responsibilities, and complexities of child rearing in an attempt to deglamorize parenthood. The teens expressed interest in continuing their affiliation with each other and ECC, and a weekly Girl Talk program grew out of the first babysitter training session.

Phase II—Building Capacity of Staff and Residents Through Modeling, Training, and Connections to Resources

Building the capacity within the community to provide itself with parenting education was the next step in this process. This included mentoring, raising the confidence and skills of local staff and residents, and building organizational capacity to access funds that would sustain parenting activities. The CPO supported and guided staff, volunteers, and community residents who were assuming leadership roles for community parenting. In order to build this into the program, the CPO established a parenting committee made up of ECC staff, residents, and student interns. This group assumed responsibility for all levels of the conceptualization, planning, implementation, and evaluation of the program as well as playing a role in recruiting parents and assisting with the facilitation.

Identifying and training individuals who had the potential to lead parenting education efforts in the future was done with both informal and formal training. Informally, the CPO modeled appropriate facilitator behavior and always made a point of working with staff to plan strategies and events. This served two functions: to gather input from local residents so that the event would fit into the context of the community, and to provide individuals with an opportunity to see how such an event should be planned and structured. Both of the VISTA volunteers commented on this:

> She pushed me a lot. She helped me a lot. She taught me a lot, I didn't know how to run meetings, I didn't know how to write agendas, I didn't know how to take minutes. I started off as a translator, but I got sick and tired of that, going back and forth. They have to start depending on themselves. I felt they should learn and talk for themselves. I have gotten more into a facilitating role. I am involved in

planning the workshops. I have to facilitate and work on the [actual presentation of the] workshop.

It was our idea. [The CPO] was the facilitator, [and] even though I didn't look at it that way, [then] I became the facilitator. I was facilitating without realizing I was facilitating.

The UFP provided ECC staff with the opportunity to expand their vision through site visits, seminars, conferences, and training sessions. The first such opportunity was a trip to Rochester, New York, to four successful family resource centers. The trip provided several ECC staff with a concrete vision of what could be possible through ECC parenting efforts. The executive director commented,

> First of all, it's just the fact that Urban Families Program was willing to give us the opportunity to see what's happening in another part of the country around issues that we were concerned about. The community's input is there and what we have tried to do [as a] grassroots organization to make sure that the community is embraced. It really opened my eyes to how we could provide services to the family. For my staff, it was definitely wonderful and an enriching opportunity for them to get outside of their surroundings and see that there are other people across the country who are doing things . . . [It] opened up resources for them.

The ECC parenting committee gave presentations at the National Family Resource Coalition's annual conference in Chicago and at two local conferences during 1994. Organizing the presentations provided staff with the opportunity to reflect on what they had accomplished. The experiences provided an opportunity for staff to network with others and see possibilities from across the country. These opportunities further exposed staff to the concepts of family resource centers and the parenting education movement. Following is a sample of comments from those who presented:

The whole Family Resource Coalition conference was truly amazing for us. In my wildest dreams I never even thought about us having advanced far enough to even share what we had done, what we found worked. Then there were people who really wanted to hear . . . it really empowered the staff to feel that they had done something, and that's a major accomplishment . . . those are resources that, in our budgets, are just not there . . . that was a wonderful resource. It really helped us to get focused and has moved us into the family resource center mode in terms of what we have to do to put that together.

It was a great experience, a lot of networking and sharing information. We had a lot of people in our workshop.

From each trip we came back with a lot of ideas. We were motivated and we really could see what we wanted to have [here]. It definitely helped.

Phase III—Training, Support, and Technical Assistance in a Consultative Role

ECC is committed to the expansion and future establishment of a family resource center. Currently, the Parenting Center at the ECC is operated by a former VISTA employee who is now the community parent organizer funded by the Urban Families Program, and a community parent facilitator employed through VISTA. The USP supported a graduate assistant who worked with the core group of community parent facilitators to conduct parenting workshops twice a week at the ECC parenting center. In the last year, the core group moved beyond the ECC into the broader neighborhood and implemented an 11-session parenting education series for the local Headstart program, and a 7-session series in the Chaldean Church Center. Several groups of teens have received the babysitter training at ECC, and some of the trained babysitters provide child care for participants in the parenting workshops at ECC and for the parenting education conducted at the Chaldean Church. The USP collaborative group, especially the Urban Families Program partner, supported formal training in group facilitation skills and content areas for the student interns, the graduate assistant, and the community parent facilitators.

Emergence of Operating Principles

Both the university and the community learned from the experience of working with the ECC to stimulate parenting initiatives. We have identified several operating principles that emerged from the experience:

- **Community as an equal partner** The community must not be perceived as a blank slate—both the university and community organizations were equal partners in the process of building a parenting initiative. This provided a productive working relationship that was viewed as mutually beneficial throughout the project.

- **CPO's role as "bridge person"** The CPO's role evolved as she moved back and forth between the university partners and the community to articulate goals (needs) and operating reality (resources available and policy constraints) to each other. Through a constant process of informal and formal communication, a common understanding of goals was negotiated at the university and community levels specifically for the parenting efforts. At the university level, the CPO set out to understand what meanings each member brought to his or her understanding of the collaborative group. This approach, while not originally expected or defined, involved and fostered a cooperative, reciprocal relationship.

- **CPO's role as a facilitator and a resource person** The role of the university should not be as the "expert." The values, skills, and knowledge of community residents need to be recognized as important elements in capacity-building models; they are different but not inferior to professional expertise. This approach must also be balanced with a respect for the separate university and community organizational identities and an understanding that the organizations have separate and distinct agendas and policy constraints.

- **Community as the final decision maker in program development** Because the community must live with the results of any project, they must have final say over the types of programs that are established. ECC achieved this by setting up a communication process that kept unrestricted information flowing both ways. In this way the activities were appropriate to the context, thus assuring the right fit between content and form and the institutionalization of the program after the grant period ends.

Conclusion

The USP collaborative group provided a combination of interdisciplinary services and activities over a three-year period. One result of the USP collaborative group initiative is the selection of ECC by the Funders Collaborative for five years of support for business and operational development. ECC also received several local grants for the parenting education and Girl Talk programs. A community-based health education program, the Village Health Workers, funded through the Detroit Health Department, services the neighborhood through ECC. In the last year, the Urban Families Program supported a community resident in Wayne State's Community Education Leadership Program for intensive community leadership training. Seven student interns from education and social work and a graduate assistant in educational psychology worked on-site at ECC. The Center for Peace and Conflict Studies also supported a community resident for a community organizing internship. The USP collaborative, especially the Urban Families Program partner, continued staff training, technical and equipment assistance (computers, a phone line), and business development training, all with a focus on building the organizational capacity of the ECC to better develop the competency of the community.

ECC staff and volunteers have gained a broader vision of the possibilities at ECC, as well as the skills and experiences to continue the process of building a parenting presence in the Emmanuel neighborhood. While the direct involvement of the collaborative group is just winding down, it appears the ECC and residents will continue a commitment to parenting education activities in their community. It is too early to tell how sustained this effort will be. However, parenting has become an important part of the ECC. Parenting is physically present, with a room dedicated to storing resource materials. Programming has continued, even with diminished resources. And several staff members received training and plan to continue efforts at the center. This appears to be an excellent foundation for future parenting efforts at ECC.

EDITORS' COMMENTS

Wayne State University researchers Barbara Gallagher and Neva Nahan describe a university-funded, bottom-up grassroots program on crime, parenting, and education that was established in one of Detroit's more diverse neighborhoods. They emphasize the important quality of ownership that community members have when they are involved at all levels of the collaboration. Research collaborations do not have to be based in one discipline or department within the university. This project was multidisciplinary—with participants coming from many departments and programs and different types of methodologies. For example, Peace and Conflict Studies trained facilitators and helped create a curriculum on dispute mediation. Geography and Urban Planning used graduate students to work on a crime prevention program. Applied sociology and anthropology methods, such as participant observation and informal interviews and discussions, were also used. Finally, the authors have identified several operating principles about research collaboration that emerged from this project.

Part IV
Health Issues Are Social Issues

The World Health Organization (WHO) defines health as an overall sense of physical, mental, and social well-being and not merely the absence of disease or infirmity. In this part of the book, the authors present us with a variety of research collaboration cases centered around issues of the health and general welfare of the population. Like WHO's definition, the definition of health in these cases is broad and includes such topics as educational programs designed to prevent violence and following mental health patients into the community after their long-term care facility has been shut down by the state. We have also included cases examining the topic of health from a variety of angles. Health involves local, state, and national public policy, direct care, and prevention programs.

Many of the health issues discussed here are connected with stigma and fears on the part of the general public. Fear and stigma about AIDS, mental illness, drug use, lesbians, and violence all contribute to the even greater need to collaborate with community groups who are sensitive to both the discrimination and unique needs of populations within our communities that are underserved or not well understood. For example, as a public health issue, AIDS/HIV is one of the most costly and deadly diseases to combat. Two of our cases (one talking about local policy efforts and the other about programs to prevent the spread of the disease) involve efforts to educate and stop the spread of this deadly disease in our communities. But it is also fear and ignorance about persons with AIDS, the mentally ill, and gay men and lesbians that needs to be combatted with effective and proactive community-based research. That is what the research cases and collaborators presented here attempt to do. Our cases also take us geographically from California to Chicago to Indiana and include an urban, suburban, and statewide focus.

Our first case takes us to the western suburbs of the Chicago area. In "Reframing Knowledge About the AIDS Epidemic," Anne Figert and Paul Kuehnert write about the collaboration between an academic-based sociologist and the medically trained director of a large community-based provider of AIDS/HIV-related services. The case of "Putting a Face to Lesbian Health Risk," by Mary McCauley, Ellie Emanuel, Alice Dan, and Zylphia Ford, explains how discrimination against lesbians by scientists, health care providers, and the general public results in a set of unique health risks and problems. Whereas a lot of attention and funding has recently been given to study women's health needs, lesbian health is an area that is still very rarely researched or talked about. Another set of problems is faced by collaborative researchers when one of the collaborators and funders of the project is government based and funded. This was the situation faced by Eric Wright, Terry White, and Richard DeLiberty in "The Closing of Central State Hospital" in the state of Indiana.

Diane Binson, Gary Harper, Olga Grinstead, and Katherine Sanstad actually present two case studies involving AIDS prevention in California. We have included two of the many studies coming out of the Center for AIDS Prevention Studies at the University of California, San Francisco, for the unique issues and populations discussed. Our final case in the health section addresses the issue of violence and the harm that it does in our society. "Grassroots Approaches to Violence Prevention," by Nancy Matthews and Anne Parry, explores the efficacy of a violence prevention program and the broader issue of how smaller community-based organizations get research and data to justify the creation or support of existing programs to outside granting agencies.

Reframing Knowledge About the AIDS Epidemic: Academic and Community-Based Interventions

ANNE E. FIGERT, *Loyola University Chicago,*
and PAUL KUEHNERT, *Paul Kuehnert Consulting*

In the United States, HIV/AIDS has had a disproportionate impact on suburban communities that have one or more of the following characteristics: large racial minority populations; large populations of persons living in poverty; large populations of homosexual men; and/or large populations of intravenous drug users. Yet even in communities with high incidence and prevalence of HIV/AIDS, the stigma still attached to the disease, as well as the fears HIV/AIDS engenders, results in denial of the problem by community members, organizations, and local policy makers. This is especially true for predominately African American and Hispanic communities (Hammonds 1987; Lester and Saxxon 1988, Quimby and Friedman 1989; Brown 1991).

Existing social, medical, and psychological services for HIV-infected and AIDS patients in the Chicago metropolitan area have concentrated in the northern part of the city of Chicago or in the northern suburbs, where the predominately gay male clientele has made use of them. Services and treatment options oriented to the western suburbs (where the clientele is both heterosexual and homosexual and racially diverse) have been slow in developing and do not have broad community acceptance. Minority group members are highly represented in the western suburbs and surrounding parts of the city of Chicago.

Lack of a local policy response and leadership involvement in the epidemic results in these social and individual costs:

- Increased risk of new infections due to lack of prevention strategies and efforts

- Discrimination against persons with HIV/AIDS and their loved ones

- Fears of discrimination on the part of community members with HIV/AIDS and their loved ones, resulting in their withdrawal from community life and isolation

- Barriers to use of community health and social services by the persons living with HIV/AIDS and their loved ones

Even if alternative HIV/AIDS-specific social services are created within these communities or extended to them, the social costs of duplicate services and the reinforcement of the stigma continue to be problems. Our project began with the shared assumption that principles of social justice and a desire for cost efficiency in the delivery of health and social services can encourage local policy makers to support extension of existing community services to members living with HIV/AIDS.

Forming a Partnership and Developing Our Research Questions

In the summer of 1993, a collaborative partnership was formed between an academic social scientist and a community-based AIDS organization that is the largest provider of AIDS/HIV services in the western suburbs of Chicago. This relationship was part of a competitive grant funded through the John D. and Catherine T. MacArthur Foundation and Loyola University Chicago's Policy Research Action Group (PRAG) to encourage research oriented toward changing local-level policy. The main goal of the PRAG program is to link academic researchers with community activists and organizations in a cooperative venture (Nyden and Wiewel 1992). This approach is consistent with recent calls within the sociological community for more collaborative and community-based research (Lynch 1993).

As Nyden and Wiewel point out, there are strong tensions in collaborative community-based research. These tensions center around the production of knowledge and facts about the community. Academics need to work within the discipline-based reward structure for publications, grants, and promotions. As many sociologists of science have pointed out, properly researched and scientifically validated data written for a scholarly audience is the most practical means by which academic sociologists succeed (Cole and Cole 1973; Long 1978). On the other hand, community-based activists and organizations need as much scientifically legitimated knowledge and information written for a lay audience delivered as soon as possible in order to increase the community's awareness and enlist their cooperation in addressing the problem being studied. Academic schedules and the demands of the scientific method often play havoc with these needs. Yet, it is precisely the "scientifically" legitimated data and research that community-based organizations seek in order to legitimate local policy initiatives (Nyden and Wiewel 1992).[1]

With these tensions and a shared political commitment to social change in mind, we proceeded with our project to influence local AIDS/HIV policy in the western suburbs. We thought it could be beneficial to mutually "use" each other and acknowledge this at the start of the project. The academic would get a research assistant from the community organization to collect data and furnish introductions to AIDS/HIV service providers and government providers in order to establish a reputation as a legitimate community researcher. Part of the small grant from PRAG and the MacArthur Foundation provided the funding for the assistant. The project would also count toward community service and research for the academic.

The leader of the community organization would be able to use the knowledge and data of a scientific study and the social status of a Ph.D. at a local university to influence policy. Letterhead from the university was used in all correspondence with the communities. This connection with the academic community was important to the community organization for two reasons: The push for a local AIDS/HIV policy would not appear as totally self-serving for the community organization, and the data/results would be seen as having legitimacy. Also, if any results seemed critical of the community, the presence of the outside academic researcher would deflect any consequences for the community organization.

---

[1]Another source of scientific legitimation for this project was its approval by the Institutional Review Board of the university affiliated with this project.

With these goals and hazards in mind, we proceeded and developed our study based on these specific research questions:

1. Can community-level variables be identified that predict the local HIV/AIDS policy response?

2. What are the local policy issues that must be addressed in western suburban communities in relation to HIV/AIDS?

3. Can a peer-led intervention with local community leaders have a positive (that is, more just) impact on local HIV/AIDS policy?

In order to understand and work toward reframing knowledge about HIV/AIDS, we targeted eight geographically clustered (western) suburbs of Chicago. Each of the research questions and the ways in which we attempted to address them is discussed separately.

Community-Level Variables

Our primary research question guiding this part of the study was *Can community-level variables be identified that predict the local HIV/AIDS policy response?* With the help of a research assistant funded through PRAG, we identified six major social areas by which to address and predict whether or not a local HIV/AIDS policy response is put into place in the community:

- **Demographic characteristics** Using 1990 Census Bureau data, the demographic composition of each community was collected along the following dimensions: physical size; density; population size; racial, gender, and age distribution; per capita incomes; and educational level. We used these variables to make descriptive and predictive distinctions within each of the communities.

- **Degree and nature of "religiosity"** We collected lists of churches and ministries using the following sources: listings in telephone books, whether or not there was a ministerial alliance to check our list against, and whether or not a gay and lesbian church group was listed in the gay and lesbian newspapers, telephone directories, or advertisements. A numerical and denominational accounting of the numbers of communities of faith was also collected. We noted whether or not a ministerial alliance was formed in the community and whether or not there was religious outreach to the gay and lesbian community. A more diverse religious community, a strong ministerial alliance, and some degree of religious outreach to the gay and lesbian community would predict that a local HIV/AIDS policy response had been made.

- **Extent to which the community is considered "gay friendly"** This area was measured by whether or not there are public and listed gay and lesbian organizations or establishments, whether or not there is a town ordinance protecting the sexual orientation of its citizens against discrimination, whether or not the police department has a program of gay/lesbian sensitivity training, the number of books in the public library under the headings of "gay," "lesbian," or "homosexual," and the number of articles published on these subjects from 1988 to 1992 in the local newspaper. A "gay friendly" community is more likely to have made a local HIV/AIDS policy response.

- **Extent to which the community is "HIV/AIDS friendly"** This measurement was composed of the following: number of HIV/AIDS-specific service agencies or programs, data on public service or personnel policies on HIV/AIDS, the number of books in the local library on HIV/AIDS, and the number of articles in the local newspaper on HIV/AIDS from 1988 to 1992. Only agencies or programs of agencies with an address in the respective town were listed. Some agencies' or programs' catchment areas included other towns within the study. Hospital and health care programs were included in these numbers. An "HIV/AIDS friendly" community is more likely to have made a local HIV/AIDS policy response.

- **General community health indicators** We examined the morbidity and mortality statistics compiled by the Cook County Department of Health, the Oak Park Department of Health, and the Illinois Department of Health and looked for indicators of the reported cases of sexually transmitted diseases (including AIDS cases), and the number of health care centers, physicians, and social service agencies. The prediction was that a community with a higher number of sexually transmitted diseases, and more health care facilities (this figure includes hospitals) and physicians, is more likely to have made a local HIV/AIDS policy response.

- **Degree to which school and youth HIV/AIDS policies are addressed in the community** We collected information on the number of school and youth programs, whether or not there is HIV/AIDS and gay and lesbian training and policies in the school districts, and whether or not universal precautions are observed for their staff. The extent to which a community is addressing HIV/AIDS in the schools and in youth programs would predict whether or not that community has made a local HIV/AIDS policy response.

Each of our findings, listed here, indicates ways in which communities can respond positively to the existence of AIDS/HIV among their citizens.

- There is a direct relationship between the education level of the community and a progressive or proactive response to the disease at the policy and the program level.

- There is a direct relationship between the number of health and professional services and a proactive response to the disease at the policy and the program level.

- There is a direct relationship between the number of library volumes on HIV/AIDS, gays, and lesbians and a proactive response at the policy and program level.

- There is a direct relationship between the number of gay and lesbian organizations and a proactive response at the policy and program level.

- There is a direct relationship between the number of religious communities and a proactive response at the policy and program level.

This information was conveyed to participants at the conference that we held and in a final written report to local government officials and community leaders. We realize that local AIDS/HIV policy is not put into place quickly; however, it can be built by identifying and incorporating important variables such as we have identified in this study.

Local Policy Issues

In order to better address what local policy issues existed in the western suburbs, we formed an advisory board of local community activists, persons living with HIV/AIDS, and health care and AIDS/HIV service providers.

This board met and identified major policies (educational, housing, service needs, political) affecting these communities. Board members also helped to formulate and plan the best ways to address specific concerns about the AIDS epidemic, education and prevention, and business/employment issues in the peer-led intervention discussed in research question 3. As Lynch points out, a planning committee is essential to understanding and learning about different needs and perceptions concerning a problem within a community (1993, 126). Our planning committee helped formulate the important areas of need and pretested interview/questionnaire schedules. Involvement of a planning committee also spread out the workload of planning a conference, allowed for a greater expanse of network contacts in terms of speakers/knowledge, and brought a larger audience to the actual conference.

Peer-Led Intervention With Local Community Leaders

Our final research question dealt with the question, *Can a peer-led intervention have any effect on local HIV/AIDS policy?* We addressed this question by conducting a half-day seminar for business, educational, and community leaders on HIV/AIDS in the western suburbs. With the help of the advisory board (discussed earlier), we located an accessible west suburban location and arranged for a variety of speakers addressing three main areas (overview of west suburban AIDS/HIV issues, education and prevention, and employment issues). We chose speakers from a variety of health and community-based AIDS/HIV intervention programs as well as individuals living with HIV/AIDS from the communities involved. Over 60 community leaders atten-

ded the program. The results of a postconference evaluation indicate that the leaders found the program to be informative, but maybe more important, *practical and helpful* in their work and for networking purposes. Most agreed that they would attend another conference on practical issues related to HIV/AIDS.

Conclusions: Doing Good While Doing Good Social Science

Recent writings on AIDS and AIDS activism have called for a more democratic science, one in which scientists and persons with AIDS work together to shape the knowledge about the disease (Epstein 1991). From this collaborative project, we wanted to extend the notion of democratic science to include the social sciences. Together, social scientists and members of community-based organizations can actively shape and influence the community's assessment and perceptions of persons living with AIDS and help the community more effectively respond to the growing and changing nature of the AIDS epidemic.

Collaborative research is a good way to combine political commitment with solid, empirical research. There is one caveat: The research has to be "good science" in the methodological sense, or the entire project is undermined. Social scientists who believe in the social and constructed nature of science should not abandon the notion that their own science can have a very real effect on the social world. The actual social science conducted should be no better or worse than a pure "academic study." One could argue that the methodology is improved because it is more valid and democratic—based on actual community members' lives and their input.

Social scientists must become aware of the needs within communities and respond to them—not by "just going into the communities and studying them" but by actively collaborating with persons and organizations within those communities. This ensures that community participation and better data can evolve through a more democratic social science. Feminist scholar Donna Haraway points out that the AIDS epidemic involves scientists very intimately in ways that "natural scientists and biomedical scientists [are] changing their sense of what counts as knowledge—their epistemological positioning, their political positioning, their sense of science as culture and social practice" (as quoted in Darnovsky 1991). Social scientists involved in community research about HIV/AIDS have to take this to heart about themselves and the knowledge that they produce. Like natural and biomedical scientists, social scientists must begin to examine the epistemological nature of knowledge. Legitimated knowledge about the physical and social effects and needs of persons living with HIV/AIDS is just as important in the lives of persons in a community as whether or not AZT really is effective in slowing the development of HIV or finding a cure.

Social scientists are not the only ones who need to focus on the experience of persons living with HIV/AIDS in the community. Community members also need to own up and recognize that their next-door neighbor, their postal worker, or members of their church may have HIV/AIDS. Explicitly asking community members whether they know someone living with HIV/AIDS, and having a panel made up of residents living with HIV/AIDS address them, makes the disease much more real. It becomes something individual and personal—as well as a tangible part of the community.

The equal relationship of the academic researcher and the community-based organization leader demands changes in the way participatory social science research is conceived of and accomplished. The first step is the explicit acknowledgement and agreement of what each partner is doing in the project—engaging in participatory and democratic social science.

EDITORS' COMMENTS

In this case, Anne Figert, Assistant Professor of Sociology, and Paul Kuehnert, then the Executive Director of Community Response of Oak Park, write about one of their research collaborations. The ultimate goal of this research project was to influence local AIDS/HIV policy in the western suburbs of Chicago. Both researchers started with the assumption that the lack of a local policy response and leadership involvement in the AIDS/HIV epidemic has many social and individual costs. With this shared political commitment to social change in mind, they were able to find funding for a research assistant to identify factors in the community that might promote an effective HIV/AIDS policy. With the further help of a community-based advisory board, they then created a practical informational conference attended by local community leaders. Their conclusion is that local AIDS/HIV policy is not put into place quickly but that it can be built and influenced by researchers willing to identify and communicate their findings and practical information to community leaders.

Putting a Face to Lesbian Health Risk: A Collaborative Research Project

MARY MCCAULEY II, Howard Brown Health Center–Women's Program,
ELLIE EMANUEL, University of Wisconsin–Stout, ALICE DAN, Center for Research on
Women and Gender, and ZYLPHIA FORD, Chicago Department of Public Health

The Lesbian Community Cancer Project (LCCP) was founded in October 1990. Nancy Lanoue, a breast cancer survivor and a caregiver to her life partner who had died of pancreatic cancer, helped organize and run the meeting after being consulted by a number of recently diagnosed women in need of information and support. Over 40 women gathered at a meeting to talk about the issues affecting lesbians with cancer and the profound lack of information about available alternative treatments. The gathering attracted survivors of a variety of cancers, newly diagnosed women, women undergoing chemotherapy, as well as feminist scientists and health activists.

Many of the women attending had intimate knowledge of the current treatment protocols; all of them had opinions about the way things *should* be done. Some of these women wanted user-friendly information about breast cancer, treatment options, and prognosis. Others wanted nonjudgmental information about treatment options that went beyond traditional Western medical approaches. Still others just needed general information about their cancer as a result of discrimination in the health care field. Many women reported that once they came out to their physicians as les-

bians, basic information about their cancer and treatment options was never discussed—the doctor just left the examining room.

As part of a nationwide informal network of grassroots groups and organizations now approaching cancer with a feminist perspective, LCCP is committed to challenging the various forms of discrimination that exist in both mainstream and alternative cancer establishments—lesbophobia, sexism, racism, ableism, ageism, and classism. This discrimination affects the funding and interpretation of research, the attitudes of health care providers, and women's access to medical treatment. LCCP provides support, information, education, advocacy, and practical services to lesbian and heterosexual women living with cancer and to their self-identified families. The name of the organization was chosen both to attack the invisibility that lesbians face in the world and to let it be known very clearly that this was a safe place for lesbians.

In November 1992, the Advocacy Committee of the Lesbian Community Cancer Project, Chicago, Illinois, met to formulate its 1993–94 goals. At the urging of two founding members—then Executive Director Mary McCauley and breast cancer survivor Ellie Emanuel—the committee decided that in order to advocate for services and programs specifically for lesbians, the agency would need to have clear data on the status of lesbians and cancer in metropolitan Chicago. As a representative of the committee, Emanuel contacted Dr. Suzanne G. Haynes, Deputy Director of the National Cancer Institute, to find out whether the institute had any interest in funding research on lesbians and cancer. The committee was informed that lesbians were not currently viewed as a minority group apart from their status as women and therefore required no special research or other funding. Dr. Haynes recommended that we undertake local field research to study similarities and differences between lesbian and heterosexual women relative to cancer. Such a field study could favorably influence the National Cancer Institue to consider future funding of research at a national level.

As a result, McCauley and Emanuel recommended that a field study be conducted within the Chicago metropolitan area to investigate lesbians and cancer. The Advocacy Committee of LCCP accepted this recommendation and proceeded with the development of the project described in this paper. Simultaneously, McCauley started looking at the backgrounds of the LCCP volunteers to see whether some of them were affiliated with universities that might undertake a partnership in conducting this field study. LCCP ran up against two problems at this point: Many academics perceived the organization as a group of radicals and did not want to work with the group; and academic women were afraid that affiliation with a group of women who were blatantly putting the word *lesbian* in front of people would hurt them professionally— whether or not they were lesbians.

McCauley then started looking at who was attending the meetings and participating in the coalitions that LCCP was concerned about to see who shared concerns and vision. Alice Dan was the only university-affiliated individual who attended the monthly meeting of community-based women's health groups, and she was working with LCCP and Greenpeace to convene the first-ever conference on breast cancer and the environment. Dan is the director of the Center for Research on Women and Gender (CRWG) at the University of Illinois at Chicago. McCauley approached Dan to see if the CRWG might be interested in collaborating on a women's health survey and was assured that this type of collaboration was consistent with the goals of the Center.

Background of Academic Institution

The Center for Research on Women and Gender is a multidisciplinary unit on the Chicago campus of the University of Illinois. The Center's mission is to promote collaborative research, with the following goals: (1) stimulate and increase knowledge about women and about gender as an explanatory category in research; (2) study and evaluate the impact of policy related to women and gender; (3) improve the dissemination and use of new scholarship on women and gender; and (4) create alliances with outside organizations sharing interests in women and gender-related issues. These purposes support the involvement with a variety of community groups in collaborative research efforts.

When representatives from LCCP and CRWG met, it was clear that both groups were approaching research from a similar standpoint, being totally aware of the traditional problems—trust issues, confidentiality, and respect for the culture of the community being studied. Issues of legitimacy and credibility are clearly important when undertaking collaboration, and these work both ways. For some groups or individuals, seeing that a university research center is involved in a project adds to their credibility; while for others, the involvement of the community group is the key to legitimacy. This also holds for funding agencies: Sometimes the institutional connection with the university serves to heighten the chances of funding, and sometimes funding is only available to the grassroots group. In either case, the collaboration adds flexibility in seeking resources of all kinds.

Facilities for managing data were perhaps the most significant resource offered by the research center. These ranged from the capability to accept and store hundreds of questionnaires in a secure location, to data entry and analysis. In addition, the university's Institutional Review Board was available for human subjects review, providing protection for research participants on the one hand, and for the researchers as well, should any questions arise.

Development of the Survey

It seems obvious that the research center would bring scholars with research expertise to a project, and this was indeed the case. However, a number of researchers associated with the Women's Health Survey were not from the University of Illinois. The range of expertise in this group was truly impressive, including not only health conditions per se, but also mental health, substance use, relationships, vocational and disability issues, women of color, and other useful backgrounds. This commitment by a total of 12 members of the research team seemed to create a better balance of power in negotiating; that is, the research center never held all the cards. It also necessitated the creation of a "Survey Use Agreement," clarifying

many aspects of ownership and acknowledgement and providing procedures for use of the survey instrument and data. A scholar from Brazil attended one of our meetings where the language for this agreement was discussed, and she could not believe the level of collegiality and the amount of respect each member of the research team showed the others. She said she was most impressed with the fact that egos seemed to be left at the door and the primary concern was only to benefit this work.

From January 1993 through February 1994, a research team developed the Chicago Women's Health Survey. The team was composed of lesbian and heterosexual women from universities, community agencies, and the community at large who had experience in nursing, rehabilitation, gender studies, marketing, business, teaching, sales, and research. Individual members selected topic areas and reviewed the available literature and other surveys to develop each section of the survey. We found that there were many subject areas about lesbian health with no available literature.

In the spring of 1993, we submitted a proposal to the Chicago Foundation for Women for funding support of the study in the amount of $10,000. The grant was funded at the requested amount in June 1993. We received $5,000 in additional funding from the Chicago mayor's Office on AIDS Prevention, specifically for the information on women and HIV.

The research team then reviewed the initial drafts, made changes, and invited two focus groups of lesbians of color to take the survey in order to ensure that the survey was inclusive of all women. Thirty Latina, African American, and Asian lesbians participated in the focus groups. Each group took the survey and then discussed the content and process of doing the survey in an open forum facilitated by LCCP's executive director. We reviewed the information garnered from these groups and made changes to the survey. We worked on language usage, clarity of questions, question modification, additions, and deletions.

Next, the team met with a research consultant, Dr. Ann Pollinger Haas of City University of New York, Lehman College. Dr. Haas has extensive research experience and a particular interest in lesbian health. Dr. Haas reviewed the survey and focus group commentary and proposed an alternative methodology for the project. After listening to her question, "Do you want a nice little lesbian survey, or do you want to do something really big?" the research team made additional changes to the survey using the focus group information. We created a second draft of the survey, including these changes and recommendations from Dr. Haas.

The new methodology suggested by Dr. Haas allowed for direct comparison of lesbian and heterosexual women based on similar work roles. This methodology was developed to strengthen two aspects of the survey design. First, the lack of a comparison group in previous lesbian health studies was addressed by pairing lesbian and heterosexual women who shared the same work roles. By including a comparison group, we were able to study whether there are any appreciable differences that would merit further investigation. The dimensions that held constant for both groups were training, socioeconomic status, salary, general job responsibilities, and job stressors.

The second aspect of the new methodology that enhanced the study pertained to the fact that previous lesbian health studies had only included self-identified lesbians, who were typically white, middle class, and well educated. In many cases, surveys for previous lesbian studies were distributed in bars, which are primary social meeting places for many women around the country. The research team

felt this skewed the results regarding alcohol consumption. The weaknesses of these studies were addressed by having the research team conduct the survey with both "out," self-identified lesbians and "closeted" lesbians who represented a wide range of work roles. The team decided to accept the new methodology and create a third group of possible respondents—a sample of nonpaired lesbian and heterosexual women who had heard or read about the study and wanted to participate.

At this point, the team once again reviewed the literature and other surveys before making further revisions to the survey. Since the survey was still very long (40 pages), we started weeding through the questions. The decision to include or exclude a question was based on two points: Is an area of risk being defined, and will someone do something with the data. As an example, we had some really good questions about environmental risk factors, but no one on the research team knew anyone in the Chicago area who could do something with the information, so the questions were omitted. This draft was then reviewed by two other academics who had knowledge of the research experience in the area of lesbian health. The research team met two more times and made final revisions based on recommendations from these academics and other studies. Ultimately, the final survey instrument was 24 pages with a variety of question styles.

Distribution of the Survey

The research team was responsible for the distribution of the survey. We engaged in a sampling method known as "snowball," which means going to organized groups of women with many lesbian members and asking them to recruit additional women. This method is often used in working with under-studied groups because individuals trust people they know, and members of a community know how to reach their own people. As Singleton, et al., point out, there is a "process of chain referral: when members of the target population are located, they are asked to provide names and addresses of other members of the target population, who are then contacted and asked to name others, and so on" (1993, 164). This ensured both time efficiency and accuracy in describing the project to study participants. Members gave the survey to lesbians in a wide variety of formal and informal settings, such as potluck dinners, bookstores, softball games, lesbian coffeehouses, social support groups, therapeutic centers, musical events, domestic abuse shelters, informal gatherings of friends and co-workers, and bowling teams. At these events, the women were given a second survey (a duplicate of the original printed on different colored paper) to distribute to a woman (work-role mate) to complete and return by mail to LCCP. The researchers did not specify sexuality of the work-role mate, hoping that we would get at least 60 percent nonlesbian respondents.

The survey was distributed from March 1994 to June 1995. By April 1995, 400 of 850 surveys had been coded and entered into an SPSS computer file. We ran a distribution frequency to ascertain where further distribution of the surveys should be done. For example, although one third of the surveys distributed had been distributed to women of color, the number of completed, returned surveys from these women was very low. There is difficulty inherent in the distribution procedure, since many of these groups are meeting specifically for social reasons for a limited amount of time, and completing a survey for 30 minutes isn't the highest priority. The research team de-cided to continue distributing the survey until June 1, 1995, in an effort to increase the number of participants among women of color. We then added these returned surveys to the data set. Our total number of returned surveys was 450.

Challenges

Although there was an ever-increasing bond of trust developing between the Center for Research on Women and Gender and LCCP, that relationship was strained when the arrangement was formalized with a contractual agreement. A representative of CRWG met with the University of Illinois contract department to inform them of the project, the nature of our working relationship, and other information that would affect the contractual agreement. After the university's contracts department felt satisfied that *their* concerns were being met, they sent an outside working agreement to LCCP. This created considerable problems when LCCP did not feel that their interests were being fully considered in the contract. For example, the university initially declared ownership of everything—surveys, data, and finished product. This was not at all acceptable to LCCP, so calls and edited agreements went back and forth to clarify LCCP's position. The university explained that the contract they were submitting to LCCP was the standard contract they used for agreements in the engineering or computer areas, and it needed to remain the same. LCCP explained that this relationship was probably different from arrangements the University of Illinois might have with an engineering firm. Although it seemed all was understood as the phone was hung up, each time a new edition of the agreement was forwarded to LCCP, it was clear that there was still a problem.

It seemed as if LCCP was banging its head against a brick wall with the university's contract department. Finally, both parties felt that they needed to clarify where the project stood. Because members of LCCP and CRWG had been working together intensely on this project for more than a year, all was not lost. The question of the hour was definitely, What is going on? Once both sides shared an understanding of the current situation, directors McCauley and Dan realized that the basic agreements still existed. After comparing notes, it was clear that the difficulty rested with the listening ability and bureaucratic rigidity of the contract department. Although both groups had told the lawyer the same thing, the university had set up the agreement from its own narrow frame of reference.

It became a major part of the project to educate the contract department of the university to the nature of the university's participation in this project—as collaborator/consultant, not originator. Although Dan, CRWG's director, was donating much of her time, the university was being paid for some of the work. However, LCCP was the organization that received the funding for the project. Those two points seemed to be the deciding factor for the legal department's final understanding of their relationship with this research.

A related issue, the protection of research participants, also created problems for this collaborative research project. The survey was lengthy and included some open-ended questions. While there would be little chance that a participant could be identified, and no specific identification was requested, a faculty member at CRWG was unwilling to allow the raw data (original returned questionnaires) to be removed from the research center. At first, LCCP saw this as conflicting with its ownership of the project. It took several discussions of the

issues before it became clear that *both* organizations agreed that once the data was entered and "cleaned," and all handwritten comments transcribed, the original questionnaires should be destroyed to protect the confidentiality of participants in the survey. The difficulty had arisen because both groups wanted to make sure that the original questionnaires would not fall into unknown hands. The solution of destroying original questionnaires satisfied all parties.

Recommendations

As a result of our work on this project, we propose the following guidelines for collaboration:

1. Openly and honestly examine why both the researcher and the collaborating community are participating in this research. What and whose interests are being served? Collaborators need to know this about each other to decide whether the project is something they want to pursue.

2. Involve community collaborators at *all* levels of the project, especially project planning and development (it's here that they're often left out). Community people will know what the population's concerns are, how best to reach and recruit potential participants, what's been tried before (successfully and unsuccessfully) in their communities, and what innovative interventions might be used.

3. Openly recognize your own assumptions and their origins.

4. Develop a two-way, trusting relationship between collaborators: Be honest, keep promises, and listen.

5. Recognize the strengths each party has to offer the collaboration. In particular, aca-

demic researchers need to respect and value the knowledge and expertise community people bring to the discussion and planning.

6. Don't study only what is deemed deficient in under-studied communities. Examine also what works (for example, don't assume that the primary social outlet for all lesbians is at bars or that most lesbians are depressed).

7. Develop a contract to prevent misunderstandings and miscommunication. Periodically reassess the contract and project, with particular sensitivity to educating the community agency about the process of academic research.

8. Work with your collaborators on organizing focus groups to identify issues of concern before developing project proposals—your concern may not be a concern in the community you planned to study.

9. Recognize that cultural competence is needed to conduct research within certain populations; having bilingual questionnaires and interviewers is not enough. Participation of people who know the community and are known and respected by the community is extremely important.

10. Examine the definitions used in the study, and determine the root of any assumptions (for example, "noncompliant").

11. Meet the community's needs in terms of economic development (job opportunities, sharing grant funds) and staff development (providing technical assistance and ongoing consultation with the collaborating agency's staff).

12. Recognize and nurture common bonds.

13. Acknowledge and address the issue of mistrust and the effects of factors such as sexism, racism, poverty, patriarchy, and homophobia.

14. Understand that the research study developed in collaboration for the community agency will most likely be used for programmatic development and community interventions rather than for more purely academic reasons.

Finally, the collaboration, like the study, is a creative process in which at least two things must occur: The collaborators must be continually flexible in shaping their respective roles, which may not look exactly the same as described in the contract; and the collaborators will serve as ambassadors to their respective organizations (university, entire agency), representing the welfare of the project, and generating change in the structures or policies of the sponsoring organizations. Each organization should periodically evaluate its own learning as to its effectiveness as a project partner. If each organization has decided that collaboration is one aspect of their organizational culture, this should consistently be present regardless of personnel changes.

EDITORS' COMMENTS

The number and range of institutions of the authors on this case study represents just how collaborative this project was. Mary McCauley II was a founding member of Chicago's Lesbian Community Cancer Project and was its first Executive Director. Ellie Emanuel is an Associate Professor in the Department of Rehabilitation and Counseling in the Stout Vocational Rehabilitation Institute, University of Wisconsin-Stout, Menomonie, Wisconsin. Alice Dan is the Director of the Center for Research on Women and Gender at the University of Illinois-Chicago, and Zylphia Ford is at the Chicago Department of Public Health. Each of these women had a personal or political commitment to make this collaborative project of lesbian health concerns and needs work in spite of many problems and obstacles. By working together to create the Chicago Women's Health Survey, a team of community members and academics were able to survey both lesbian and heterosexual women about their health needs and problems and compare the two groups.

Collaborative research is not without its challenges, and this project in particular faced a variety of conflicts between the researchers. For example, university-based legal contracts do not take into consideration the jointly owned nature of intellectual property that results from these ventures. Debates about the ownership of the data and the protection of research participants (especially in situations where respondents could be potentially harmed by their identities being revealed) were only two of the issues that needed to be resolved in this project. The authors conclude their case with a list of guidelines for any academic and community-based collaboration.

The Closing of Central State Hospital: An Alliance of Academic and Government Collaboration[1]

ERIC R. WRIGHT and TERRY F. WHITE, *Indiana Consortium for Mental Health Services Research, Indiana University, and* RICHARD N. DELIBERTY, *Indiana Division of Mental Health*

Over the past four decades, thousands of people with serious mental illness have been discharged from large state psychiatric hospitals to smaller and more diffuse treatment programs in community settings (Grob 1994). This policy of deinstitutionalization occurred gradually during this period but gained the strongest momentum during the late 1960s and 1970s (Gronfein 1985). More recently, this "transfer of care" has gained renewed support as state governments have been forced to reconcile serious budget crises with the large budgets needed to support state mental hospitals (Brown 1985). Political debate has intensified with the recent resurgence in state efforts to downsize and close additional state mental hospitals, and with claims by many mental health advocates that deinstitutionalization has proven to be a failed policy (Isaac and Armat 1990). While researchers have been instrumental in documenting both the intended and unintended consequences of this policy (see Mechanic 1989 and Brown 1985 for comprehensive reviews), much of this work fails to inform current policy directed at reshaping America's state mental hospital system.

The closing of Central State Hospital (CSH), the oldest state mental hospital in Indiana, offered a significant opportunity for public policy makers and academics to work together to study many critical and still unanswered issues about the policy of deinstitutionalization. This case study provides a brief overview of a collaborative research effort launched between researchers at Indiana University and the Indiana Division of Mental Health shortly after the decision to close CSH. Over the course of the project, the team faced a number of significant challenges that had to be resolved in order to stay on track and ensure the success of the study. Here we recount briefly some of the sociopolitical circumstances surrounding the closure of CSH and the implementation of our research project (known locally as the Central State Hospital Discharge Study). With this background, we

[1] A version of this paper was presented at the International Field Directors and Technology Conference, Tampa, Florida, May 1995. The authors gratefully acknowledge the generous financial support of the National Institute of Mental Health (Grant No. MH51669) and the Indiana Family and Social Services Administration (Contract No. 49-3-009).

highlight two particular challenges that shaped our work and the overall organization of our study. Specifically, we focus on the importance of forging a balanced partnership and the mechanisms to do so; and the strategies we employed for ensuring the scientific integrity of the data. We conclude with a brief discussion of how future public-academic collaborative research projects could be improved.

Background: The Decision to Close Central State Hospital

Central State Hospital, located on the west side of downtown Indianapolis, opened its doors in 1848. By the mid-1960s, it had grown to house over 2,500 patients. Following a series of well-publicized patient deaths at the hospital in 1991 and 1992, Governor Evan Bayh ordered admissions to the hospital to be frozen in March 1992 pending a systematic investigation into the problems that led to these tragic deaths and a review of the overall quality of care being provided at the institution. At that time, CSH was staffed by 658 employees who provided care to 409 patients. While the majority of patients were diagnosed with serious mental illness (mainly schizophrenia and affective disorders), 20 (4.9 percent) held a primary diagnosis of a substance use disorder, and another 86 (21.2 percent) were developmentally disabled. Later that year, on June 23, 1992, Governor Bayh announced his decision to close the hospital on June 30, 1994.

In the subsequent months, through a series of reports to the governor, government officials outlined their plans to close the hospital and to use this as an opportunity to build additional community-based services and continue Indiana's long-term efforts toward deinstitutionalizing people with serious mental illness

(IDMH 1993; Richardson, Dyer, and Conner 1993). State officials asserted, "In the 1960s, over 16,000 people lived in state hospitals and developmental centers. Today that number is approximately 3,300" (Richardson, Dyer, and Conner 1993, 1). These reports also summarized the guiding beliefs of government officials: that the hospital did not provide the best possible care, that institutional care was more costly than community-based care, and that new services and treatment systems are now (or soon would be) available, making community care more viable. To facilitate the closing of CSH, a special "transition fund" was created to finance the process of moving patients into community-care settings, and an oversight and coordination committee of officials from various state agencies and CSH was formed. Late in 1993, an employee assistance program was added to aid CSH staff who were being dislocated by the closure.

Not everyone agreed with the plan to close Central State Hospital. Politicians, the media, and the general public feared that former clients would end up homeless and in jails. The local newspapers, in particular, took a keen interest in the decision and regularly published articles describing public and professional concern that the current community system was already overburdened and that persons with mental illness constituted a high proportion of those who are homeless. Not only was there concern about the conduct of former patients, people were worried that the burden of the cost of care would not be covered in community settings and that costs might actually rise rather than be reduced, as the governor and state officials asserted.

A serious practical problem for government officials in both planning and responding to the criticisms expressed by advocates and journalists was the overwhelming absence of concrete, practical data on the process of closing and downsizing mental hospitals, or representative data describing the long-term outcomes of deinstitutionalized mental patients.[2] In this politically charged environment, discussions occurred between senior staff members at the Indiana Division of Mental Health (IDMH) and researchers from Indiana University during the initiation of the closing of CSH (see McDonel et al. 1993). These discussions focused on the critical need to establish some sort of tracking program and mechanisms to assess the outcomes of this decision. With the financial support of the IDMH, these researchers assembled a steering committee to develop and design a comprehensive study of the closing of Central State Hospital. The committee was composed of 22 individuals, including academic researchers from three different universities, public advocates, and government policy makers.

The Central State Hospital Discharge Study

Early in the collaboration, it was clear that government policy makers and academics held different goals for the research. Government officials saw the project primarily as a "tracking" project that would provide them with regular and timely information on the

process of deinstitutionalization. This information, they maintained, was and would continue to be critical for them to effectively monitor the outcomes of the decision and to intervene proactively as problems were identified in the process. In contrast, the academic researchers saw this as an exciting opportunity to conduct an in-depth study of the *outcomes* of deinstitutionalization for mental patients, their families, and the community. Recognizing that the bulk of research on the impact of deinstitutionalization is based on unrepresentative samples of former mental patients, the academic researchers felt that this study would constitute a major scientific contribution. During the initial series of steering committee meetings, discussions focused on outlining the major research questions of the committee members and developing a study-design and procedures that could effectively address these divergent, and frequently conflicting, agendas.

Because the IDMH was funding the research and participating in the design phase of the project, many critics and legislators vocalized concerns about the "objectivity" and "scientific adequacy" of the research. For this reason, the planning, design, and oversight activities of the steering committee were organizationally separated from the field operations and data analysis.[3] This structure protected the IDMH from criticisms of using "biased" data to evaluate a politically controversial policy and allowed a more stringent application of scientific standards of data collection than is frequently found in evaluation

---

[2] While there are a number of published studies on the long-term trends in deinstitutionalization (see Brown 1985, Gronfein 1985, and Mechanic 1989 for reviews) and studies of unrepresentative samples of former mental patients, there have been few, if any, systematic efforts to study an entire cohort of individuals deinstitutionalized from the same institution. The absence of such studies makes it difficult to estimate accurately the number of patients likely to end up homeless, in jail, or in other dire circumstances. More practically, in the absence of comparative policy studies of different hospital closings, decisions regarding the best way to downsize or close hospitals are being made without empirical guidance.

[3] The steering committee was intentionally inclusive. Anyone concerned about the impact of the closure or interested in the study was invited to attend. In fact, many of these "interested parties" suggested a number of important research questions and analytic strategies that were incorporated into the overall plan.

research. This organizational structure, however, has also increased the pressure on the academic researchers, as they were viewed as the only "neutral" observers of the process in a very politically charged environment.

The study itself consisted of two major data collection efforts: (1) a monthly tracking survey and (2) a program of in-depth, face-to-face interviews with samples of people affected by the closure: patients, their families, and hospital employees. The tracking survey focused on the entire cohort of 389 patients who were enrolled at Central State Hospital on the day admissions were frozen by the governor (March 23, 1992).[4] Each month, the primary clinicians of each of these consumers were surveyed either by phone or by a written questionnaire. The instrument queried informants about the location, service status, and clinical functioning of clients. Additional data was collected on episodes of inpatient care, contact with law enforcement, and the costs of community care. Practically, this survey has been very difficult to implement and manage (see Wright et al. 1994). Hundreds of providers had to be taught how to provide tracking information. Further, because community mental health workers are often overburdened and difficult to reach by phone (they are frequently in the community working with clients), many of our clinician-respondents had to be reminded frequently to file their reports with our office. Concerns regarding data security also meant that data management staff had to devise special procedures to protect the data. One unanticipated challenge was the volume of reports we received from anonymous callers and interested parties "reporting" issues and concerns. The field staff accepted these calls and pieces of information

graciously, but they were only included in our database when staff could independently verify the account provided. Nevertheless, this turned out to be an important source of tracking data.

The interview portion of the study, while relatively straightforward from a survey research point of view, was also more difficult than usual because of the complexity and volume of the research questions asked by the team and because of the practical difficulties imposed by the closure process. While the interdisciplinary team provided for a more holistic conceptual framework of the closure process, the instrumentation and interview protocol took several months to design and pretest in order to adequately accommodate the team's many concerns (see McDonel et al. 1993 for the theoretical framework guiding this research). In the end, the final interview schedules were approved for the three study populations (patients, workers, and family). Each interview averaged one and a half hours.

The closure process also created special practical difficulties for the research team. At the beginning of our field period (August 1993), we were provided with a complete listing of all patients and workers who were living and working at the hospital. Over the course of that year, state legislators continued to debate whether the governor had the legal authority to close the hospital. Consequently, many hospital staff and community mental health professionals voiced their reluctance to implement the closure process because of the chance that the legislature might order the hospital to stay open. Our original protocol design was to conduct the patient baseline interview within 30 days prior to discharge. This protocol, however, required that we know in advance the discharge plans for each patient. As the closure date approached, communication both in the hospital and with the community facilities

---

[4]Those who held a diagnosis of substance abuse (N=20) were excluded from this research at the request of IDMH officials.

began to happen more rapidly and unpredictably, making it nearly impossible for us to know who was leaving the hospital when. In December 1993, when it became clear that the closure was imminent, we relaxed our protocol and launched an all-out effort to interview every patient and staff member who was still at the hospital. Cooperation from the former patients was often easier to obtain than cooperation from staff members and providers in other settings who continued to view the researchers with suspicion. In one informant's words, the atmosphere was "paranoid," and it felt like the hospital was "imploding." The emotionality of the environment made it extremely stressful for the research staff as well. Interviews often ended in tears and pleas for help. The continuing media attention on both the closure process and our research has only added to the charged environment and made the field staff's efforts to establish rapport with the research subjects more difficult.

In the end, we completed interviews with 88 patients and 124 workers by the official closing date of the hospital (June 30, 1994). In 1995, we launched our first wave of interviews with family members and conducted the first follow-up interviews with both the patients and workers one year after the closing of the hospital. In retrospect, the relative success of our project was dependent on the research team's, and particularly the field staff's, ability to forge partnerships with all of the major advocacy groups and balance the demands for timely results with the need to ensure scientific integrity of the study.

Forging Balanced Partnerships

The political nature of the decision to close CSH and the closure process itself meant that many people had vested interests in the results of our study. Indeed, part of the initial motivation in creating the steering committee was to

be inclusive of those with policy and/or academic research interests. In reality, however, the interdisciplinary management team structure was not enough. Over the course of the first year of the project, and several months *before* IDMH awarded any funds to support this work, the principal investigators and field staff began attending meetings with the various parties involved in the closure process, including legislators, patients and their families, union representatives, advocates, and staff from various governmental agencies. While this was a very time-consuming process, it did provide a vital perspective on the variety of opinions regarding the decision and on the bureaucratic process surrounding the situation. More importantly, by being present and demonstrating a deep appreciation of the complexity of the issues, over time we succeeded in defining both the project and the field staff as "insiders" in the process.

Establishing the study's impartiality, however, was also dependent on our building a special working relationship with IDMH—the major funding agency for the project. On the one hand, the field staff needed quick and ready access to existing data and information about the closure process, and this required frequent and close contact with key IDMH staff. On the other hand, we also needed to ensure that IDMH staff could not control the design or outcomes of the study. Because of fundamental differences in academics' and policy makers' views on the goals of research, building this relationship was often frustrating, required frequent discussions, and involved making strategic compromises on both sides. For example, early in the implementation of the tracking program, the field staff encountered resistance to participating in the study by the clinical staff at the community mental health centers to which the former CSH patients were being discharged. IDMH staff's response upon hearing this was to suggest that IDMH mandate participation in the study by including it in their contract with the state for funding.[5]

The academic researchers, concerned about the quality of the data, recommended that a better strategy would be to take the extra time to "prep the field" and garner these providers' support for the study on a voluntary basis. IDMH consented, but included contract language mandating participation as a "plan B" solution in the event that field staff could not garner adequate participation. It took over six months of meetings and training sessions to convince the staff in the six community mental health centers across central Indiana to participate in the process; but, in the end, both IDMH and the clinical staff felt more confident in the quality and objectivity of these data because of our field staff's efforts.

Balancing Science and Timeliness

Rossi and Freeman describe evaluation research as "the systematic application of social research procedures for assessing the conceptualization, design, implementation, and utility of social intervention programs" (1993, 5). Our experience with the CSH project has been that, practically speaking, this is not an easy task. In contrast to traditional survey or experimental research in which the researcher has more control over the conditions of the study, our evaluation of the closing of a hospital was like studying a moving target. Indeed, while government officials, the legislature, and the media

[5]Each mental health center that was to receive one of the discharged CSH patients was responsible for developing a special contract that IDMH would fund to cover the costs of providing care to this special group of patients. The "Community Transition Fund" provided the money for this special funding stream.

frequently voiced frustration at the slow pace of the project, the academics were overwhelmed by the quick turnaround expected on the research for it to be deemed "relevant" and "timely." The demands for speedy results posed important threats to the scientific validity of the data collected. Similarly, public and governmental reactions to the speed of the research also cast doubt on the wisdom of IDMH's commitment to continue their financial support of the project.

At the beginning of 1994, a compromise was established. Each month, we agreed to provide a short update to IDMH staff on the location and service status of the 389 clients in the tracking study. On a semiannual basis, the field staff agreed to develop an expanded summary report, again for IDMH to distribute, that would describe more completely the overall functioning of the entire cohort of consumers. These reporting procedures satisfied the IDMH and other government officials' need to know what was going on while also allowing the academic researchers more time to review and study the interview data in detail.

A major factor in our being able to strike this balance was that the field staff took time to outline the scientific issues for the nonacademics involved. Specifically, the principal investigators met frequently with advocates and policy makers to discuss their information needs and to translate their concerns into applied research questions. We tried to highlight the data needs for answering specific research questions as well as the rationale for various segments of the study. In particular, we made a special effort to clarify the limitations and validity of particular questions and data. By engaging in these types of discussions, the academics succeeded in enlisting various interested parties in setting priorities and focusing the research agenda while also being able to maintain higher standards of scientific validity of the overall study. Over time, the team hopes that the in-depth outcome analyses can be linked with the process data being documented in the tracking study to provide a deeper understanding of the deinstitutionalization process that will be of use to *both* mental health policy makers and academic audiences.

Conclusion

Many of the problems we faced in the CSH project are characteristic of public-academic research collaboration in the area of mental health (see Gilchrist et al.1994). We feel that we have had and continue to have many successes with this project. There are also several areas where (if we had known more what to expect), we could have improved our project both practically and scientifically. First, the academic researchers could have benefited from being brought into the planning discussions so they could have reviewed the goals of the research much earlier in the closure process. Evaluation research aimed at studying the guiding assumptions of specific policies requires a deep understanding of the rationale and logic of the policies being implemented (see Rossi and Freeman 1993). While our team of academics was familiar with the broad scientific research on deinstitutionalization, the late implementation of the research meant that the academics had to learn "on the job" the details of the case after the decision had been made and plans were well under way. Had the academics been involved earlier in the process, the research design could have been more carefully tailored to test systematically the assumptions guiding the closure process.

The ambiguity and tension inherent in public-academic collaborative ventures also suggest a need to incorporate these issues early in the research planning process. As mentioned earlier, policy makers and academics had different agendas for our study. While we have been able to combine these agendas into a "win-win" situation, it took significant amounts of time, and many frustrating discussions, to clarify the divergent agendas and needs of the public and academic actors involved. Indeed, early in the relationship, many of the public officials involved in the project became convinced that the project would not yield the "practical" information they had hoped. At several points, their frustrations directly threatened the continuation of the project. Nevertheless, because of the persistence of a few key public and academic team members in confronting the difficult problems, the field staff were able to shape the project in ways that specifically and effectively addressed the needs of both parties. In particular, we developed a list of key products (for example, specific technical reports and code books; see Wright et al. 1994, for an example) that would result from the project over the contract period. Our success in this project grew out of these negotiations as they heightened awareness of the differences in the environmental context of our public and academic team members' project-related work.

In many ways, government officials see research as an intermediate step to improve planning, to test new policies, and to respond to their critics. Their audience is the public, lobbyists and advocates, and other governmental officials. Academic researchers, in contrast, orient their research toward their own professional circles. Recognizing these interests at the beginning and integrating them into the planning process would greatly enhance future projects.

Collaborative researchers face a unique set of problems when one of the collaborators and funders of the project is government based. This was the situation faced by the authors in this case study. Eric Wright and Terry White are academic researchers based at the Indiana Consortium for Mental Health Services at Indiana University, and Richard DeLiberty is Deputy Director of the Indiana Division of Mental Health. Central State Hospital was the oldest and largest state mental hospital in Indiana before it was scheduled to be closed in 1994. The scheduled closure created fears among politicians, the media, and the general public that the patients would end up homeless or in the criminal justice system. As a result, senior officials at the Indiana Division of Mental Health approached researchers at Indiana University with the proposal to develop a comprehensive study of the closing of Central State and to track the former patients as they moved into the community.

A problem facing this type of collaborative project was the different goals, concerns, and information resulting from the study. For example, the academic researchers found it difficult to meet the demands of state officials for "relevant" and "timely" data without jeopardizing the scientific nature of the project by rushing the data collection and analysis. A compromise that satisfied both the academic researchers and the government officials was reached, but not without a major effort on both sides. With the experience that both sides have had in this project, the authors also outline recommendations for further academic-state policy-making collaborative ventures.

The Center for AIDS Prevention Studies' Collaboration Program: An Alliance of AIDS Scientists and Community-Based Organizations

DIANE BINSON, *Center for AIDS Prevention Studies, University of California, San Francisco,* GARY HARPER, *Department of Psychology, DePaul University, and* OLGA GRINSTEAD *and* KATHERINE HAYNES SANSTAD, *Center for AIDS Prevention Studies, University of California, San Francisco*

Technology transfer and feedback between behavioral and social science research and prevention efforts must be improved, increased, and accelerated.

—National Commission on AIDS, 1993

Social science research is a key element in the battle against AIDS. Its effectiveness, however, is directly related to its success in changing practice and policy. This is particularly true in the field of AIDS prevention, in which research and service are usually performed by different groups of professionals. The work and reward structures for researchers and service professionals are quite different and often create barriers to sharing knowledge and practices. Researchers are rewarded for publishing in professional journals; providers are rewarded for the number of clients they serve. Researchers often appear to have much greater resources to conduct studies than providers do to offer services. The primary objective of research is furthering theory and method; the primary objective of service is meeting client needs.

In an effort to dismantle these barriers, the Center for AIDS Prevention Studies (CAPS) at the University of California, San Francisco, has created a program, Technology and Information Exchange, that creates innovative links between social science researchers and community-based organizations. In addition to the direct interchange of ideas, research expertise, and innovative HIV interventions between CAPS scientists and the staff of community organizations, the Technology and Information Exchange program disseminates research findings related to HIV prevention and provides a forum for consultation and technical assistance to researchers, prevention service providers, and policy makers. The specific aims of the Technology and Information Exchange Program are as follows:

1. Coordinate a program of community-based collaborative HIV prevention science that further develops HIV service providers' skills in program planning and evaluation and carries out research on interventions among vulnerable populations.

2. Provide an environment for consultation and technical assistance between HIV service providers and CAPS scientists that links HIV prevention research and service.

3. Disseminate HIV prevention research findings to HIV service providers through Prevention Fact Sheets, HandsNet, and the Internet.

4. Inform policy makers by providing research summaries and analyses to legislators, public health officials, and funders.

5. Provide news and analysis of HIV prevention science through the media.

The Technology and Information Exchange Model

Service providers, policy makers, and the public all have a stake in knowing what works in HIV prevention. Service providers and those who set program funding policy need to know how to implement prevention programs. Service providers also need skills to plan, evaluate, and improve programs. At the same time, researchers need contact with high-risk populations, exposure to how prevention programs are conducted in the field, awareness of promising prevention approaches, and feedback from service providers in order to design timely and relevant research. The Technology and Information Exchange program has developed a model for technology and information exchange that uses a mix of information and interaction in an effort to integrate practice among researchers, service providers, and policy makers, and to inform the public. The model is designed around the following activities (see Figure 1):

- Seek information and know-how from both research and service

- Forge links between research and service that improve prevention programs

- Interpret and disseminate HIV prevention information

- Gather feedback from service providers and researchers, which is used in the development, implementation, and interpretation of prevention research

Community-Based Collaboration Program[1]

During the last three years, the collaboration between CAPS' scientists, Bay Area community-based organizations, and Northern California Grantmakers (NCG) has involved 16 organizations—5 in 1992–93 and 11 in 1994–96. (Table 21.1 lists the 11 organizations currently working with CAPS).[2] They represent a wide range of target populations, agency sizes, types of HIV interventions, and research experience. The focus of these projects is HIV intervention, and the primary purpose of the collaboration with CAPS' scientists and NCG is to build an evaluation component into the intervention effort. The program involves monthly meetings for all participants as well as individual project meetings between staff of the community organization and CAPS scientists. This case study describes two of these collaborative projects, the Marin AIDS Project, which provides AIDS prevention programs at San Quentin prison, and the Tri-City Health Center's Youth Action Project, which focuses on AIDS prevention among adolescents.

---

[1]This program is funded jointly by Northern California Grantmakers and the National Institute of Mental Health with evaluation funds from the Ford Foundation.

[2]For more detail on how these collaborations were established see "The HIV Prevention Evaluation Initiative: Model for Collaborative and Empowerment Evaluation." Cynthia A. Gomez and Ellen Goldstein, in *Empowerment Evaluation: Knowledge and Tools for Self-Assessment and Accountability*, (Eds.) Fetterman, Wandersman and Kaftarian. Belmont, CA: Sage, 1995.

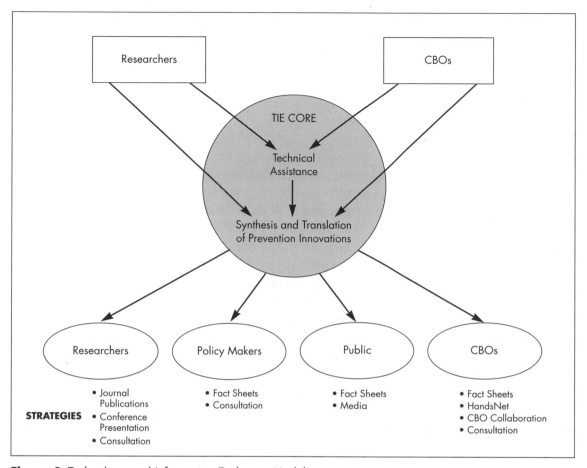

Figure 1 Technology and Information Exchange Model

The Marin AIDS Project

The Marin AIDS Project has been conducting HIV prevention programs for inmates at San Quentin prison since 1987. The first collaborative project with CAPS' scientist Olga Grinstead involved an evaluation of their ongoing peer education projects for incoming inmates. San Quentin is a reception center; inmates from all of the Northern California counties are processed at San Quentin and then sent to other prisons in California. For this reason, San Quentin is the ideal location for such a pro-

gram, which serves thousands of inmates every year. The intervention consists of an hour-long discussion led by a trained HIV-positive inmate who reviews the basic facts about HIV/AIDS and discusses how to prevent infection. In our evaluation we compared this peer-led intervention with a similar intervention led by a professional HIV educator who was not an inmate. Our evaluation found that inmates prefer peer education and do change their behavioral *intentions* as a result of their participation in the intervention.

TABLE 21.1

1994–1996 Community-Based Collaborative HIV Prevention Science Program (in Progress)

Coalition for Immigrant & Refugee Rights & Services—Impact of empowerment intervention on HIV risk behaviors among Latina immigrant women, San Francisco, CA.

East Bay Community Recovery Project—Impact of improvisational theater on HIV risk behaviors of substance abusers in recovery, Alameda County, CA.

Face to Face—Impact of peer-led street outreach to high-risk youth and their parents in two neighborhoods, Santa Rosa, CA.

La Clinica de la Raza—Effect of multilingual peer education program for Latino youth and their parents, Oakland, CA.

Marin AIDS Project—Effects of peer-led intervention for incarcerated men delivered at entry and before release vs. intervention upon entry only, San Quentin, CA.

Mid-Peninsula YWCA—Peer- and adult-led prevention interventions with in-school youth, Santa Clara County, CA.

National Task Force on AIDS Prevention—Impact of 13-week community outreach and intervention with African American gay, bisexual, and transgender men, San Francisco, CA.

The New Conservatory Theater Center—Effects of school-based theater intervention on parent-child communication, Chico, CA.

STOP AIDS Project—Effects of STOP AIDS small group meetings for gay men in preexisting social groups, San Francisco, CA.

Tri-City Health Center—Impact of outreach and small group prevention intervention with high-risk youth, Alameda County, CA.

Youth Advocates—Impact of 10-session prevention intervention for high-risk youth, San Francisco, CA.

We are currently conducting three projects at San Quentin State Prison in collaboration with the Marin AIDS Project. While our first project showed that peer education could change behavioral intentions, we wanted to know if we could influence inmates' behavior after they leave prison. In this project, we randomly assigned men leaving the prison to receive or not to receive a one-session peer education visit prior to their release. Men are being traced after they leave prison and asked about their actual sexual and drug-using behavior since release. A natural extension of our interest in inmates' behavior after they leave prison was to consider the needs of their female partners on the outside. To pursue this interest, we are currently conducting a study of women visiting male prisoners. The study includes a needs assessment and an exploratory study of whether the peer education model can be transferred to meet the HIV prevention needs of these women. Finally, we are currently developing a pre-release class specifically designed to meet the needs of HIV-infected inmates leaving prison. HIV-infected inmates have been serving the prison for many years as peer educators. As a result of this project, we will have the opportunity to offer them a post-release intervention to facilitate their utilization of community resources. The goal of this project is consistent with all of our other projects at San Quentin: to prevent new HIV infections among members of the prison community, which includes inmates and all of their intimate partners outside and inside the prison.

It would not be possible to conduct this research at San Quentin prison without our collaboration with the Marin AIDS Project. Having worked in the prison for many years, the program staff at the Marin AIDS Project have developed relationships with the prison administration, correctional officers, and other organizations serving inmates. The academic researchers at CAPS, on the other hand, were situated to provide the research expertise to design evaluation studies that inform program staff of the effectiveness (or ineffectiveness) of their interventions and of what interventions are most urgently needed next.

The collaboration of academic researchers and community-based organizations is critical to meeting the HIV prevention needs of disenfranchised communities. Who can better define the intervention needs and critical evaluation needs of disenfranchised communities than those who have been working to prevent HIV in such communities since the beginning of the epidemic? Who can better develop evaluation research questions and produce manuscripts, reports, and presentations that inform project staff as well as administrators, funders, and policy makers than academic researchers? Research collaboration between community-based organizations and academic researchers works because each of us is able to do what we do best. In the world of AIDS prevention, time is always of the essence. Collaborative research is efficient: Important research questions are addressed in a timely way, and the results go immediately to the individuals most likely to use them.

Tri-City Health Center's Youth Action Project (YAP)

One of the things we know about adolescents who do not attend school or who are chronically truant, is that compared to their in-school counterparts, they participate in higher rates of HIV risk behaviors. In addition, these high-risk adolescents are typically not reached by traditional school-based HIV prevention programs. Tri-City Health Center's Youth Action Project (YAP) is a multilevel, community-based HIV prevention program that targets a variety of high-risk adolescents, including homeless, runaway, chronically truant, and gang-affiliated youth. The research component consists of evaluating YAP's effectiveness in lowering the rates of HIV risk behaviors among the study participants. It was designed in collaboration with Tri-City Health Center's Lisa Carver and CAPS' scientist Gary Harper.

In order to assure that YAP is culturally sensitive and relevant to the needs of high-risk adolescents, members of the target population are involved in all phases of the program. The first component of the project involves the distribution of HIV prevention information and supplies (such as condoms, lubricant, bleach) to high-risk adolescents in parks, on street corners, and in other public areas where they congregate. At the same time, interested individuals are invited to attend a safer sex workshop, which is the second component. The workshops are interactive sessions that teach self-protective skills through activities, peer modeling, and role plays with guided practice and corrective feedback. The primary content areas of the workshops include consequences of high-risk sexual activity, sexual communication skills, sexual decision making, effects of substance use on self-regulation, condom placement skills, and erotic alternatives to high-risk sexual activity. The third component of the program is a monthly meeting of the adolescents, who participate in additional prevention activities and receive social support for positive behavior change. The fourth component is a series of weekly open office hours during which the participants are free to drop in at the YAP office. The office is decorated with youth-generated posters regarding safer sex activities; a bulletin board with information on jobs, social services, cultural events, and HIV-related events; and baskets of free condoms, bleach, and lubricant. During office hours, adolescents can talk with the project staff and peers in a relaxed environment and receive social support for positive behavior change.

Impact on the Community and High-Risk Adolescents

The YAP-CAPS collaborative research effort has had an impact on both the community and on the population of high-risk adolescents served by the project. On the community level, the research has helped to make community government aware of the high-risk adolescents (who are runaways, homeless, chronically truant, or involved in gangs) in their suburban neighborhoods and in desperate need of an array of services. Although we are still collecting data for this project, the number of target population youths involved in the project so far has been a clear indication that an entire population of high-risk adolescents, heretofore "invisible" in the eyes of the community, lives in these suburban areas.

The impact on the target population has been by far the greatest. Because of this collaborative project, high-risk adolescents now have a safe place to congregate and to receive a range of services. The outreach component of the collaborative effort has provided preven-tion services to a wide range of adolescents and has served as a way to educate members of the target population about services that are provided by YAP. In the first eight months of operation, over 1,600 youths were contacted through outreach activities, and approximately 450 contacted or visited the YAP office to receive additional services. The participants in this project have responded favorably to the research component. The majority take their time when completing pre- and post-test measures and have been inquisitive about the various aspects of the project. Many adolescents have encouraged their friends to get involved in the project and have personally brought them to the center or told them about filling out a survey during street outreach. This enthusiasm has helped with follow-up data collection, as the participants are generally quite interested in completing the various measures. Since the questionnaires give the adolescents a chance to tell about their life experiences, many participants see the research component as a way to let others know about the difficulties with which they are struggling. Many of these young people have had multiple, negative interactions with adults and authority figures who have suppressed their self-expression. The questionnaires allow the youths to have a voice that they know will be heard. Our continued contact with the participants through reminder/check-up calls, birthday gift packages, and outreach contacts demonstrates to the youths that their input is important to the study and helps to assure them that we are truly interested in what they have to say. Many youths have been surprised when they are called for follow-up or when they are contacted to receive a birthday package, and they have indicated to the staff that such contact has given them confidence that YAP is genuine and sincere.

Methodological Issues

The challenging methodological issues that have arisen during this project have mainly centered around sampling and data collection. One primary research question that we are attempting to address is the differential impact of having high-risk adolescents participate in either mixed gender or single gender HIV prevention workshops. We initially wanted to assign participants randomly to one of these conditions. But since all of our participants are recruited through street outreach, we were concerned that if friends who were "hanging out" together were assigned to different conditions, they would not attend. Another concern was that since several of our participants are affiliated with gangs, we did not want to risk the chance of violence due to the mixing of rival gangs. These assumptions were corroborated by our youth workers and other youths from the target populations.

Our solution was to use each outreach site as the unit of randomization instead of the individual participant. We were concerned that this restriction of the number of experimental units (21 outreach sites) would prohibit us from obtaining adequate balance across the experimental groups on demographic factors that might affect the outcomes of the study. The primary variables that we were concerned about were ethnicity and type of high-risk youth (runaway, homeless, truant, gang affiliated). We collected preliminary demographic information from youths at all of our sites and then blocked them according to the type of adolescents who frequented the sites. When this was done, ethnicity was evenly distributed within each block. Sites within a block were then randomized to either the single or mixed gender condition. This modified randomization procedure resulted in a balanced mix of participants across the experimental conditions.

The methodological challenge regarding data was related to the types of data we are collecting. In our initial plans, the majority of the data was going to be quantitative in nature, derived from a series of pre- and post-test questionnaires that were developed specifically for this study. As the project was being developed and pilot tested, we saw an increasing need to expand our scope to include other types of data. One change was to develop a contact log to record the number and types of contacts made with each participant. This data will be used to determine the "dose-response" relationships and will help to give the community organization an indication of what components of the project are most frequently used. The project staff are also recording qualitative data in the form of field notes. This information will be beneficial in determining ways to modify the program and to help make recommendations for future program development.

New Resources for the Community

The implementation of YAP has resulted in the development of several services aimed at high-risk adolescents. Since these adolescents are confronted with a variety of life stressors that may affect their ability to practice safer sex, the services extend beyond traditional HIV prevention. Many of the new programs have been developed in response to the participants' needs and with their input. Following are detailed descriptions of the services currently being provided through YAP—all of which will continue even after the completion of the research project.

■ The first component is the street-based outreach that provides HIV prevention materials and supplies to high-risk adolescents in the places where they congregate and socialize. Outreach contacts also serve as a way to inform youths about the YAP drop-in center and about the range of services provided by the project. As the study has progressed, the number of outreach sites has increased, and more adolescents from the target population have been contacted. Educational materials distributed during street outreach are all developed by youth workers involved in the project, which allows for the development of population-specific messages that are delivered to adolescents in their own language and style. Since the initiation of this collaborative effort, our youth workers have developed educational materials on an array of prevention topics that can be used in other programs as well.

■ The YAP drop-in center is another new resource that was developed as part of the collaborative effort. This is a safe, drug-free environment where youths can come to relax and talk with project staff and other peers and/or receive a range of services, including HIV/STD prevention, family planning, tutoring, job search assistance, and resume development. In addition, youths in need of additional social services get help with all phases of obtaining such services, and project staff make follow-up contacts to assure that the youths' needs are met. Services are provided in a youth-focused and nonjudgmental way, and project staff members work to empower the youths to take control of their lives. Participants have the opportunity to educate other adolescents through the design of educational posters and flyers. Youth educators are available during all office hours for participants who may feel uncomfortable working directly with an adult.

■ The final service developed as part of the collaborative research effort is a comprehensive HIV prevention workshop. The workshop is an interactive session that teaches self-protective skills through activities and peer modeling, and further enhances them through role plays with guided practice and corrective feedback. The workshop deals with consequences of high-risk sexual activity, sexual communication skills, sexual decision making, effects of substance use on self-regulation, condom placement skills, and erotic alternatives to high-risk sexual activity. The curriculum and activities for the workshop were developed specifically for implementation with this project but will now be available for use in other projects and agencies.

Student Involvement

Students have been involved in this project at two different levels. One college student has consistently served as a research assistant, primarily involved in data management. This individual has received general training in the conduct of research in community settings and has learned about the differences between community-based and laboratory-based research. He has also received training in various methods of data collection and in the development of research questionnaires. Working on this project has not only exposed him to community-based research but has also helped to increase his understanding of the material presented in his psychology courses at the university. He has remarked that he now takes a more analytic approach to reading research articles and delves deeper into the methodology used in studies. Since he now has a better understanding of the "nuts and bolts" of research, he pays more attention to the types of data collected and has a greater appreciation for the amount of work that goes into research.

High school students and one college student have also served as our youth outreach workers. These individuals represent a range of ethnic backgrounds and have all been involved in activities that would place them in the target population. They have benefited in different ways from participation in the project and have become more aware of the issues that confront youths living in their community. They have displayed higher levels of maturity as the project has progressed and have become known by their peers as "experts" on issues related to sexuality, sexually transmitted diseases, and HIV. One of our youth workers who has been with the project from the beginning of the study stated, "I have become much more open-minded about what is going on in my community. The best part is knowing that I'm helping other youth and that they're getting something out of it." Another youth who has been involved with the project from the start also talked about how he has become more "open-minded" and stated that he is now "bursting with knowledge." This young man has also remarked on the personal benefits of his participation in the project: "It gives me self-esteem. I am more sure of myself, and I now know what I need to do to take care of myself."

Youth workers have also had the opportunity to gain recognition for their efforts at a community level. As a result of a recent youth candlelight vigil that the workers helped to organize in observance of World AIDS Day, one of our youth workers had her picture on the front page of a community newspaper, and another had an interview with a reporter that was televised on the nightly news. These events gave the young people a greater sense that the community is invested in the work they are doing and cares about how they are reaching out to each other.

Impact on CAPS Scientists

As the CAPS scientist (Gary Harper) on this paper, my own experience with this collaborative project has given me a greater understanding of and appreciation for the tireless work conducted by many workers in community-based organizations. I have gained greater insight into their daily work lives and have witnessed the multiple stressors that confront service providers in these settings. This information is extremely valuable to researchers who collaborate with these organizations, for without knowledge of the multiple demands placed on the workers, the researcher may formulate unrealistic expectations for the project and staff. The researcher must realize that the primary focus of community-based organizations is to provide services, and even when they are engaged in collaborative research, the needs of the target population are paramount. With this understanding, I have learned to be more flexible in my approach to collaborative research and to watch more closely for early signs that modifications will need to be made in the project.

While some researchers may view the sometimes fluctuating nature of community-based organizations as an impediment to research, I have seen it as an opportunity for discovery and growth. It has forced me and the organization's project coordinator to strike a balance between maintaining enough scientific rigor to produce valid results and allowing enough flexibility to provide the services that are truly needed within the target population. One way to do this is to develop one or more research questions that will remain stable throughout the project, while allowing for the development of secondary questions as the project progresses. The primary questions are not dependent on all components of the study, which allows for changes that may occur based on the target population's and organization's needs, and does not destroy the scientific integrity of the study.

When using such a strategy, the need for rigorous documentation is increased in order to determine which services were received by participants and how these different services were related to the outcomes of interest (the "dose-response" relationship). The introduction of secondary research questions often increases the relevance of the study findings for the target population and the service providers since these hypotheses are generated with input from these individuals as the project develops. So far, involvement in this collaborative project has also resulted in several presentations at academic conferences. These meetings have afforded me the opportunity to talk with other researchers about the benefits of conducting collaborative research, while also cautioning them about the special circumstances and difficulties that may arise. When disseminating this information, it is important to incorporate the perspective of the community-based organization and to caution researchers against taking advantage of their resources and then leaving them without any beneficial products.

Vicissitudes of Collaboration

Many factors have contributed to the success of this collaborative research effort. Primary among them has been the match between the university researchers and the collaborating organization's project coordinator. Our shared commitment to helping high-risk adolescents and prior experience with this population has helped to strengthen our working relationship and has given us a common language. In addition, even though we are employed by very different institutions, we are both dedicated to reducing the spread of HIV. Since we share these common goals and interests, we have been able to bypass potential conflicts that might have arisen due to differing philosophical perspectives. We've also taken the time to learn about each others' work environments and about the different demands placed on us by our respective institutions. This inquiry has also extended to learning about our respective talents and areas of expertise related to both the target population and to HIV prevention. I think that this relationship-building process has strengthened our work and has given both of us an appreciation and respect for the other's unique talents and strengths.

The other aspect of this project that has helped to make it a success is the involvement of youths from the target population. We sought input from these young people during each phase of the project, making both the research and service components relevant to the needs of high-risk youths. This has been especially important with regard to the wording of questions in our assessment questionnaires and the messages in our youth-generated outreach materials. Since we are speaking to the adolescents in their "own language," they are more likely to take the questionnaires seriously and to listen to the outreach messages. In addition, since youth workers are present during all phases of the project, participants have the option of talking with an adult or with a peer. When participants see the amount of input from other youths like themselves, it often helps to increase their comfort with the program, and they see that YAP is truly an advocate for young people.

Impediments to the collaborative relationship have been mostly structural and organizational. On the most basic level, the geographic distance between the university and the collaborating organization has made it difficult to have as much face-to-face contact and site visits as were desired. The community coordinator and I have had meetings at other locations to compensate for this, but the distance has made it difficult to be present during the implementation of the various project components. The organizational components have mostly been related to the way this particular collaborative relationship was established. As described earlier, the organization involved in this project is one of a number of community-based organizations that are conducting research in collaboration with CAPS' researchers, and a private agency is providing the majority of the funds for the endeavor. Even though this overall effort is designed to be a three-way collaboration between community organization, funder, and university, the community organizers have felt that the structure is "not a triangle, but a pyramid" and that they are at the bottom. The people from the community feel that their voice is not as loud since they do not control the money or the scientific resources to complete the research.

Impact on Social Policy

Even though the final data is not yet ready for this project, community leaders and policy makers are already looking forward to the results. The collaborating community organization's project coordinator spoke about the needs of the adolescents involved in our project at a public hearing that was held to review a draft of the HIV prevention planning committee's report. Following her testimony, both city officials and county HIV administrators asked her

to forward the findings from the project when they are available. Many of these individuals were not aware of the number of high-risk youths living in their community. As more data becomes available on these youths and more people become aware of their needs through this project, it is hoped that policy changes will occur that will lead to increased resources.

Emerging Insights and Implications for Future Research

Even without collecting and analyzing all the data, some themes are already very obvious. Primary among these is the need to expand existing models for changing HIV risk behavior as they have been applied to high-risk adolescents. Since HIV risk behaviors do not occur within a vacuum, prevention efforts should not be presented in a vacuum. Instead, programs should be sensitive to the variety of contextual factors affecting adolescents' lives and actions. This is especially important for young people who are struggling with life stressors that require more immediate attention than worrying about a disease, such as AIDS, which may not affect them for 10 years or more. Some of these youths are confronted with daily challenges to their basic survival, such as being "kicked out" of their homes or stalked by rival gang members. Even if they are not struggling for survival, normative adolescent development indicates that adolescents typically have a poor future time perspective and are most concerned with issues that have immediate consequences. Programs that focus on HIV risk reduction without considering other situational and immediate factors may not meet the needs of high-risk adolescents. Instead, comprehensive HIV prevention programs for high-risk adolescents should be developed that either provide adolescents with additional social services or incorporate an effective mechanism to do so.

The method and location of delivery of HIV prevention services to high-risk adolescents is also crucial. Messages need to be delivered to youths in various modes in their communities, and program developers must take the time to assure that sites where prevention activities take place are in convenient and safe locations. If the project is conducted in an area where there is gang activity, it is essential that these sites be located in a gang-neutral territory and that participants are not required to cross rival gang lines in order to receive services. Sites should also be close to public transportation and should be in inconspicuous locations so youths who do not want others to know they are attending can maintain their confidentiality.

Another theme addressed in this project is the importance of using adolescents from the target population in all phases of program development and implementation. This helps to increase the likelihood that participants understand and appropriately respond to both research questionnaires and prevention materials. The inclusion of target population adolescents can also help participants to feel more comfortable and encourage them to return for follow-up assessments. When participants see the extensive inclusion of the youth perspective in all phases of the prevention program, they are more likely to feel empowered to be part of the solution as they go forth into their communities and become active agents of change for other adolescents.

Evaluation of CAPS' Collaboration Program

An evaluation of the collaboration between CAPS' scientists and the community-based organizations and NCG (conducted by an independent research consulting firm) reported that all participants found the collaboration both taxing and rewarding. The collaboration was not without difficulties. The work took more time than was allotted. On average, community participants dedicated 30 percent more time than anticipated to the project; researchers spent nearly double the time anticipated. Also, six community organizations had staff turnover and five had management changes that slowed progress when information was not passed along to new staff. On the other hand, the organizations were "very satisfied" with their researchers' understanding of the project, and with the amount of access to the researcher. They valued the availability of funds for program evaluation. One participant commented, "It's given us the opportunity to measure change due to our project. We're looking more in-depth into our program, formalizing and documenting it." They also valued the support of other organizations struggling with similar issues: "It is good to hear community-based organizations voice their problems and solutions—it's good for networking and increasing resources." A CAPS researcher noted, "The benefit is that this keeps me in the field. Being able to work in the community through a local organization and not on my own is an advantage."

For CAPS scientists, the community organizations taught them what is feasible and what is real. A community participant said, "There are mutual benefits. . . . Researchers have access to populations we work with and a chance to do relevant research. Also, organizations can learn so much. This process says to us, we'll stick with you for the long run. It's the only way it can work." All the community participants agreed that research and program evaluation is a time-consuming and often frustrating process. Many of the staff in the community organizations did not have research backgrounds and many had not been involved in evaluations in the past. However, they indicated that involvement in this process has resulted in a change in their approach as an agency. In spite of the difficulties of research, they have plans to conduct more in the future, viewing it as a necessary part of their organizational culture.

EDITORS' COMMENTS

This case study by Diane Binson, Gary Harper, Olga Grinstead, and Katherine Haynes Sanstad actually presents two projects involving AIDS prevention. We have included two of the many studies coming out of the Center for AIDS Prevention Studies at the University of California, San Francisco, for the unique issues and populations discussed. The first study, the Marin AIDS Project, provides AIDS prevention programs for prisoners and their families at San Quentin prison. The second project, the Tri-City Health Center's Youth Action Project, focuses on AIDS prevention among adolescents. What makes each study of particular interest for this book (besides their populations) is the method of using peer educators and peer-led interventions. In both populations, peer-led interventions were essential to the success of working to prevent the spread of HIV. In the youth project, students in high school and college participated both as educators and youth outreach workers.

The researchers suggest that future studies should allow for some flexibility in the development of secondary questions as the projects progress. During the course of one of the research projects, the methodological scope of the study was also expanded to include both quantitative and qualitative data collection, which has led to valuable policy and health intervention strategies.

Grassroots Approaches to Violence Prevention: Rainbow House's Choosing Non-Violence Institute

NANCY A. MATTHEWS, *Northeastern Illinois University,* and
ANNE PARRY, *Rainbow House*

Rainbow House began as a shelter for battered women on the near south side of Chicago. Originally, their primary concern was domestic violence against women and children. In 1986, they started a violence prevention program. They began with outreach to high school students, educating them about how gender roles contribute to patterns of male violence against women and children. They found, however, that by high school, youths' ideas about what was normal behavior between girlfriends and boyfriends, women and men, were already pretty set. Girls often expressed their hesitancy ever to have a baby because they were afraid they would abuse a child due to their short tempers. When asked about violence in their relationships, girls admitted that they often initiated violence because of their partners' unwillingness or inability to express their feelings, which then led to a violent outburst. Teens involved in lesbian relationships also experienced violence. Others spoke of the sexual as well as physical abuse they experienced at the hands of parents or guardians. Boys already had strong notions connecting masculinity with violence, not only to be used to control girls, but to prove themselves on the street. Girls had accepted the gender socialization that led them to tolerate and even encourage some of the precursors to violence, such as jealous and possessive behavior by boyfriends.

Convinced of the value of working with youth and teaching them about healthy relationships without violence and how to recognize danger signals, Rainbow House had some difficult decisions to make about where to put their very limited time, personnel, and resources. They began to focus more on younger children—three-, four-, and five-year-olds participating in the Head Start and Child Care programs throughout Chicago. It quickly became clear that this was an age where one could effectively influence children in the area of problem solving and conflict resolution. Rainbow House had a plan for such an education program. They would train classroom teachers in the approach they developed for working with young children, which has come to be known as Choosing Non-Violence (CNV). Teachers would then implement the plan in the classroom. However, there was resistance to this plan by teachers—reluctance and discomfort serious enough to impede implementation. Rainbow House staff realized that a process designed explicitly for adults was also needed to enable them to work through their own definitions and experiences of violence and put them in a place in their own lives which would allow them to help children do the same. That has become the core of the CNV training.

Anne Parry, the director of the program, developed a curriculum that focuses on raising awareness of the pervasiveness of violence in American society. This curriculum relates violence to developmental issues affecting young children, explores the meaning of discipline, and offers alternative approaches to dealing with stress and conflict in everyday life, whether in the classroom, at home, or in public. Violence is such a volatile, personal issue that a 3-hour in-service workshop is inadequate to meet the actual need. However, the 8–10 hour program has been offered in a variety of models to meet individual groups' needs and circumstances. Single sessions on specific CNV concepts are provided as well as overview sessions. In response to the hundreds of calls from educators, administrators, and groups as diverse as employee assistance programs, church ministry groups, and health care professionals, Rainbow House formed the Rainbow House Institute for Choosing Non-Violence. Parry and Rainbow House have published a book, *Choosing Non-Violence: The Rainbow House Handbook to a Violence-Free Future for Young Children* that outlines the ideas and ways to put them into practice, and Parry has recently coauthored *Caring for Children in Dangerous Times: A Protocol for Responding to Violence* with the Chicago Department of Human Services, Children's Services Division. In addition, Take Ten is an action plan that offers the CNV ideas to older children and adults.

The Beginning of the Collaborative Research Project

Our collaborative research was facilitated by a nascent network of feminist activists and scholars. In the fall of 1994, Parry met Nancy Matthews, a sociologist with a background in studying feminist organizations, at a conference on bridging the gap between community activists and academics held at the University of Illinois, Chicago. Parry was already in touch with a network of academics she consulted with about doing an evaluation of her program, and people in that network knew Matthews was interested in this kind of work. Matthews and Parry met to discuss what Rainbow House needed and agreed that Matthews would design a research program to evaluate the Choosing Non-Violence training. Rainbow House had applied for and received a grant for this work, which was used to pay Matthews and a collaborator, Deborah Zapalik, to create the research design and conduct a small pilot study. Zapalik, an early childhood education specialist, had worked with the Choosing Non-Violence Institute for some time.

This arrangement was mutually beneficial to the community organization and the researcher. Rainbow House needed to know more about the impact of its training programs on its audiences in order to know "what directions to nibble in." The program has developed and evolved over eight years, and seems poised on the edge of becoming a model for similar programs nationwide. A February 1994 visit by Secretary of Health and Human Services Donna Shalala sparked increased commitment to gathering the data so that CNV could demonstrate more widely what they had to offer as a model. And generally, Rainbow House needed information that documented and legitimated their work if they were to continue receiving funding from various sources. For the researcher, this was an opportunity to continue research related to issues of violence against women, and particularly violence prevention.[1]

---

[1] The researcher also anticipated making a career move out of academia into freelance research, so this was a chance to enter the field of policy-relevant collaborative research with an eye toward this professional step.

One of the attractions between this researcher and community activist was the potential for applying qualitative methods to the study at hand. Traditional quantitative approaches had been attempted in the past and were not very effective at evaluating this program. Most traditional approaches to evaluation research assume that which needs to be understood (Patton 1990). That is, they assume that a program is created and implemented, and then its effects can be measured. Our approach has been to study the process of implementation as well as the reported effects of the program on its audience.

The Research Question

At the simplest level, the purpose of the research was to collect the stories about how CNV training has affected the people who took it and the places they work and live. Another goal was to provide legitimate social science documentation of the value of this program that would be respected by people who might be interested in taking the training, gatekeepers at funding agencies, and officials who might be in a position to promote CNV as a model program. In addition, Rainbow House was exploring a new approach to CNV training and needed to evaluate it. We decided to use the new approach as a pilot study, along with collecting data on the way trainings have typically been done in the past.

The approaches to CNV training have been shaped both by what Parry and her colleagues know is effective and by what fits with specific audiences who are interested in having the training. As the work of a nonprofit organization, Choosing Non-Violence has to be either self-supporting or attractive to grant-making agencies to survive. State-supported early childhood education programs, such as Head Start and Title XX-supported child care centers, have been the primary audience with the resources and the need for CNV. Each year the Children's Services Division of the city of Chicago Department of Human Services purchases a number of CNV trainings for staff of Head Start, Child Care, and School Age programs. The department then recruits 25–30 participants for each training from all over the city. This "scattershot" approach has its advantages and disadvantages. When staff from different sites come together for the training, their level of professionalism is elevated. Sharing takes place on neutral ground and their perspectives are broadened by meeting other child care professionals committed to similar goals from all over the city. Trainers frequently hear comments like, "I wish my director could take this training"; "I wish all of my co-workers could go through this"; and "I wish our parents could get this information." The present design does not allow for concentrated participation from one center or neighborhood, but only spotty representation, with the hope that individual CNV participants will carry the message back to others at their center.

Rainbow House received good feedback from those who attended. They were often invited to make smaller scale presentations for an entire staff at a single site. However, individuals who had completed the training felt some frustration as they attempted to implement it in their classrooms without the administrative support and enthusiasm that was generated by the training. They were trying a different approach to relating to children and colleagues, but no one else was. In particular, when administrators had not taken the CNV training, their approaches to relating to staff were sometimes at odds with the CNV model. This is not an unusual problem; in fact, it is a common obstacle to social change. When only a few people take new ideas and approaches into a setting that has its own structure and culture, and where power relations are already at work, they have limited impact.

Out of this problem with implementation, Rainbow House began to develop an alternate model for CNV training. Instead of having a group from a scattering of sites go through a training and then disperse back to their sites, they decided to try an intensive approach at a single site. One of the core ideas of CNV is the creation of "violence-free zones"—safe places where practicing nonviolent skills in solving problems and addressing conflicts is possible. Children and adults know about violence. What we understand less is the meaning of nonviolence and the role nonviolence could have in our collective lives. Thus, to create spaces—whether it is the classroom, the playground, the school, the home, or the community—where nonviolence can be practiced, involves building a shared commitment in a group or community to choose nonviolent approaches to relating to each other. One of the problems with the scatter-shot approach to training is that individuals have a hard time creating these spaces effectively if others do not share that commitment and want to cooperate. The intensive approach could overcome this problem.

Thus, the research question for the pilot study was to examine how this intensive approach might work. For the initial pilot study, Parry readily identified an agency that was interested in trying out an innovative approach to the Choosing Non-Violence training.

The Fellowship House Case Study

Fellowship House is located in the community of Bridgeport on the south side of Chicago and is part of the Chicago Youth Centers (a large agency with sites all over the city). Fellowship House includes a Head Start program and School Age program, with a strong parent component. The community that uses Fellowship House is ethnically diverse, including Hispanics, Chinese, African Americans, and European Americans. Parents speak English, Spanish, Cantonese, and Mandarin, and parent meetings are conducted in all languages.

Fellowship House's involvement with Choosing Non-Violence began when the education coordinator of the Chicago Youth Centers (CYC) invited Anne Parry to do a two-hour training with the entire child care staff of CYC. The Head Start director at Fellowship House was so impressed, she pushed for a full training for the staff at her center. Parry recruited them as partners to develop an intensive model of CNV training. The leadership of the center seemed enthusiastic and supportive of the program. When Parry visited, they had already included some activities from the short CNV training in the center, such as posting the "Violence Free Zone" signs and doing classroom activities with the children.

This pilot program involved developing a community partnership around choosing nonviolence. All of the Head Start and School Age staff members (about 12 people) went through a five-session CNV training that was spread over three months. In addition, three sessions of CNV training given for parents were attended by about 25 mothers, and conducted in English, Spanish, and Chinese. The plan also included a community outreach component that has not yet been implemented. A Choosing Non-Violence team of youths, teachers, parents, and a member of the Rainbow House staff will visit the elementary schools in the Fellowship House catchment area. In addition, there will be outreach to other parts of the community, such as churches, businesses, clinics, and dentists.

Method

The method employed in this study is ethnographic. Ethnographic data collection that focuses on process is especially appropriate for a small-scale, action-oriented, experimental program such as this pilot project (Patton 1990). Qualitative data collection allows for studying the *process* of the program—investigating how the program operates informally as well as theoretically, its strengths and weaknesses, and experiential aspects (often unanticipated) of the program that may be useful in deciding whether a program is a good model that can be transplanted to other settings. Rainbow House is particularly interested in these kinds of questions, as there has been some interest in using CNV as a model for violence prevention programs elsewhere. Matthews conducted observations of trainings followed by interviews with individuals and groups about the perceived effects of the training, and observations of interactions at the site. More structured forms of observation were also included.

Deb Zapalik, the early childhood education specialist, developed an instrument that systematizes data collection about classroom environment and interaction relevant to CNV. She used it in conducting observations of the classes at Fellowship House. This allowed a pretest for examining changes after the CNV approach was introduced and implemented. After the training Matthews conducted interviews and focus groups with most of the participants. She asked them to talk about their reactions to the training, what they found important and memorable, and about implementation—that is, what changes they have made or would like to make based on the training, and how supportive an environment they have for making changes. A short written instrument was used to collect reactions to specific topics in the training.

After six months, we plan further classroom observations and interviews. We will use the classroom observation instrument developed and include observations of classroom environment and teachers' interactions with the children. We will also ask teachers about how the program is working with adults at the center and find out how supportive the administration is in implementing CNV.

Preliminary Findings

Teachers find the training very moving. It not only affects their lives as teachers, but as wives and mothers. Several talked about the changes they were making at home, for example, in relating to their own children, or with their spouses and parents. When asked to recall what was the most important part of the training, interviewees commonly mentioned the general issue of violence around us in everyday life and the effects of stress on children. Matthews used a list of topics covered in the training to refresh their memories and asked them to mark the most important topics and those they felt needed more discussion. The following were the most common responses:

Topics deemed most important or significant:
  worst and best childhood memories
  stress
  kids and stress
  cycle of violence
  domestic violence
  feelings
  coping with stress at work
  discipline

Topics thought to need more discussion:
  children and stress
  coping with stress
  giving children space to express
    themselves

gender stereotypes
incorporating choosing nonviolence into
   all interactions
implementation

A striking theme in the discussions was the participants' own desensitization to violence and how the CNV training resensitized them. For example, one teacher recounted observing a crisis situation in which a youth was brandishing a gun on the street outside the center. When he accidentally shot himself in the hand, she found herself laughing. She took this as an indicator of how desensitized she had become and credited the CNV training with renewing her sense of outrage and caring about the frequent violence she was witnessing. The Head Start teachers told about a day they came to work and found bullet holes in their classroom windows. One of the teachers (a white woman) was pretty upset and wanted to call the police, while the others (two Latinas) were outwardly nonchalant about it, pointing out that it had not happened while they were there, and what were the police going to do about it? They talked in the focus group about what this meant—that they were too used to violence being a normal part of life. This turned into a discussion of how to have an impact on the neighborhood outside their classroom doors—starting with painting the "Violence-Free Zone" logo on the outside doors of their building. This discussion is an example of the kind of community-building orientation that CNV aims to engender.

The issue of stress factors and how they contribute to violence was also an important topic for these teachers. In particular, they were very interested in learning about emotions, stress, and children. The training presents the idea that children experience the effects of stress in ways that often make them act out inappropriately and invites teachers to give children the space and language to express their feelings. This goes beyond the usual preschool levels of "happy and sad," to get at the realistic range of emotions that children, like adults, experience. The idea is that feelings are legitimate, but in the interest of having alternatives to violence as an emotional outlet, it is necessary to teach the use of language to express them and allow space (literally as well as figuratively) for individuals to be different and get their varying needs met. This approach challenges teachers to have a different kind of relationship with children. It includes addressing the issue of power in a relationship between an adult and a child, as well as an examination of what constitutes abuse of power in such a relationship. Teachers are asked to model talking about feelings, but also to do more listening than adults often do with young children.

Conclusion

Although this collaborative pilot study is still in progress at this writing, several valuable outcomes have already been found:

- Development of the classroom observation instrument that has several applications, both for program evaluation and self-reflection by training participants

- Development of a training topics instrument that can be used in ongoing program evaluation and audience research

- Discovery of some of the challenges of the intensive model that would need to be addressed if this were to continue as a primary model of offering CNV training. Although the scattershot approach has limitations, the intensive site-based model requires extraordinary organizational commitment that has to be fit in with existing agendas. Also, the reality of uneven commitment remains an issue

■ Discovery of the range of reactions to CNV training in a single group. Participants' responses to the training depend partly on what background and experience they bring into the situation. Further evaluation work needs to examine this more fully, and CNV program design needs to incorporate ways of taking this into account in the trainings.

Based on this collaborative experience, Rainbow House and the researcher plan to continue working together to complete and expand on this project. Rainbow House wants to explore seeking currently available funding as a research and demonstration site for violence prevention. Such grants help community organizations build the legitimacy of their programs and also provide a needed funding base that allows experimenting with optimal styles of programs, rather than being locked into the structure of the local grants economy.

EDITORS' COMMENTS

The final case in the health section expands our definition of health to include physical and mental safety from violence. Nancy Matthews, an Assistant Professor of Criminal Justice, and Anne Parry, Executive Director of Rainbow House, explore the efficacy of a violence prevention program. Perhaps the larger or more important issue in this case is how and why smaller community-based organizations need research and data to justify the creation or support of existing programs to outside granting agencies. Rainbow House, a community-based organization and shelter for battered women, needed legitimate social science documentation to demonstrate the efficacy of their violence prevention program in order to qualify for future funding. Because of their limited resources and social science expertise in the area of research evaluation, Rainbow House turned to Matthews, an academically based researcher, to create a collaborative research project.

What makes this research collaboration unique was that, unlike most studies of community groups, this collaboration was qualitatively based. Traditional quantitative approaches had been attempted in the past but did not turn out to be very effective at evaluating this type of program. Parry and Matthews agreed that ethnographic methods should be used in order to understand more effectively both the process and the outcome of the violence prevention program implementation. The data collection methods involved observation of the training sessions of teachers and staff at a local youth center, interviews, surveys, and focus groups. Future observations in the classrooms and student-teacher interactions are planned in order to determine how well the violence prevention program has worked.

Finally, suggestions for doing future qualitative work with community groups are outlined by the authors, who found that collaborative research is very helpful for small community-based organizations in expanding their programs and providing the necessary documentation to gain further funding bases for innovative programs.

Part V
Community Control and Voice

We end our case studies with this part, titled "Community Control and Voice." By saving these cases for last, we want to highlight both the need for community members and groups to take an active role in defining and controlling the research done in and about their communities and the frustrations they may experience when they do this. In almost all of these cases, funding and control over funding of research grants is a significant issue and a source of contention. In most collaborative research projects, the issue of control over the research questions is also important. This is not a small issue or conflict when the research funds can involve thousands or even millions of dollars. Another major issue addressed in these cases is how collaborative research can influence or shape government policy at the local, state, and national levels. Changing policy at any level is a slow process—often too slow for individuals and community groups frustrated by institutional resistance to policy reformulation and change.

Our first case, by Warren Friedman, examines how a coalition of community groups, with the help of academic research, successfully pushed for and developed a new form of thinking about policing in Chicago. There are many definitions of what constitutes "community policing." But Friedman points out that community policing is effective only when all parties—from city hall, to police officers, to community members—change their notions about what police work is and should entail.

The wary relationship between community activists, academic researchers, and city officials over the definition of programs such as the newly created Empowerment Zones is explored even further by Wanda White and Doug Gills. They include another actor in the mix—the federal government as a major player—as parties try to negotiate and struggle over the creation and implementation of these programs. But not all collaborative research efforts are wholly successful. The highs and lows, the successes and failures of this type of research are echoed in Randy Stoecker's contribution to this volume. The infusion of federal money to housing and community planning struggles in Toledo, Ohio, brought with it conflict, division, and some degree of failure to collaborative research attempts.

Collaborative research can be a model of scholarship and activism applicable to all parts of the world, not just North America. Gasper LoBiondo and Rafael Pleitez describe a community-based, north-south dialogue research project carried out in the country of El Salvador, which is spreading to other Latin American countries. In some cases, collaborative research needs to be ongoing and more than just one project. Our final case ends with tales and cautions about sustaining effective collaboration between academic researchers and community members over an extended time frame. Kenneth Reardon describes a variety of efforts and projects that have taken place for close to 10 years between the University of Illinois and community groups in the East St. Louis area, and what it takes to overcome the mistrust and wariness that often accompany the involvement of large universities in community-based research projects. This piece is an exemplary case of what can go right in academic-community research projects.

Research, Organizing, and the Campaign for Community Policing in Chicago

WARREN FRIEDMAN, Chicago Alliance for Neighborhood Safety

"The police don't care about our neighborhood."

"They just drive through."

"They don't show up when we call 911."

"They don't respect what we are doing."

The comments quoted here were made by block watch and other community crime prevention participants in church basements, living rooms, and community organization offices around Chicago in the mid-1980s. The sentiments and the realities of police-community relations underlying them set the stage for a research project and an organizing campaign (described here) to actively change the Chicago police department and to make Chicago's neighborhoods safer.

Overall, this campaign has been successful. Between 1987 (when the meetings were held) and the summer of 1995, Chicago and the Chicago police department *have* changed. The police department's mission statement now speaks of partnership with the community. Patrol officers are beginning to be anchored in their "beats" for the first time. Officers are being trained in problem solving and how to work with the community. City services are being prioritized in terms of their potential impact on crime and disorder. Officers and community residents meet regularly on each beat, discuss crime and disorder problems, participate in strategy sessions, and are begin-

ning to develop a division of labor and ways of talking and working together. Thousands of community members are being trained for their role in community policing.

Progress is always fragile and reversible—often threatened by a backlash of unrealistic expectations, impatience or the fear of change, loss of power, and the issue of "too much" community participation. All is not rosy, to be sure. Many beat meetings turn into poorly run gripe sessions. Many have low community attendance. A major issue of contention revolves around the issue of who controls these meetings, the police or community members. The police department has also reversed itself on several important reforms, and resistance and cynicism in parts of the police department and in the community persist. At a time when federal dollars for 100,000 police officers encourage police departments around the country to call whatever they are doing *community policing*, Chicago probably has the most significant experiment in this area in the nation.

Improvements have also taken place—especially in two of the high-crime, low-income districts. Community members perceive a decline in major crimes and drug and gang activity. In addition, people perceive a reduction in the aggressiveness with which officers treat law-abiding citizens in two of the highest crime districts in Chicago. Trust between officers and the community has increased. City services have improved. People told interviewers that they were more optimistic about their neighborhoods and policing. The city and the police department deserve credit for these developments. But much of the credit also goes to a community group, the Chicago Alliance for Neighborhood Safety (CANS). CANS made community policing a public issue, led the way in putting it on the city agenda, and is working to make it succeed. Change does not appear out of nowhere, and CANS members spent eight years working for their goals. Like many community organizations, CANS went through several stages: there was discontent; research was done to define the problem more precisely and suggest a solution; community leaders were educated about the solution; organizing and education took place to get public and governmental acceptance of the solution; and community policing was started in five prototypes. At present, thousands of people are working for safer neighborhoods as community policing is instituted citywide.

Transforming CANS

The link between the report's recommendations and the present reality is found in CANS' history. It came together in 1980 with federal funding as the Urban Crime Prevention Program (UCPP) and is a coalition of community organizations. The goal of the UCPP was to build the crime prevention capacity of community organizations and create a public-private partnership for community safety—a partnership in part embodied in community-police cooperation. Chicago's UCPP was transformed into CANS in 1984 with the establishment of a board composed of board members of community organizations.

During its first few years, CANS worked with community organizations and residents to develop block, apartment, and school watches and helped to design strategies on how to combat drug sales and crime hot spots. CANS acted as a provider of resources, technical assistance, and information to community groups. It also gathered information that would keep the organizations informed about what was happening elsewhere in the city and the country. The purpose was to provide community groups with the most promising crime prevention strategies available.

The organizations were supposed to take these resources, organize residents, develop action plans, and when necessary, work with the police to make the neighborhood safer. This was the original grant's version of community crime prevention. However, there was no hint of police participation or institutional change. With the lack of police cooperation, this strategy began losing credibility. CANS had to change its mission in order to be credible and survive. It evolved in response to the clear limits of its community safety strategy and its interest in being useful to the communities it served. Eventually, these needs moved the organization from a training and technical assistance operation to an organization that could also organize and mobilize people. This capacity provided the critical bridge between the research and the campaign, between good ideas on a page and thousands of people working to make those ideas a reality.

The Role of Research

The first CANS-sponsored meetings with community participants resulted in surfaced grievances, a tentative definition of the problem, and a search for solutions. But most people went into these meetings accepting the prevailing, traditional policing model that maintained a largely passive role for citizens, despite their involvement in neighborhood crime prevention activities. Citizens thought of their role as merely the "eyes and ears" for the police. Police were viewed as "the professionals" who took the information and dealt with crime. In accepting this model, participants turned their concern to what they perceived to be the heart of police-community relations and crime fighting—the emergency response system. They were troubled by slow or no response from patrol cars to their calls to 911, discourteous treatment by dispatchers, and the constant possibility of being publicly identified as callers by officers when they arrived. The initial charge to CANS was to find a way to fix the system.

Talking to experts and reading studies of traditional policing convinced us that the problem was deeper and more basic than the emergency response system. We concluded that the twin pillars of traditional policing—rapid response and preventive or random patrol—were ineffective. In fact, researchers on a 1974 Kansas City project found that visible cruising police cars were not a deterrent to crime, nor did their visibility significantly reduce citizens' fear of crime (Kansas City Preventive Patrol Experiment). Compounding the problems for traditional policing was the irrelevance of rapid response to over 95 percent of calls-for-service. Only a tiny fraction of the calls to 911 were deemed "hot calls," that is, calls in which a quick response by police would make a difference in the outcome of the incident. Thus, building a police strategy around rapid response is not an effective foundation for public safety.

In fact, it is a barrier. This kind of strategy requires keeping officers in their cars so they can be ready to respond to calls. As a result, they are out of touch with the community they are supposed to serve. Many of the commu-

nity's complaints at the Chicago meetings support these findings. The department operated in a way that required officers to spend most of their time in cars, driving through the neighborhood. If officers were concerned about a situation (and most were), they had no way to act on that concern. The absence of contact and cooperation was responsible for many of the complaints community people had about the police service they received.

CANS released its report, *Police Service in Chicago: 911, Dispatch Policy and Neighborhood-Oriented Alternatives*, in 1988. The report was done in-house, with the aid of an intern from Loyola University Chicago (who also became a VISTA volunteer while the research was in progress). During the writing of the report, the authors called on technical assistance from other Chicago area universities, spoke frequently to criminal justice experts around the country, and relied heavily on studies funded by the National Institute of Justice. Our research enabled us to place the numerous community complaints in a new, more complicated context. We began to see that, in general, there were two kinds of concerns: complaints about 911 and the more numerous complaints about what traditional policing did to community-police relations and neighborhood safety. These were less focused and articulate. Part of the reason for this was that most people believed that traditional policing—with officers in cars, racing to calls, taking reports, and going on to the next call—was the only way policing could be done.

We concluded that even with a courteous, perfectly functioning 911, efficient rapid response, and officers visible in their cars, any gain in a community's safety and quality of life would be marginal. Since only about 3 percent of the over 3 million calls each year to 911 were hot calls, time spent on answering these calls could be better used. If officers were freed from many of these calls (which take 45 minutes each on average), they would have time to work with communities reducing crime and solving crime-related problems. Time could also be freed by reducing the number of calls to which cars were sent. Instead, these calls could be handled in other ways, including, for instance, taking reports over the phone, which requires an average of only 13 minutes per call.

In making this judgment, we did not respond to the charge to fix 911. We chose to address the complaints that implicitly questioned traditional policing and its assumptions. We developed an analysis that connected the critique of traditional policing to the possibility of thousands of police officers with time freed to work with residents. We had the vision of a different kind of policing that would contribute to neighborhood cohesion and safety by bringing neighbors together and encouraging them to hold the police and each other accountable.

The Audience for the Report

We wanted *Police Service* to be read by the police, elected officials, scholars, and reporters. We wanted those who normally have an influence on policy to take it seriously and, ultimately, to support our recommendations. At the same time that we wanted influential allies, we didn't want to rely on the long-term commitment of people not directly affected by the crime and disorder that stalked many of Chicago's neighborhoods. Nor did we believe in the power of ideas separate from the power of an organized constituency that supported and advocated for those ideas.

Because advocacy and action were seen as an outcome of the report's recommendations, we directed the report to an audience that was considerably different from the audience ad-

dressed by most criminal justice research. A critical part of our audience were residents who had made or were likely to make a commitment to working for their community's safety. The report had to be accessible and useful enough for these community leaders to translate it to *their* constituency; to spread the word and mobilize their neighbors to take action. To be useful to us, the research had to yield recommendations that could be presented as an incentive to participation. If we wanted to pull people from their private lives, there had to be a plausible expectation that the recommendations would be implemented and, if implemented, that neighborhoods would be safer.

We needed to create a core of community experts who believed in the power of organizing and who understood the reform for which they were advocating. This was also crucial to a sustained effort. We told people, "It'll take 10 years to build a real partnership between the community and the police." Without a substantial amount of time, we could not overcome the resistance we expected in the police department. Nor could we fashion a democratic version of community policing: one in which people influence the direction of the department, hold the department and their officers accountable, have significant say in selecting the crime priorities to be dealt with in their neighborhoods and a major role in solving those problems.

Members of this initial audience became the leading participants in the campaign. Overall, participants came (and continue to come) mainly from high-crime and at-risk neighborhoods. Whatever the local crime rate, all were concerned with actual or potential neighborhood decay, with drugs and gangs, crime and disorder. All were frustrated by their relations with police, and all would benefit from and be empowered by a more decentralized police structure that placed partnership with the community and responsiveness to its concerns at the center of its mission.

We slowly convinced enough people that the problem wasn't 911; the entire model of policing had to be changed. If they wanted safer neighborhoods, the issue had to be changing the basic strategy of traditional, reactive policing. Even more slowly, we convinced them that we could actually change the Chicago police department. Over time, anger and frustration were redirected from 911 and transformed into a positive agenda for change. But convincing people wasn't easy. Indeed, even at our victory celebration, many campaign participants confessed to each other that until the city publicly committed, they had not believed we had a chance of winning.

The Campaign

Our vision of implementing community-police partnerships and neighborhood safety activities depends on one condition. Large numbers of people must get involved, be challenged and excited, and take responsibility. It was clear that unless CANS was committed and involved, no one else would be. CANS' long-term involvement was a condition of the *Police Service* report's relevance. The campaign persisted through two mayors and two police superintendents. It went forward, made converts, got attention, ran low on energy, stalled, and revived. The campaign got its final impetus in spring 1991, when a group of people— mainly from eight low-income, high-crime, African American communities—gathered at CANS' office. They were concerned about the prospects of a violent summer in their communities. Some were sending their children out of the city for the summer. They wanted to know what else could be done. We argued that there were no quick solutions. We explained community policing.

Out of that meeting we formed CANS' Community Policing Task Force. It became a loose coalition of about 100 community-based organizations. Like the varied momentum of the campaign, the numbers of participants expanded and contracted around a core of 20 to 30 organizations. After a series of discussions that were animated by a growing camaraderie, hope, and impatience to get started, the expanding group decided to seek a meeting with the police superintendent. Our plan was to ask him to choose a representative to work with us to design a pilot project for community policing. After initial rebuffs to our requests, we began visiting meetings of Chicago's police board.

By law, the superintendent had to attend these public meetings. The meetings took place in an auditorium sprinkled with community people. They had a variety of concerns, including police misconduct. CANS' Task Force participants called on the superintendent to meet with them. They also used their time at the microphone to explain the benefits of community policing to police board members and others at the meetings.[1]

We eventually got our meeting with the superintendent at a well-planned and high-energy gathering at CANS' office. He was aggressive and stole the initiative from the chair. He pointed to a gray-haired woman and asked her, "What's this community policing?" She gave the first of half-a-dozen firm, passionate, and well-informed replies. Apparently, the crowded room, the thoughtful answers, and obvious determination convinced him that we would persist. He threw up his hands and asked, "What do you want?"

---

[1] The police board is composed of civilians charged with adopting "the rules and regulations for governing the Police Department," reviewing and approving the annual department budget, and dealing with police disciplinary matters.

The well-rehearsed response came: "A liaison to work with us on a community policing pilot project proposal." We reached an agreement with the superintendent. He appointed a widely respected district commander as his personal representative to the community. When the proposal was completed, we agreed to submit it to the superintendent, and he agreed to respond.

The Task Force worked with the commander, learned about police work, taught him about community concerns, haggled over language, and pored over drafts of the document for four months. We finally agreed on a proposal designed to institute community-police partnerships by using officers belonging to district units already exempted from responding to 911. This was a first step in trying out the strategy. We didn't want to push immediately for major changes in the department. Our constituency wasn't broad or deep enough. And we weren't powerful enough to get it. Nor did we know enough about what we wanted. Even if we had gotten the superintendent to accept overly ambitious policy recommendations, there was every likelihood that they would fail in the implementation and that it wouldn't lead to a changed police department, empowered citizens, or safer neighborhoods.

We were prepared to be patient following the submission of the proposal. We wanted the document to get serious attention and wanted the pilot programs to be well considered and receive whole-hearted support. We knew the superintendent was a busy person, but we were not just waiting for his response. We spent time talking to city council representatives, a majority of whom co-sponsored a hearing on community policing. We filled a city council hearing room with tales of victimization, of noncooperation by the police, of community policing's importance to Chicago's neighborhoods. Representatives of CANS and the Task

Force made presentations to the editorial boards of Chicago's two major daily newspapers. In addition, we conducted dozens of workshops and presentations in communities around the city, spreading the report's analysis and recommendations, stressing the limits of traditional policing, introducing the idea of community policing and *always* arguing that an organized constituency was powerful and could change things.

During this time, CANS also conducted the Leadership Institute for Community Policing with funding from the John D. and Catherine T. MacArthur Foundation. The Institute provided participants with six sessions in the history and theory of community policing and community crime prevention, using experts from the National Center for Community Policing, the Police Executive Research Forum, and Loyola University.

The sessions were followed by field trips to New York and Seattle to see their versions of community policing. Seventeen people went to Seattle, 19 people to New York City. In Seattle, we were hosted and transported by the police department. In New York, the co-hosts were the New York City police department and the Citizens Committee for New York. The excited, racially diverse group from troubled Chicago neighborhoods met with police officials and officers, city officials, community people, and scholars.[2] Institute participants saw more clearly the promise of community policing and learned many details about its implementation and the barriers to progress. They also gained a context for judging what they were asking of Chicago. Most evenings, before breaking up to see the sights, we met to discuss what we had

[2]Also along on the trips were the Chicago police department's Director of Research and Development, now chief of police in Joliet, Illinois, and the commander of Chicago's 15th district, the superintendent's representative in the pilot proposal's development.

seen and heard that day. Over and over, the question was raised, "Where's the community?" In both cities, Chicagoans saw that little thought had been devoted to or investment made in community participation, education, or training. When they returned to Chicago, they had confirmed the belief they had gone with: Community involvement and partnership needed to be a central idea in Chicago. Throughout the Leadership Institute, people's enthusiasm was high. Most of the participants had flown infrequently, if at all, let alone on a policy-related, fact-finding mission. The anticipation and excitement of the trips obviously made an important contribution to the spirit of the group. People from around the city were sharing the experience of studying topics that would help them influence the direction of the city's largest agency, and make their lives and their communities better.

After several months of silence and evasive answers from the superintendent's office, the group's patience finally ended. The report was released at a well-rehearsed press conference. The group had initially submitted the proposal to the superintendent, and journalists had asked to see a copy. Following considerable discussion at the time, the group turned them down, saying they didn't want press coverage to confuse the negotiations. Over the months, the press called frequently to find out the status of the proposal. Growing increasingly curious, they turned out in large numbers at the press conference to get a copy of the proposal and to hear the community describe the response it had gotten from the department.

Task Force volunteers—people from the community who had participated in developing the proposal, who had made presentations in communities and had gone through the Leadership Institute—spoke briefly through the media to hundreds-of-thousands of their fellow Chicagoans. The report's basic ideas,

enriched by the new voices, embodied in a practical proposal, had reached its largest audience. The need to change the way neighborhoods were policed had become a public issue.

After the press conference, members of the media went to city hall to get the mayor's response. In a year that was breaking records for homicide and other violent crimes, a year of fearful headlines and against the background of editorial support for our proposal, it was hard to resist a mobilized community with recommendations for its own safety. The next day, the news media reported the mayor's support for community policing. Shortly thereafter, a new and sympathetic police superintendent was appointed, and a management consulting firm was hired to help the department figure out how to make a large-scale transition. When the mayor of Chicago announced his commitment to community policing, thousands of people had participated in the effort. It was a victory won by people from low- and middle-income, high-crime, and at-risk neighborhoods. They had worked together, developed a vision, and brought it to the city. It was a bottom-up effort built on education, turnout, testifying, and media work, always involving people from different communities, racial and ethnic backgrounds. Much of the power of the Task Force and many of its accomplishments in initiating community policing were possible because community policing, as a response to neighborhood safety issues, reached across community, class, and racial lines. Crime, so often a divisive issue and a racial code word, became a unifying issue.

Research and Organizing

Research, its dissemination, and the choice of audience are all crucial factors to consider for organizations that seek to enlist the energy of citizens in changing some portion of the way the world is run. But taking these factors into account is only the beginning of the process. From the writing of the report, *Police Service,* through the conduct of the campaign, whatever we did was seen as an attempt to influence policy decisions, and a learning experience for CANS and campaign participants. Throughout the campaign and the prototype experiments, our vision of community policing (of how free time could be used and what the community's role should be) gained depth and complexity. Though much in the original report seems timid and out of date, the larger goal of freeing officers' time to work with the community remains the same.

There is not yet enough time freed, but it is also true that the conditions for productive use of this time have not yet been established. Officers and community members must learn how to use the time. They must overcome decades of socialization in roles that have created distrust and defined them as unequal participants in the maintenance of neighborhood safety. When the group designed the original proposal to free up officer time, it had not asked with any precision what would be required to prepare officers and community people to use the time productively.

When the prototypes were announced and plans for training officers were being made, we began pushing for training for the community. If this was to be a true partnership, both parties had to be trained and ready to play their role. Investment in the community was crucial. When CANS and the city signed a contract, the Joint Community-Police Training project was launched. Over the first year, the training has been delivered to roughly 6,000 people.

CANS is seeking to integrate two roles for itself in the next stage of this project: (1) its city-wide training responsibilities, which involve it in partnership with the department in developing curricula and delivering training and (2) its role as policy advocate and monitor of departmental progress. These different roles and responsibilities generate tension and some confusion in staff, leadership, community participants, the city, and the police. And this tension will not end soon. But as it delivers training, CANS' staff and Task Force leaders are beginning to talk to people about barriers to progress and steps that can be taken to improve community policing in Chicago. This discussion, supported by further research, will most likely result in another report and recommendations. It is also clear that the issuing of another report and doing what it takes to make it a reality will impose a whole new set of transformations on CANS.[3] But if CANS, the Task Force, and their allies can continue to learn and defend the gains that have been made, they can continue to push the community and the department forward and make a valuable contribution to neighborhood safety.

---

[3]In early 1995, CANS released *Young People and the Police: Trust, Fear and the Future of Community Policing in Chicago.* The study, based on interviews with 969 public high school students, found that relations between youth and police were troubled. Following the release of the report and amidst considerable controversy, CANS began organizing young people and adults to work on defining a role for youth in community policing and improving relations between youth and police.

Warren Friedman is the Executive Director of the Chicago Alliance for Neighborhood Safety, which is a coalition of neighborhood groups. His paper richly describes the long and often tedious process involved in changing not just the way people think about policing but the actual nature of police work. Traditional police responses to crime involved two methods: a rapid response to crimes committed and the use of preventive or random patrols in automobiles. CANS' research concluded that these methods of traditional policing were ineffective and called for new methods of "community policing" in which officers are trained to work with a community in which they are regularly anchored. These "beat" officers learn more about the neighborhood and its residents, meet with residents on a regular basis, and learn to work together to form a partnership to reduce crime. In this case, researchers and community members did not want just to change the nature of the often strained police-community relations (often in low-income neighborhoods). Using research and political lobbying, CANS redefined their goals about the types of changes they wanted and would not settle for anything less than implementing changes to the actual nature and practice of policing itself.

The Chicago model for community policing has been successful in both reducing the crime rate and in creating better relationships between the police force and community members. However, like most policy changes affecting the nature of work done by an established and influential group, this implementation was and is not easy. City of Chicago officials and police officers continue to be wary of citizen involvement in policing. Friedman ends his paper with the warning that the gains achieved in this project could just as easily recede as a result of proposed budget cuts, reduced community activism, and complacency.

In fact, as this volume goes to press, Mayor Daley has moved coordination of key elements of community policing from CANS to the Chicago Police Department and the Mayor's office. CANS has been battling city hall over this issue. While a change in coordination would not necessarily eliminate community policing in Chicago, this change and the potential reduction of an independent community voice in community policing, underscores Friedman's point that the need to protect citizens' control of community policing is a never-ending battle.

Chicago's Empowerment Zone and Citizen Participation

Doug Gills, University of Illinois–Chicago, and
Wanda White, Community Workshop for Economic Development

This case study focuses on citizen involvement and community participation in the various stages of the development of the federal Empowerment Zone (EZ) Initiative. The EZ Initiative was established under the leadership of the Office of the President as a pilot urban policy demonstration initiative of the Clinton-Gore Administration. It became law in 1993. The U.S. Department of Housing and Urban Development (HUD) is the lead agency to coordinate the EZ Initiative through an interagency task force combining the urban programs of several federal departments and intergovernmental agencies.

EZs are based on four major principles: (1) addressing individual, family, and community impoverishment by creating economic opportunities for EZ residents and marginal businesses; (2) pursuing sustainable communities such that enduring viability emerges, resulting from the infusion of government resources and private sector reinvestment, coupled with community innovation, creativity, and collective efforts addressing the causes of economic distress and impoverishment; (3) creating sustained collaborative partnerships between business, government, and the organized community agents, with grassroots participation throughout the process; and (4) developing a strategic vision of social change aimed at addressing the sources of poverty and altering the way government does business with its citizens, so that basic relations between the people and public authorities are "reinvented."

The roots of the EZ process can be traced to the community development movement, which includes both economic development (capital needed for business building) and human resource development (human capacity-building). This movement focuses on the local level, but there has been considerable national networking between local activists. It embraces the local level through the various levels of partnership-building, including the municipalities, the affected states, and the intergovernmental agencies of the federal administration; and it emphasizes collaborative research and action with social and community development objectives within and upon various aspects of the overall policy formation implementation process.[1]

---

[1] In the larger study that we are undertaking, we have used interviews with participants, incorporating official documents produced by various public and private entities involved in, or related to, the Empowerment Zone process at the federal, state, and local levels into our analysis. We have coupled data with our own observations as participants-activists in the process from its initial inception. We have supplemented these interviews with other secondary materials and accounts on the historical antecedents of the Empowerment Zone process.

Because of this, the EZ Initiative will have greater significance at the local levels of the policy development process than at the national level. It creates significant "windows of opportunity"[2] for activists on both sides of the policy reform spectrum. Also, the modes of interaction required in the EZ process offer opportunities to advance collaborative research and action between academicians, policy advocates, and community activists. Together they can press for progressive reforms that both facilitate development of greater democracy and work to alleviate poverty.

How the Chicago EZ Process Got Started

Chicago is noted among U.S. cities for its strong network of community economic development (CED) groups. Community groups in Chicago can also lay considerable claim to advancing the political concept and practice of community empowerment to a high standard, as well as the related notions of community-building and capacity-building (United Way of Chicago 1993; Kretzman and McKnight 1993; and Community Renewal Society 1993). Chicago's housing, economic, and employment development coalitions have all served as models on which groups of activists in other cities have patterned themselves. Part of this tradition is rooted in the fact that Chicago is a city of neighborhoods—neighborhoods organized around a collective identity of ethnicity, nationality, race, as well as class. Another part of this has its

recent origins in the civil rights, black power, and antipatronage movements of the 1960s and 1970s (Akalimat et al. 1986, 1989; Brecher and Costello 1991; Fisher and Kling 1993). Despite the episodic lapses into turf battles, the coalitions phenomena have been a unique, if not dominant, feature of Chicago's community politics and public policy arena, particularly over the past 20 years. There are nearly a dozen stable coalitions in Chicago that are dominated by community-based organizations.

Early Empowerment Zone Planning Activities in Chicago

During late spring and summer 1993, the Clinton-Gore transition and governance organization held several national economic and community development conferences involving human services activists and community and economic development practitioners. These meetings included persons from Chicago and other cities. Many of the ideas found their way into the formulation of the central policy thrust of the Clinton-Gore urban and domestic development agenda. One of these ideas centered around what is now known as the Consolidated Plan (Con-Plan) for interagency coordination. The aim of this plan is the creation of an interagency, coordinated continuum of care to drive local urban constituent service delivery and direct involvement of community-based organizations (not just city hall) in developing and guiding local policies. Specifically the plan included the following:

- Community-directed development in which citizen constituents drive the process of redevelopment and participate in the planning and development process as equals with the private and public sector

---

[2]We use this phrase to suggest that the EZ process creates openings in the policy-making structures of government for social activists to initiate reforms that increase the quality of life and living standards of ordinary citizens via collective action.

- Multidimensional accountability whereby the service recipients are held accountable, but the service providers—public or private—are held accountable by the service recipients

- Comprehensive and multifaceted service support in order to address the problems of poverty, economic and social distress, and alienation

- An understanding that the object of comprehensive support services is not to maintain impoverishment but rather to reduce poverty through programs that address the systematic causes of poverty and social distress

- Community and citizens' participation throughout all aspects of the policy development process—planning, implementation, oversight, and assessment

- Sustained collaborative partnership

- An assumption that poverty cannot be alleviated without asset accumulation at the individual, family, and community levels

- An acceptance that shared power is an essential component of community empowerment

These principles clearly established the need for a collaborative practitioner-researcher relationship if Chicago's application for an EZ was to be approved. Recently, academically trained urban and community planners and economic development specialists have become a prominent feature in community development organizational practice. Influenced by academic researchers who have themselves been involved in community-based social movements in Chicago and elsewhere, more and more Chicago university departments and programs are incorporating community development courses into their curricula.

Chicago was able to mobilize quickly for the EZ application process and to frame the progressive character and content of the HUD application. One reason Chicago's social action researchers and community-based practitioners could respond so quickly to the application was that so many preexisting networks, collaborations, community-based coalitions, and partnerships had already been established. These formations provided spaces for scholars, researchers, and practitioners to come together, to exchange ideas, and to work through problems. For example, the Community Workshop for Economic Development (founded in 1982) brought all CED agencies in the city together and provided comprehensive technical assistance to them. It was also instrumental in coordinating the community input for Chicago's successful application for an EZ.[3]

The Selection Process and City Council Sanctioning

In early March 1993, Chicago Mayor Richard M. Daley appointed an Interim Empowerment Zone/Enterprising Community Coordinating Council, a 15-member body charged with the responsibility of selecting the census tracts that were to be included in the HUD application. With the support of the University of Illinois Center for Urban Economic Development, the University of Illinois Great Cities Program, the University of Chicago, and several consulting firms of lawyers and urban designers, the interim Coordinating Council selected the

[3]*The Chicago Empowerment Zone Strategic Plan* (1994) is the document produced by this community-city government collaborative planning process.

tracts to be included in the EZ and developed the full proposal to be sent to Washington. The mayor's office and the city council members stayed relatively clear of the selection process, at least from the public side.

One of the important struggles was over whether or not to include public housing within all zone boundaries. Most members of the coordinating Council felt that if they were to represent those who were truly unempowered, then public housing residents should be at the top of the list. However, inclusion of all public housing developments would eliminate other persons in need. A compromise was reached to request a waiver to treat all public housing residents as resident beneficiaries. The other major issue was over how to assure the inclusion of "economic engines" within each designated area. Economic institutions that would act as anchors, as well as industrial tracts, should be available to stimulate employment and potentials for asset accumulation.

Thirty-three distinct groupings of communities submitted applications to be included in the plan being drawn up by the Coordinating Council. After the submission deadline in early April 1994, applicants had to make a presentation of their strategic conception. Most groups presented collaborative presentations, suggesting that community-community and university-community collaboration had taken place as part of their planning processes. The proposed EZ map was then presented to the mayor in mid-April 1994. The mayor introduced this map into the city council, which approved it in May 1994.

The approved EZ contains approximately 200,000 people living in just under 19 square miles of Chicago neighborhoods. The poverty rate in these neighborhoods exceeds 40 percent. With the ultimate approval of Chicago's plan by HUD, $100 million in government funding will be provided to the city. This will support activities over a 10-year period starting in 1995. Local officials and business leaders project that this federal money will leverage an additional $2.5 billion in private investments in the EZ communities.

Goals and Strategic Objectives

Despite some of the shortcomings of the planning process, the EZ coordinating body developed seven policy and action areas for the EZs:

- Economic opportunity/economic development
- Affordable housing
- Human and organizational development
- Health and human services
- Youth futures
- Public/community safety
- Cultural diversity

These are designated as activity areas in which proposals submitted by community organizations for EZ money are focused.

Who Is Involved in the EZ Research and Development Process?

Other than the Community Workshop for Economic Development, the most active supporters of the EZ in Chicago were the Urban Land Institute, the Chicago Jobs Council, and the Chicago Initiative. Other agencies were active, such as the Center for Neighborhood Technology, the Neighborhood Capital Budget Group, and the Neighborhood Institute. Most of these organizations are community research institutes that are independent of universities. The involvement of university-based researchers happened on an individual basis rather than on an institutional basis. This is in large part because of the community participants' conscious decision to discourage formal university links to the EZ development process.

There is also concern about the limited outreach resources of the EZs to residents of the communities. The managers of the formal process provided no assistance and no support for aggressive mobilization of residents inside the "Zone," as it began to be called, referring to the overall EZ process in Chicago. There were few foundations that made funding available to the EZ outreach, to EZ volunteer organizers and facilitators, or to the local community cluster operations. The city was slow to provide educational materials that were indicative of a broad partnership within the communities. Moreover, the city gave no support to initiatives undertaken by the local Zone community cluster organizers when they attempted to hold meetings, conferences, and informal educational forums for citizens and businesses within the EZ in Chicago. Only for a brief period following the submittal to HUD, did the city provide any technical staff assistance to the fledgling community cluster organizations. In short, the EZ cluster organizations were pretty much left to their own devices and support resources by all but a few institutional entities, following the HUD submittal.

Whither the EZ Process Now?

After the submittal of applications to HUD, the city administration focused most of its outreach resources on the corporate business community, primarily the banking community. This was not wrong; it was just too exclusive, and it neglected the broad mobilization of the resident base within the Zone. On the surface, this commitment of lending institutions seems progressive. However, some critics think that the unregulated redevelopment of the physical aspects of Chicago's poorest, most distressed neighborhoods may accelerate economic displacement and gentrification within the EZ communities. EZ community activists have asserted that the best means for averting this outcome is to ensure that community residents and their representatives are full partners in the implementation, monitoring, and assessment of the EZ process, as well as in its initial planning.

After the hoopla surrounding the initial mobilization for Chicago's participation in the national EZ competition process, participation (if not interest) waned in much of the nonprofit research and policy community, and support for the work of communities in preparing for the Chicago EZ implementation diminished. Some commentators indicated that the overall planning process had been messy and confusing. Others thought that the process would not result in being designated as an EZ. Still others thought the process was dominated by machinelike politics.

It is our contention that the democratic process *is* political. It is often messy and confusing; especially as it relates to the demand for shared power between public officials, who have it, and social agents who do not have it. While many agents from institutions of higher learning were sensitive to the need for mass outreach, most felt overwhelmed by the task of attempting to sustain the involvement of thousands of potential Zone resident activists. Even when it came to the task of responding to the demand of EZ-based community organizations to establish computerized electronic networks, the major educational and research institutions in Chicago responded partially and unevenly. While some EZ-based groups were able to go on-line, the majority of the community groups were not linked electronically.

The main forms of links between community organizations within the Zone remained the traditional ones; although new links have been established by local community clusters with groups, institutions, and associations outside as well as inside the Zone. Those groups with a tradition of grassroots organizing and with some outreach capacity were able to assume the responsibility for bringing the constituent base of the EZ's cluster into the process.[4] Thus, the difficult task of maintaining constituent participation of EZ activity at all levels—from community to regional levels—to be slanted toward the mobilization resources base that Zone facilitators could tap. In one region, the most aggressively active sectors were the local political ward organizations. In another, the local business organization and chambers were more active. Therefore, this involvement tended to reflect the orientation of the regional and subregional clusters that emerged in the EZ process. In other regions and in their subregions, ward politicians and business groups were less involved, all for various reasons. In these communities, the Zone activists had to rely principally on the church or the traditional form of community organization. Thus, resources varied across the Zone that the organizers had at their disposal.

Over an 18-month period, all but the most committed and conscientious wavered, being taxed by the brutally long EZ development process. In the EZs, there has been a constant taxing struggle to sustain participation among those who are recruited into the process. They wage a major internal battle to get the diverse aggregation of participants to remain collectively focused on the ends of the process and for individuals to avoid being caught up in diversions that take their toll over periods of protracted struggles.

On Sustaining Citizen Participation and Collaborative Activity

In addressing the question of collaborative citizen participation, it becomes clear that we are now talking in relative, rather than absolute terms. We have observed that two conditions must prevail if there is to be a sustained, collective commitment to community empowerment politics and the extension of democratic practices. First, the anchor group must have access to the resources to initiate and maintain sustained outreach and contact with the community. Without these resources, the anchor organization will resort to mobilizing tactics that rely on the constituent networks close to it. Involvement might be intense, but it will not be broadly diverse or extensive. The costs will be limited participation of broad sections of the community; and the pursuit of desired diversity will suffer.

Second, local community groups must be independent from the traditional political leadership. Politicians and government policy makers tend to restrict access to power in decision making. Local government is not going to give up power willingly, and as the EZs move ahead, this has become a major source of conflict. The EZ process, as set up in Washington, calls for the creation of community-based input independent of city hall. While this was present in the early stages, city hall now is taking more control of the process. We expect that the tensions between the community-based initiators of much of the EZ plan and city hall will con-

---

[4]*Cluster* is the informal popular name that the sub-Empowerment Zone community organizational form has taken in Chicago. Currently, the Zone at the community level is composed of six cluster organizations supporting the participating entities in the Chicago EZ process. Some of the Zone subclusters are further subdivided into community area subclusters called *assemblies*. The south side Empowerment Zone subcluster, called the "South Side Empowerment Zone Cluster, Inc.," is, perhaps, the most decentralized and elaborately organized of the six Zone clusters.

tinue; although this may be constructive tension, if the community is able to prevail in some
areas. Once the community-control genie is out
of the bottle, it is hard for even the most powerful politicians to put it back in.[5]

In Chicago's EZ process, collaborative partnership has been most vibrant and progressive
in the aspect of planning. However, the establishment of the permanent governance process
has been one of the most regressive from the
standpoint of sharing power and assuring the
community's participation in the formal structures of deciding *who* will make policy about
how the money is spent. Moreover, the political leadership of the city does not want to share
responsibility for mutual accountability for the
goals statement and central initiatives being
adhered to by the managers of the EZ process.
For community-directed development to be

sustained, democratic characteristics and traditions must be present. This is not something
that will be given to us by politicians in power,
it is something that must be taken and used by
the community. That is the struggle we are
seeing right now in Chicago.

The bottom-up process has to be built by
those with a self-interest in seeing it develop. In
the EZ communities, typical voter turnout is
less than 35 percent of the voting population.
We must then have realistic expectations of EZ
involvement. These are communities whose
residents have been disappointed time after
time. Most of those who will become involved
first will tend to be those already involved in
some aspect of volunteerism and civic participation. For many others, it has been their first
time to meet and work in a collaborative nature
with others who are committed to rebuilding
some facet of their communities. Participation
will increase among local residents when they
are able to see and work on activities that
improve their quality of life, when they feel
threatened, and when they think they can win.

---

[5]This process of pitting community groups against local
government is not new. During the 1960s, President Johnson used a similar strategy of funding local community
groups, as a way of challenging the political resistance of
many city governments to the War on Poverty program.

EDITORS' COMMENTS

Doug Gills of the University of Illinois–Chicago and Wanda White
from the Community Workship for Economic Development describe
their experience as participant-activists and researchers in the development of Chicago's Empowerment Zone. The Empowerment Zones
(EZs) developed as a result of a Clinton Administration initiative
toward community and economic development. When the federal government and millions of dollars are involved, what happens to community groups and their collaboration? This case explores the
successes and failures of the Chicago Empowerment Zone coalition of
community groups, researchers, government officials, and policy
makers. One reason why Chicago was able to mobilize successfully
and quickly to create this EZ was that a large number of academic-
community collaborations, and community-based coalitions and partnerships, already existed.

The authors include recommendations for future efforts that are more inclusive of community groups. One of the major concerns about the Chicago EZ was the limited outreach resources available to residents of communities due to the decision by city of Chicago officials to focus their outreach resources on the corporate business community. Gills and White conclude that for the democratic process to continue, city officials and academic researchers need to think and act beyond the traditional outreach linkages and be more committed to citizen participation in the implementation of EZ funds and initiatives. As they state, "For community-directed development to be sustained, democratic characteristics and traditions must be present. This is not something that will be given to us by politicians in power, it is something that must be taken and used by the community."

The Imperfect Practice of Collaborative Research: The "Working Group on Neighborhoods" in Toledo, Ohio[1]

RANDY STOECKER, University of Toledo

From 1989 to 1994, neighborhood-based redevelopment in Toledo went from the doldrums to the modern age. That happened through the creation of the Working Group on Neighborhoods (WGN—pronounced "we gone"). WGN is a coalition of community development corporations, neighborhood-based organizing groups, local foundations (including the Local Initiatives Support Corporation), government officials, and the University of Toledo Urban Affairs Center. I was a member of this coalition through the Urban Affairs Center.

WGN is the fruit of an ongoing collaborative research[2] project, and partly the victim of it. This paper tells the story of WGN as a collaborative research project, tracing its rise and demise, its successes and failures, its sense of community and perhaps necessary factionalism. My community collaborators lack the

time to coauthor this paper, which they see as less directly beneficial than the other tasks demanding their attention. Thus, I am writing this paper in the modified collaborative style with which I conducted much of the WGN-related research. I do the research and writing, with community collaborators as guides and reviewers.

Collaborative Research and Its Implications

In the WGN project, I encountered three kinds of dilemmas facing collaborative research, which were resolved imperfectly. These involve role specialization, factionalism, and power and influence.

Role Specialization

In the form of collaborative research known as "participatory research," community control is ideally the paramount concern. The community decides the research question, designs the research methodology, and even does the research. The argument supporting this research process is that when community members actually do the research they reduce their alienation from research technology, and

---

[1]Thanks to Dave Beckwith for his insightful comments on an earlier draft of this paper and for his continuing mentorship.

[2]There are a lot of terms floating around to describe research involving community-based groups and academics, including participatory research, participatory action research, collaborative research, and many others. I have used both participatory research and participatory action research to describe some of my work, but the working definition of collaborative research also applies.

reduce their dependence on technical experts. They learn how to learn (Hall 1992; Lynd 1992; Gaventa 1991). But many collaborative endeavors do not meet this ideal, perhaps for good reasons. When community members lack the time or interest, or when doing the research will not produce new skills, a sensitive researcher may specialize in doing the research, with the community still determining the question and the final product. Additionally, when there is no coalition of community members available to guide the research, the researcher may need to organize the coalition through the research process—using research itself as an organizing tool (Nash 1993).

Factionalism

Collaboration with a "community" also means that one is working with a less than perfectly formed consensus. Eventually, the question arises of whom one is really collaborating with. The academic researcher may end up collaborating with one faction against the other—especially when factions develop within the community. At what point should the collaborative researcher become an advocate for one faction or another, or maintain distance from both factions? In general, collaborative research with grassroots groups eventually has to confront the reality that empowerment of grassroots groups will threaten power holders, making collaborative research on one level adversarial research on another level (see Brown and Tandon 1983; Simonson and Bushaw 1993).

Power and Influence

What if the researcher does occupy a central role in the research process? Could the researcher become so powerful that he or she actually decides the research question and the final product? How does one maintain accountability to the "community"—however that is determined? Collaborative researchers often feel stuck between saying nothing to avoid unduly influencing the community, or using their expert status to direct the community's decision-making process. Avoiding the roles of both unquestioned expert and mere technician is a difficult balancing act, as the collaborative researcher tries to find a status as one contributor among many around the table. Community members will often show researchers what their role is, but in other cases either the researcher's role is ill-defined or there are multiple definitions floating around. These situations can pressure the researcher into roles ranging from pawn to power broker (see Zuniga-Urrutia 1992).

The Rise and Fall of the Working Group on Neighborhoods

I began my career with the University of Toledo in the fall of 1988. I occupied a joint position as an assistant professor of sociology and a research associate with the university's Urban Affairs Center. Ohio is unique in funding research and service centers at each of the state's urban universities to study and solve local urban problems. The University of Toledo Urban Affairs Center assigned its half of my time to work with Dave Beckwith, a community organizer from the Center for Community Change, who at the time was also employed half-time with the Urban Affairs Center. Dave had begun the collaborative process before my entrance onto the scene by surveying community organization leaders to establish a community research agenda. The survey generated about a dozen ideas, out of which I favored doing a needs assessment of the community-based development and organizing groups in the city, since I was most familiar with the concepts, issues, and methodology involved.[3]

This project was near textbook-perfect collaborative research. Dave helped me organize a core group of about six leaders and staff from community-based organziations who guided the entire research project. Over numerous lunch meetings, we developed the categories of information we wanted (budget information, project information, staff and board skill levels and training needs, and community characteristics). I wrote a draft interview guide that the core group critiqued, and then began the data collection process. While I did the actual research, I was not collecting information using techniques or data sources unknown to any of the research participants. They in fact told me where and how to get the information we sought. Consequently, my labor did not deprive community members of any knowledge or expertise, and it helped me establish contact with organization leaders and members.

I followed the method of research I had developed with the CedarRiverside neighborhood in Minneapolis (Stoecker 1994). I asked community representatives to review the information and findings that I had collected about them and asked them to correct errors and "reframe" information before it went public. I then asked everyone who participated to review a draft of the research report. Only a few of the 20 organizations responded with further information or comments, but the process seemed to generate good will and helped support further involvement.

[3]See Stoecker and Beckwith (1992) for another discussion of the earlier phase of this project.

The advantages of role specialization became apparent during the production of the research report. Doing the research left me depressed, as I found Toledo's community-based organizatins to be thoroughly disorganized, underfunded, underskilled, and unproductive. I knew neither what to do with the information, nor how to present it in any way that would lead to positive change. My community organizer mentor, Dave, saw the opportunity in the data, and established a tradition that lasted through two more research projects. He organized a half-day research conference that brought together community organizations, funders, government officials, and corporate officials. My research report was the catalyst of the conference. After I presented the research, which included information about the individual organizations and about the "state of the art" in Toledo, Dave sent the funders and officials to one room and the community organizations to another room. Funders and officials were to decide what they would want from community organizations in exchange for increasing their support of them. The community organizations were to decide what they would be willing to do in exchange for getting increased funding. Both sides agreed that the organizations had to become more productive and accountable in exchange for more funding.

Out of this conference we formed the Working Group on Neighborhoods (WGN)—a coalition of government officials, foundations, corporations, and community organizations. It began as an informal group sponsored and administered through the Urban Affairs Center. Since increased funding for community organizations was the issue that brought the groups together, that became WGN's main focus. WGN next commissioned two research projects: a study of funding models for other cities (undertaken by a WGN subcommittee) and a study of philanthropy in Toledo (which I conducted). The funding model research project occurred without incident. Rather than a formal scientific study, the main task of this piece of research was to gather information on how a few well-known cities (Cleveland, Pittsburgh, and others) funded their community organizations.

The complications of collaborative research soon became apparent in my project, which was to study the giving patterns of Toledo's foundations. One main difficulty was deciding who was a "participant" in the project. The feel-good atmosphere of WGN, where the corporate/foundation/government "wolves" lay down peacefully with the community organization "sheep," gave all of us the idea that a study of philanthropy could bring more funders into WGN by involving them in the research. But only three Toledo foundations participated willingly—and they were already involved in WGN. The rest refused to return phone calls, answer letters, or even provide information they were legally obligated to submit.

As a consequence, the project turned into something more like an adversarial research model (Brown and Tandon 1983). I had to learn how to maneuver around foundation blockades to get their tax returns and other information. As with the previous project, a core group guided the research process, but they were unable to guide me to information sources. Thus, I developed skills and knowledge of how to access foundation information that the core group members could only learn about secondhand.

Another conference followed these two research projects and eventually led to extra funds approaching $1 million. These funds were procured with the help and efforts of our local member of the U.S. Congress, Marcy Kaptur. It was at this point that tensions began to develop within WGN. Distributing the money—a combination of federal and local matching funds—shifted WGN from an advocacy role to a management role as a subcommittee formed to oversee the newly christened Toledo Fund for Neighborhood Development (TFund). The Urban Affairs Center created a staff position to administer the growing work of WGN, which had also expanded into research, education, training, and service programs. Disputes arose over who would control the TFund. Would it be foundations, corporations, the government, or community-based organizations? Disputes also arose over who was in control of WGN itself and especially its budget. Would it be the Urban Affairs Center or participating members? There was no clean break between the grassroots groups and institutional actors. Intense individual personalities muddied the waters further, but the structural conflicts built-in between poor communities and powerful institutions exacerbated the conflict.

The collaborative research model broke down amid these growing conflicts. I was becoming increasingly disturbed by what I saw as the attempts of the Local Initiatives Support Corporation (LISC) and city government to divert, or at least rigidly control, funds supposedly destined to the community organizations. I was also concerned, with the community organizing groups (a minority in WGN), by the overwhelming emphasis on physical redevelopment rather than community organizing with the coalition. I had always felt more sympathetic to the activists in the group, and saw them getting shut out of the agenda.

At this point I proposed a study of two major community organizing efforts, one in

Minneapolis and one in Toledo, which became transformed into development projects. I got the Urban Affairs Center director (Dave Beckwith) and the community organizing activists in WGN to support the project. This was not officially a WGN-sponsored project, but it became attached to the organization and became the focus for the third annual community conference, which also included a panel of community organizers who stressed the need for increased focus on their vision of urban redevelopment.

This piece of research was to show the crucial importance of community organizing, and the disruptive effect of development activities on community unity and power. I again conducted the research, making sure that community members in the two research sites reviewed both specific parts of the research report and drafts of the final copy. As with the first project, community members knew much more about my research than I did, but I got the benefit of piecing together all the separate personal histories of these two neighborhood movements, editing information in perhaps a different way than community members would have.

This final community conference was a disappointment. In contrast to the other conferences, which led to high energy and subsequent action, this one ended with no action plans except to establish a WGN organizing subcommittee. By this time it was evident that powerful foundation, corporate, and government actors were in control of WGN with the support of a couple of the more powerful community development corporations.

Attracting the participation of minority communities was becoming more and more difficult. But the community activists that remained involved became more and more vocal, as did I, over attempts by LISC and city government to exert a stranglehold on the

increased funds—by this time totaling over $2 million—coming in to support community-based organizations. The growing grassroots protest within WGN was not enough to transform WGN, but it was enough to destroy its presentation of unity and expose its heretofore hidden structural conflicts, eventually leading to the disbanding of WGN itself in early 1994.

It is unclear how much my drift from a collaborative research model influenced WGN's trajectory. My final research project certainly gave voice to a neglected and much more controversial perspective on urban development. But my voice was not the loudest to protest the direction WGN had taken. I had also chosen to collaborate with a faction of WGN, feeling that I had to fight being coopted by the institutional actors. Was that my role or my right as a collaborative researcher? I still don't know. I certainly could not have continued down the path WGN was headed. On the other hand, perhaps the more ethical option would have been to exit. But my commitment has been, and continues to be, grassroots empowerment, and to simply exit would have meant forsaking that mission.

Conclusion

The wounds of this experience are beginning to heal. Enemies are beginning to talk to each other again. I am involved in a new collaborative effort extending beyond Toledo to link with the other urban universities and neighborhoods across Ohio's seven major metropolitan areas. And I have learned some lessons that may guide collaborative researchers. They relate to the three issues discussed at the beginning of this case study.

First, role specialization may not be the worst thing that can happen. The ideal is to have the community engaging in the research itself. When that is not practical, however, a strong community core group can still direct the research and hold the researcher accountable with useful benefits. This is especially the case when there is nothing useful to learn from the research process itself. Until we can write grants that pay community members to take time off from work, obtain child care, and reduce the other demands on their time, researchers will have to do more of the labor. However, that does not absolve us of finding ways to provide community members with those resources.

Second, the researcher has to be very careful in determining whom the community is. Communitarian models (see Etzioni 1993) that deny or at least ignore the existence of structural antagonisms between the haves and have-nots are unrealistic at best, and dangerously coopting at worst. Eventually, real empowerment of grassroots groups will be threatening to power holders. Researchers must eventually decide with whom they are going to collaborate (haves or have-nots) and on what they are willing to do research (safe or controversial issues). I have opted, for the time being, to collaborate with grassroots groups only, and not institutional power holders.[4]

Finally, while the researcher may not be able to exert undue influence, she or he may do too little of value by not following the collaborative model strictly enough. Part of the obligation of the collaborative researcher is to seek out the research ideas floating around in the community. We followed that strategy in our first research project, but a relatively small group in WGN conceived of the second project, and I pretty much developed the third one. Had we conducted a community research needs survey each year, and drawn our research projects from that through a more democratic process controlled by grassroots groups, we may have had a more satisfying outcome. Had I also been more conscious of my political perspective, we could have then negotiated the research agenda more.

None of this is to call WGN, or the collaborative process that led up to it, a total failure. There are more community-based organizations in Toledo today that are more productive, better trained, better funded, and more energetic.[5] There is a remaining coalition of community development corporations in place. There was enough latent organization to allow me to bring community-based organizations together around our new collaborative efforts. But enough also went wrong to allow me to learn something, which is what an ideal collaborative research project should do anyway.

[4]In his comments on an earlier draft, Dave Beckwith refers to this as "choosing not to pick a partner but to pick an arena."

[5]This information comes from Dave Beckwith's September 1, 1994, memo, "Review of Our Work with Neighborhood Groups."

EDITORS' COMMENTS

Randy Stoecker writes about a series of collaborative research projects in Toledo, Ohio, called WGN. What happens when relationships in a collaborative research project do not always work out perfectly? Stoecker's observations summarize three dilemmas that often face collaborative research projects: role specialization, factionalism, and power and influence. Role specialization occurs when community members do not meet the ideal of fully participating in the research, and the academic often takes over—as exemplified in Stoecker's statement that he is the only author because his community group collaborators didn't feel they had the time to write this case study. So, Stoecker writes this piece in a "modified collaborative style" in which his community collaborators have served as guides and reviewers of the ideas and he has taken on the specialized role of communicating its findings.

Factionalism among collaborators occurs when there is tension between academics and community members and among community members themselves. What side does the academic researcher take when community members are fighting among themselves or are divided on issues facing the collaboration? Finally, how does the researcher come to terms with the fact that she or he is influential and powerful enough to control or decide the research question and final product? How does the researcher negotiate this tenuous balance? In evaluating his own experience with WGN, Stoecker highlights both the successes and failures of the projects. More importantly, he reminds all of us that collaborative research and decisions surrounding it are often done imperfectly—even with the best of intentions.

Microenterprise Development in El Salvador: Lessons for Both Sides of the Border[1]

GASPER F. LOBIONDO, S.J., Woodstock Theological Center (United States), and RAFAEL A. PLEITEZ, Jesuit Universidad Centroamericana (El Salvador)

El Salvador, a country of almost 5.5 million people, is still emerging from 12 years of bloody civil war. Between 1988 and 1990, the proportion of households below the poverty line in metropolitan San Salvador went from 46 percent to 49 percent (Briones 1992, 50). At the same time, microenterprises (very small businesses with five or fewer employees) have mushroomed throughout the country. In this post-conflict scenario, microenterprise development is coming to be viewed as a potentially powerful tool for alleviating poverty, creating employment, and contributing to the success of national reconstruction.

For these budding microentrepreneurs, access to credit and training is a sine qua non under circumstances in which local economies are increasingly affected by international competition. In order for this kind of initiative to succeed at the grassroots level, it needs to be financed in a way that fits the conditions of the borrowers. In response to this need, community-based, nongovernmental organizations

(NGOs) are emerging. These NGOs become conduits for the supply of international capital being made available by international agencies. They in turn make credit and training available to prospective microentrepreneurs who cannot borrow from commercial banks because the amount of startup capital they need is too small and because they cannot provide collateral on their own. The NGOs are providing resources through newly created, unconventional lending methods such as village banks and solidarity groups.

In order to meet an increasing need among the poor for startup capital, Catholic Relief Services in El Salvador (CRS/ES) coordinates a national microenterprise development program. It channels development aid through 11 Salvadoran NGOs that manage community-based lending programs, 92 percent of whose participants are women. The CRS/ES does this through its own type of "village banking" approach to credit and savings. "Village banking" refers to the particular form of cooperation among borrower/savers that structures the delivery of financial services to individuals through social support groups. CRS/ES distinguishes groups according to three levels of borrowing. Each group has progressively higher entry levels for borrowing and saving, in a

[1] "Microenterprise Development in El Salvador: Village Banking, Changing Values, and Informal Education," was funded by the University of Miami North-South Center. A version of this study has been previously published by the Universidad Centroamericana in San Salvador in the March-April, 1995, issue of *Realidad*.

series of four- to six-month credit cycles over two to three years. Stepped access to progressively higher levels of financial risk and return are possible through:

- Village banks, which receive initial loans of $50 and average approximately 25 members
- Subsistence groups, which begin with loans of $125 and average 6 members
- Simple accumulation groups, which start with initial loans of $780.

Need for Informal Economic Education

More than money is needed for this kind of community-based economic development to be sustainable. Lending mechanisms had to be complemented because "additional assistance is necessary in order to help women entrepreneurs develop their businesses beyond subsistence levels" (Holt 1994, 161). The village banking model was designed to include a technical assistance or education component because CRS/ES found that a "minimalist" approach to training—which downplays training—is less effective in programs whose beneficiaries have comparatively lower levels of education (McKean 1994, 205).

In other words, credit is only one among several components that are necessary for sustainable microenterprise development. Other factors, such as access to technical, management, and decision-making skills, are also necessary if fledgling firms are to achieve healthy growth. Moreover, while the techniques of new financial instruments for providing access to startup capital to individuals have advanced dramatically, corresponding techniques for training and technical assistance have not. Development aid policy experts have considered these as costly and cumbersome. Some have even concluded that financial sustainabil-ity of microenterprise programs is possible without investment in human capital—that is, without training programs designed to meet the educational needs of borrowers.

In order to address this problem, CRS/ES began to implement an informal education program in its field operations in fall 1994. CRS/ES called this new component "popular economic education" (PEE) (Thys and Painter 1994, 17). PEE, which is oriented primarily to pre-literate microentrepreneurs, teaches them to reflect on their business decisions. It is predicated on the notion that the more a training program adjusts to the requirements of strategic microenterprise decisions, the more adequately it will meet real needs and result in sustainable development. PEE requires a "curriculum" that can adjust and adapt to the order and magnitude of dilemmas that the microentrepreneurs encounter. Therefore, CRS/ES needed to develop and improve the design of its PEE program. Recommendations for this design emerged from community-based research.

Woodstock Study: Conceptual Framework

The Woodstock study responded to the research need for this "more careful analysis of the potential of different types of nonfinancial forms of assistance" (Boomgard 1989, 83). Its purpose was to provide CRS/ES with some general guidelines for designing and implementing its nascent PEE program. The study deals with the learning process by which microenterprise development can become self-sustaining. This is possible when development is looked at as an increase in practical knowledge rather than the accumulation of capital (Razeto 1990, 150). Thus, the more we knew about community-based learning, the better we could design PEE to be suited to real needs.

Crucial to the formulation of the research problem was the way in which the training needs of microentrepreneurs were conceptualized. If the skills needed were seen as merely technical operations, programs would need to emphasize content. However, if problem-solving skills were sought, programs should put more weight on decision-making skills. Consequently, these programs would emphasize process. The latter approach was taken in this study.

The study established a conceptual relationship between training needs (informal education) in the CRS/ES village banking program, and the changing values. The question became, What kind of experience-based knowledge best serves microentrepreneurs? Knowledge, here, is understood as information that changes the microentrepreneurs themselves so that they can make conscious decisions that result in wealth creation, empowerment, and greater freedom (Drucker 1989, 251).

Change comes from replacing the kind of habit that "consists of decisions in which what we decide has such an overwhelming value for us that we usually are not even conscious of the alternatives" (Boulding 1985, 77). To the extent that microentrepreneurs build their knowledge on the consideration of alternative courses of action, they are changed because their values are changed. Thus, the variable in the title of the study: "changing values." In the group-learning context of village banking, this assumption meant that PEE would be a function of consciously shared changing values, not of static transcultural business skills that exist somewhere outside the consciousness of microentrepreneurs.

Our assumption was that the search for data about the learning process would contribute to the design of PEE. When human beings are attentive to new information and data, squarely face the questions, and come to a new understanding of their situation, they reorder priorities that are based on a judgment that is autonomous, responsible, and free (Lonergan 1993, 36–38). People learn to resolve their business problems successfully when they improve their reasoning process and learn how to take the most important factors into consideration.

The Research Question

The unifying research question was whether or not and to what extent the reasoning behind strategic enterprise decisions made by microentrepreneurs in the course of several village banking credit cycles was economic. A PEE program designed to meet the needs of microentrepreneurs would need to base its curriculum on the extent to which economic reasoning was or was not operative in relation to the stepped cycles of borrowing and saving.

Strategic enterprise decisions are based on judgments about competing economic values. In order to judge among competing economic values, microentrepreneurs must comprehend the value of foregone alternative action. Economists have labeled this fundamental concept of economic reasoning "opportunity cost." Economic value judgments always involve opportunity cost; therefore a key operational research insight in this study is that reflection on business and financial choices and dilemmas hinges on the practical grasp of opportunity cost. A PEE program designed on the basis of this kind of data will be more cost-effective because it will engage microentrepreneurs at a significant motivational level.

The greater understanding one has of alternative business choices, the greater the chance of prioritizing competing values in business decisions. The design of a PEE program should then be based on data about the way in which questions involving this kind of economic reasoning arise at different stages of the credit cycles in the three different levels of borrowing. The practical grasp of opportunity cost takes place in strategic enterprise decisions, comparisons of costs and benefits, and the corresponding decision regarding the allocation of resources. Strategic decisions that relate to these costs can be financial, productive, administrative, and commercial.

Research Methodology

The qualitative data for the report came from 112 semistructured interviews in eight different parts of the country. CRS/ES and NGO field personnel played a crucial part in arranging these interviews and ensuring that researchers from outside could be trusted. A survey consisting of 53 questions produced quantitative data on which recommendations for the design of PEE could be made. A total of 185 microentrepreneurs were surveyed. The survey covered a sample of 33 of the 337 groupings of village banks around the country. It was administered by students of the Universidad Centroamericana under the supervision of the university public opinion research center (Instituto Universitario de Opinion Publica).

One of the positive results of this collaborative approach to community-based research was that students profited from the experience. Many had never administered surveys to the very poor. Many had never directly related to poor people in their own social and economic environment. Primary researchers provided students with special training sessions in order to prepare them for this experience.

The interview and survey questions were geared toward decisions involving a practical grasp of the concept of opportunity cost, reinvestment priorities, and factors that microentrepreneurs take into consideration in the sale of their products. We created an opportunity cost index out of several survey questions. It served as the indicator for the level of the economic logic microentrepreneurs use to make their key business decisions. This index helped gauge whether individuals were using logic that would eventually lead to self-sufficiency. A second index measured income growth, and the third measured reinvestment. These indices tested for associations between types of groups and cycles of operation. They helped determine the level of economic reasoning used in strategic business decisions.

The study also gathered demographic and training data as well as information on business experience and activities. As soon as the first results of data analysis were available, we immediately reported them to CRS/ES field staff with explanations and discussion. Upon returning to the United States, the same was done at the CRS/US headquarters. NGO staffs in El Salvador were subsequently provided with the data on an ad hoc basis.

Results and Recommendations of the Woodstock Study

We found statistically significant associations in the following areas:

1. **The type of group (village bank, subsistence groups, and simple accumulation groups) and the opportunity cost index.** Participants in the higher group levels tended to have a greater grasp of opportunity cost than those at lower levels. This would justify the way in which CRS/ES has differentiated village banks into three groups. Assuming that sustainable

development grows out of the development of human capital through increased practical grasp of basic economic logic, whatever fosters the use of this kind of logic will also contribute to a more effective delivery method. We concluded that CRS/ES could design PEE to fit these groupings and that these groupings might serve as the basis for the development of individuals' decision-making skills in the economic reasoning process.

2. **Credit cycles and the opportunity cost index.** The data reveals that this particular system of cycles is working in a positive relation with three factors: increased income, reinvestment, and employment creation. Because they play a part in differentiating the way changing values are based on practical knowledge, cycles emerge as a critical element in the design of PEE. Most village banks are in the early cycles. We recommended that designers of training programs establish a PEE matrix that relates the progressive nature of credit cycles to the cumulative nature of the participants' practical knowledge. This matrix would establish and administer training themes critical to earlier cycles, during those cycles.

3. **Credit cycles and an "index of growth."** This indicates that the program generally succeeds in moving borrowers along from one credit level to another.

4. **Credit cycles, income growth, and type of group.** This indicates a solid basis for distinguishing factors specific to the cycle and type of group in relation to decisions regarding earnings when designing PEE. The study authors recommended that designers of PEE build on the level of economic rationality that already shows itself

to be operative in the decision making of participants. The design of PEE might incorporate exercises in which the groups reflect on some of the successful and failed decisions that they have made. Tools for this reflection would include explicit reference to basic elements of economic rationality as embodied in the practical grasp of opportunity cost.

5. **Credit cycles and use of profits.** The more advanced the cycle, the greater the reinvestment of profits; hence, the importance of focusing on the specific level of practical knowledge related to each of the developmental stages of this process. Decision-making topics corresponding to each level would then be incorporated into the design of PEE.

6. **The type of group and use of profits.** Simple accumulation support groups tended to reinvest a greater part of their profits. From these associations, the Woodstock study recommended that PEE establish modules on different topics and at different developmental levels that can adjust to the circumstances of strategic microenterprise decisions. These modules could then be used in the order that the local circumstances demand.

Together these findings illustrate how learning, decision making, and changing values relate to one another. As values continue to change, they suggest that microenterprise programs of church-sponsored agencies can potentially contribute a healthy new dimension to microenterprise development. This potential can be realized when informal education is designed to respond to changing values, not made up of static ethical principles or of exclusively technical criteria. In its most practical sense, the study suggests that when

PEE programs match the progressive nature of cycles with the participants' cumulative practical knowledge, they can establish a matrix to present training themes critical to earlier cycles.

Follow-Up

Just as the role of field personnel was critical in the research process, their role is also critical in the follow-up—when the information loop is closed. The information gathered from the microentrepreneur community is given back to it by field workers who help shape and implement the PEE program. As communicators of a new type of training, field personnel link researchers, PEE program designers, and program participants. They make it possible for the research results to become a lasting resource for poor microentrepreneurs. But they do so only to the extent that they themselves participate in an ongoing reflection process with program participants, with those responsible for technical aspects of the program, and with those responsible for evaluating it.

Valuable links have been established between microentrepreneurs, grassroots development experts (agents) in El Salvador, and policy-oriented grassroots researchers in the United States. A collaborative research design and methodology is in place. It is replicable. The challenge for the future is to update data and continue with follow-up.

EDITORS' COMMENTS

Collaboration does not have to know national boundaries. This project describes a multinational collaborative research effort that involved efforts to create sustainable microenterprise development (concentrating on very small businesses). Gasper LoBiondo, S.J., at the Woodstock Theological Center in the United States, and Rafael Pleitez, at the Jesuit Universidad Centroamericana in El Salvador, describe their effort to evaluate and implement training programs in El Salvador and other Latin American countries that educated often pre-literate individuals about business skills. The program stressed technical, management, and decision-making skills of the very small business owners over the accumulation of loans and other capital-intensive community development programs.

Similar to the ideas expressed by Warren Friedman in his case on community policing, it is not just the institutional arrangements that need to be changed—our knowledge about what constitutes certain activities also has to change. For positive microeconomic change to occur in war-ravaged and economically distressed countries similar to El Salvador, we may be best served by changes in the expectations or knowledge about economic growth and business activities that people have about the world. Or, in the words of the authors, "To the extent that microentrepreneurs build their knowledge on the consideration of alternative courses of action, they are changed because their values are changed." Through community-based action research, these authors make a series of recommendations designed to change the way future educational and microeconomic efforts are conducted.

Participatory Action Research and Real Community-Based Planning in East St. Louis, Illinois

KENNETH M. REARDON, University of Illinois at Urbana–Champaign

In the spring of 1987, Dr. Stanley Ikenberry, president of the University of Illinois at Urbana-Champaign, made his annual presentation on the future of the university before the Higher Education Finance Committee of the Illinois state legislature. Following his remarks, State Representative Wyvetter H. Younge (D-East St. Louis), the new co-chairperson of this committee, challenged Dr. Ikenberry to demonstrate the university's commitment to the state's poor by establishing a community assistance project in East St. Louis. Dr. Ikenberry responded by working with the university's architecture, landscape architecture, and urban and regional planning faculty to create the Urban Extension and Minority Access Project (UEMAP).

The goals of UEMAP were to (1) fund student and faculty research on environmental, economic, and social problems facing East St. Louis; (2) encourage other public and private organizations to support the community development efforts of local residents and government; and (3) inform African American students about professional and community service opportunities in architecture, landscape architecture, and urban and regional planning.

More than a dozen UEMAP research projects were completed by university students and faculty between 1988 and 1990 on such topics as storm water management, industrial housing, local economic development, urban design, and waterfront revitalization. However, campus interest in UEMAP began to wane as few of the recommendations contained in these research reports were implemented by local officials. Growing faculty concern regarding this problem led the campus to complete a systematic evaluation of UEMAP in the summer of 1990. Forty-five East St. Louis community leaders representing a broad cross-section of the city's neighborhood, religious, and political leaders were interviewed as part of this effort. Few of these individuals were aware of the university's early East St. Louis research projects, and reaction among them to the idea of a university-sponsored community assistance project was negative. While most civic leaders expressed admiration for the university's instructional programs, many voiced stinging criticisms of its past urban research activities. These individuals believed university scholars had used the serious problems facing their community to secure research funding for projects that produced few, if any, community benefits. Local leaders viewed these academics as intellectual "carpetbaggers" who used the city's problems to justify summer salaries, graduate student stipends, and other research support for the university while offering the city nothing in return (Reardon et al. 1993).

Creating a Community-University Partnership

Only the director of a local settlement house showed any real interest in seeing the university assume an ongoing technical assistance role in East St. Louis; he encouraged the university to redirect its resources toward efforts to assist the city's growing number of community-based development organizations. These volunteer organizations were engaged in a variety of community improvement projects, including clearing illegally dumped trash from vacant lots, sealing abandoned buildings, and completing neighborhood beautification projects.

In a meeting with the leaders of the Emerson Park Development Corporation (EPDC), the neighborhood organization serving the area where the settlement house was located, the six women who ran EPDC said they were not interested in establishing a "business as usual" relationship with the university or any other so-called technical assistance provider. They said they would only work with organizations that would allow community residents to determine the issues to be addressed; involve local leaders in each step of the planning process; work with residents to implement projects contained in community plans; and promote the development of community-based organizations.

These leaders responded enthusiastically to a faculty recommendation for a program with the following goals: the use of a highly collaborative planning process based on participatory action research involving local residents and university faculty as co-investigators, co-planners, and co-designers at each step in the planning process; and the use of this process to develop a comprehensive stabilization plan in the fall of 1990 to address the neighborhood's severe employment, housing, crime, and municipal service problems (Hall 1993).

Developing the Plan

The Emerson Park leaders established a 10-person Sponsoring Committee to work with university students and faculty on the development of the community stabilization plan. This group formulated a research design to collect the archival, census, land use, building and site conditions, ownership and property tax, infrastructure maintenance, and resident perceptions data needed to complete this plan. Much of this data, such as that on land use, building and site conditions, and infrastructure maintenance, had to be collected through field surveys since it was not available from the city, which had disbanded its planning department in the late 1970s.

The Sponsoring Committee devised a work plan that required the completion of one major data collection activity each month. Monthly community meetings were scheduled to enable local residents to participate, along with the Sponsoring Committee, in the data analysis phase of the process. During the first of these monthly meetings, a young man questioned the comparison groups the university students had used to analyze neighborhood population and housing trends and encouraged them to highlight the growing social inequality in their region by comparing neighborhood statistics with those for the county minus the city in addition to those for the entire county. Residents appeared visibly pleased during the second community meeting to see the analysis revised based on a suggestion from one of their own young men. In the eyes of some residents, the university researchers earned their "licenses to operate" in the neighborhood by demonstrating their willingness to substantially revise their technical work based on community input.

Participation in these monthly community meetings increased steadily from 15 to 75 residents throughout the fall of 1990, as individuals worked with university planning students to analyze local physical conditions, economic trends, and municipal service levels. The Sponsoring Committee held a public hearing in December of 1990 to elicit community feedback on the preliminary draft of the stabilization plan. Over 140 local residents and public officials crowded into the settlement house to hear the officers of the Emerson Park Development Corporation and members of the Sponsoring Committee discuss the major elements of the plan. Local residents unanimously approved the plan following two hours of debate and scheduled a meeting on Dr. Martin Luther King Jr.'s birthday (January 15, 1991) to devise a community organizing strategy to secure municipal support for its implementation.

Implementing the Plan

The *Neighborhood Improvement Plan for Emerson Park, East St. Louis* (Adanri et al. 1991) recommended over 54 specific neighborhood beautification, housing rehabilitation and development, substance abuse and public safety, economic development and job generation, and community organizing projects. Residents, aware of the city's historic bias in favor of downtown rather than neighborhood development, understood the need to build political support to implement the plan. EPDC devised a three-pronged strategy to encourage the development of a broad base of community support for the community revitalization initiative. The organization committed itself to (1) developing a detailed community-based crime prevention plan to address the escalating inci-

dence of violent street crime in their neighborhood; (2) initiating an increasingly ambitious series of volunteer improvement projects which would demonstrate their commitment to neighborhood improvement to city residents and municipal officials; and (3) writing a Community Development Block Grant Proposal to secure public funds to correct the neighborhood's most serious infrastructure problems.

In the spring of 1991, EPDC's leaders asked the university to assist resident committees working on each of these three community development initiatives. Information regarding model community-based crime prevention programs operating in other distressed cities was collected by 15 planning students that semester. These students collaborated with local residents to create a *Community Safety Plan for the Emerson Park Neighborhood of East St. Louis* (Ali et al. 1992) that recommended the development of household and commercial security programs; a community-based substance abuse project; a citizen crime watch, escort service, and safety patrol; a crime prevention through environmental design initiative; and a community policing strategy. Local housing officials reacted to this plan by demolishing several abandoned public housing units where illegal activities often occurred and rehabilitating the neighborhood's largest public housing complex. Municipal law enforcement authorities responded by assigning several new undercover police officers to the neighborhood, and this resulted in dozens of arrests that dramatically reduced the public sale of narcotics in Emerson Park.

A second group of students helped local leaders plan and implement the first neighborhood cleanup of illegally dumped trash to be held in the city. These students completed a survey of illegal dumping sites posing the greatest neighborhood health risks, interviewed leaders from other cities that had carried out successful neighborhood cleanup campaigns, and worked with residents to develop a strategy for clearing illegally dumped trash from 10 of the worst building lots. Local residents and university students then recruited nearly 200 individuals to remove illegally dumped household trash from vacant lots adjacent to the neighborhood's primary road. Representatives from a St. Louis foundation saw a news report on this activity and awarded EPDC a $15,000 grant to expand this neighborhood-based environmental project. EPDC stretched these resources by continuing to use volunteers on this project in order to use its grant money to rent heavy equipment and pay "tipping" fees at the regional landfill.

A third group of students cooperated with EPDC volunteers to formulate a Community Development Block Grant proposal to remedy the neighborhood's most serious housing and infrastructure problems (Stills 1992). This proposal recommended spending $375,000 to repair broken sewer lines, replace missing manhole covers, install new street and traffic signs, improve street lighting, seal salvageable structures, demolish dilapidated buildings, and improve public open spaces. While the city failed to implement many of these proposals, it did replace missing street and traffic signs and restore a small playground adjacent to a now-abandoned local elementary school as called for in this proposal. In addition, the city appointed three EPDC leaders to its newly reorganized Community Development Citizen Advisory Board.

Providing a Model

The success of the Emerson Park project led four other neighborhoods to request community planning and design assistance from the university between 1991 and 1995. In what is now called the East St. Louis Action Research

Project, university students and faculty worked with leaders of the Lansdowne, Winstanley/Industry Park, Edgemont, and Olivette Park neighborhoods to complete stabilization plans and Community Development Block Grant programs (Reardon 1995). These efforts produced a series of increasingly ambitious community development projects, including the rehabilitation of an existing municipal playground, the expansion of a Head Start playground, the construction of a vest-pocket park, the establishment of a 150,000-square-foot farmers' market, the erection of a park picnic pavilion, the exterior painting of 30 homes, and the substantial rehabilitation of 8 houses. These cooperative planning efforts also served to expand the number of individuals participating as members and leaders in the neighborhood associations that sponsored these community development efforts.

Unintended Consequences

In the spring of 1995, leaders from two of these neighborhood associations criticized the university's planning model by citing the lack of training provided to residents participating in these neighborhood planning efforts. While the university offered students participating in its East St. Louis planning projects the equivalent of three college courses, no comparable formal community development training was provided to local residents. The Department of Urban and Regional Planning responded to this criticism by working with several East St. Louis leaders to devise a three-course training series on community organization, state and local government, and community development planning.

In the spring of 1995, 41 leaders representing 8 of the city's 20 residential neighborhoods completed the first of these courses, which consisted of 36 hours of community organization instruction. The second course, focusing on state and local government structure and policies, was scheduled to begin in October 1995 as part of what is now referred to by local residents as the "University of Illinois Neighborhood College." The neighborhood leaders who participated in the university's community organizing class came to realize how much they had in common with each other. As the course came to an end, several leaders proposed the establishment of a citywide coalition of neighborhood associations to address common issues too large for any single organization to confront. The East St. Louis Citizen Action Network (ESL CAN) was organized in the summer of 1995 to carry out research, education, advocacy, and organizing activities to promote pro-neighborhood policies and programs in East St. Louis. The coalition has selected "code enforcement" of the local sanitation ordinance as it relates to illegal dumping, maintenance of vacant lots, and the demolition of abandoned buildings as its first issue. ESL CAN is currently receiving community organizing, policy research, and fundraising assistance from university students and faculty through funding provided by the Illinois Hazardous Waste Research Council and Region V of the U.S. Environmental Protection Agency.

Preliminary Reflections

Most East St. Louis residents view university-sponsored community assistance projects with great skepticism. They have watched several universities use local problems to secure funding benefiting campus-based personnel, facilities, and programs without providing benefits for East St. Louis residents. They have observed the waxing and waning of university interest in urban problems caused by changes in public opinion and political attitudes. They have also witnessed the beginning and end of scores of university-initiated community projects that faltered when faculty interest faded, political controversy erupted, or outside funding ended. These experiences have caused local residents to view universities as undependable community development partners.

Several factors appear to have been critical in the University of Illinois' success in overcoming residents' cynicism to establish a strong partnership with East St. Louis neighborhood organizations. The president's decision to allocate $100,000 annually in campus funds, on a recurring basis, demonstrated strong institutional support for the project. The faculty's willingness to cede control of the project's research agenda to neighborhood leaders signaled the university's commitment to research that addressed the concerns of East St. Louis residents. The faculty's policy of not pursuing outside funding for the university's East St. Louis Action Research Project until local, state, and federal agencies were routinely funding the city's neighborhood organizations demonstrated the seriousness of the university's commitment to local capacity-building. Continuing student and faculty involvement in the proposal writing and program implementation phases of the community development process has built strong personal and institutional bonds between the East St. Louis community and the Urbana campus. The project's eight years of increasing student involvement, faculty participation, and campus funding emphasizes the strength of the university's urban service commitment to East St. Louis.

Current Challenges

Successful execution of small-scale community improvement projects has caused these East St. Louis neighborhood organizations to devise more ambitious plans. These projects, developed and implemented with university assistance, require substantial levels of municipal government support. Local officials have shown some wariness regarding the expanding memberships and increased activity of these community-based organizations. They appear threatened by the growing influence of these independent civic associations the university has helped to create. As a result, they have, on occasion, sought to undermine the credibility of these groups by making it difficult for them to acquire site control over building lots they wish to develop or to secure municipal, state, or federal funding for these projects.

The growing effectiveness of these university-assisted community organizations has led other East St. Louis groups, as well as a coalition of Springfield social service agencies and the city of Champaign, to request community planning and design assistance from the campus. The university's ability to expand its technical assistance role is limited by the number of faculty trained in participatory action research methods, promotion and tenure guidelines that provide modest recognition for community service, and federal cutbacks in applied social science research funding. The growth of the university's East St. Louis project as an interdisciplinary service-learning project has raised questions regarding where it should be located within the university's organizational structure. The project is currently operated out of the Dean's Office in the College of Fine and Applied Arts, where all major policies must be approved by the heads of the architecture, landscape architecture, and urban and regional planning units. The recent involvement of faculty from the Department of Nuclear Engineering and School of Leisure Studies has prompted some to suggest moving the project into a unit with campuswide responsibilities, such as the university's Cooperative Extension Service. Ongoing federal funding cutbacks for the Cooperative Extension Service, along with the Extension's historic rural emphasis, has raised questions regarding the viability of this option.

EDITORS' COMMENTS

We end our cases on a positive note. Kenneth Reardon, an academic at the University of Illinois at Urbana–Champaign, provides the history, tensions, and hard-won accomplishments of a long-term community development project based in a large university. The East St. Louis project has been in place at the University of Illinois since 1987. In the beginning, Reardon and other academic researchers involved in this project were discouraged because few, if any, of their recommendations contained in research reports were being implemented by local and state officials. On the other hand, individuals and community group members felt used by university researchers. In a classic scenario, members of the community felt that they and their problems were being used by academics trying to secure funding that produced few, if any, tangible community benefits. Reardon explains how these and other problems can be overcome to sustain a long-term and significant program of community-based research that most parties feel good about. Reardon suggests both structural and cultural solutions to overcome these and other roadblocks to effective academic community research collaboration.

Conclusion: Collaboration Gives Hope and Voice in an Age of Disenchantment

In reading the daily newspaper, watching the evening news, or even taking a social problems course, it is easy to lapse into the disillusionment and despair brought on by what seem to be insurmountable problems in the world around us. For some reason the media find it easier to look at the dark side of human existence and report on the accidents, murders, and tragedies. If the evening news was the only place where we obtained information about the community around us, we would hardly want to venture out into the crime-ridden and accident-prone world. Even when the typical social science course provides an analysis of society's ills, it focuses on the social practices and institutions that perpetuate the problems, not necessarily on solutions. For decades the majority of U.S. sociology departments have taught a course entitled "Social Problems." We have never heard of a course entitled "Social Solutions." To map and analyze the dimensions of social problems— crime, inequities, racism, corporate control, and environmental hazards—is seen as scientific research. To discuss and describe alternative practices and develop solutions is seen as moving more toward politics and advocacy— areas that are perceived as a threat to the objectivity of research.

We are not calling for the end to basic social research. Understanding the dimensions of social problems is a vital first step in the development of solutions. However, the traditional separation of social research from policy development and program design has produced a gap between research and practice. Research exclusively developed within the academy does not always target the issues critical to a community at the present time. Even when research is more relevant, it is not always presented in a way that is readily used by the nonacademic world. In contrast, research that is informed and guided by community needs is more likely to be actionable—that is, it is more easily used or translated into action.

We have just presented 27 different ways of using research to improve the quality of life in various parts of our society. From low-income tenants trying to preserve their homes to health care coalitions addressing serious problems related to AIDS, we have described how research and action can be linked to seek solutions to social problems. Not all of these are perfect solutions, and some of these cases do not even present long-term solutions. However, what we have seen is the ability to combine the creativity and knowledge of university researchers with the creativity and knowledge of the community. You have read about how we can combine the impressive capacities of both the university and the community to gain a broader understanding of issues and modify existing programs or develop entirely new programs to address contemporary needs.

Is collaboration just another fad? Will it die away when foundations stop putting the word in their requests for proposals? Will it fall out of favor when university administrators and community leaders tire of the word? We think not. As we pointed out in the first chapters, structural changes in the workplace, community, and university have produced an environment of austerity that now encourages collaboration. Cooperation between university and community is a way to get more capacity in an age of downsizing.

Once pushed into cooperation by these structural forces, collaborating groups and individuals discover the excitement and benefits of working together. Collaboration gets all of us to immerse ourselves in the real world full of competing interest groups as well as new alliances. Although there may be dead ends and bumps in the road on the way, collaboration creates new opportunities for all involved. By putting our minds together, we can see things from a fresh perspective and develop innovative applications of old technology in addition to finding uses for rapidly developing new technologies.

For the university, collaboration is a great educational medium; for the community, it builds new understandings and control over the policy research process. By seeing a bigger part of the picture, students get a broader view of the society around them. Rather than just seeing the community as a "laboratory" in which to do research, professors see their research being put to use and incorporated

into a community's plans for change. We all want to see that our life's work has an impact on the world around us. In collaborative projects, university faculty are not only producing a new generation of researchers and practitioners who understand the advantages of collaboration, but are helping communities build a capacity to control their own destiny. Community leaders not only gain new knowledge about specific issues, but they come to understand the research process more clearly. They understand what they can do for themselves and how to establish relationships with university researchers as partners rather than controllers of research and knowledge. This has a democratizing effect on the production of new knowledge inside and outside the university.

As we near the turn of the century, we also are seeing a redefinition of the university and of the relationship between the university and the community. Like any other change in process, we cannot predict exactly how the new institutional arrangements will look. At the same time, the case studies in this book do provide us with a glimpse into the future. Some of these cooperative efforts are bringing about changes in racially diverse neighborhoods, improving the health of children in inner-city neighborhoods, protecting low-wage workers from environmental hazards, producing scientific literacy in all sectors of the community, seeking better ways of battling the AIDS epidemic, and involving residents in decision making that affects their communities. Individually they may not all make the headlines of the *New York Times*, the *Washington Post*, or the *Los Angeles Times*, but collectively they represent a new direction for U.S. universities and communities.

These are examples of action uninfected by the fatalism produced by cynicism. "Old" researchers and activists are educating "new" researchers and activists. While we have no illusion that this model will take over universities next year, it is sowing the seeds of a new generation of teachers, researchers, and activists who know how to cross boundaries that have previously held back our capacity to solve problems. It is a movement that knows how to build bridges at the same time it realizes the need to confront powerful stakeholders and institutions that would prefer to see business as usual. It is a movement that can carry us into the 21st century with hope and new capacities to bring health, comfort, and security for all citizens.

PRAG-Supported Organizations and Projects

The following is a list of organizations and projects that PRAG has "funded" by providing paid research assistants, interns, or apprentices over the past five years. Research assistants are graduate students from the four participating universities who typically work during the academic year for 20 hours per week. Interns are advanced undergraduate or graduate students from all area universities who work for one semester or a quarter. Apprentices are individuals connected with a community-based organizations—staff members, board members, or volunteers—who are paid a stipend for six months to work on a project with a group other than their "home" organization as a way of gaining greater research skills and an understanding policy issues related to their own organization's work.

Organization	Project Description
Asian American Institute	Survey of Asian American organizations in Chicago
Bethel New Life	Tracking of job potential for participants in Bethel's recycling processing center
	Development of neighborhood computerized mapping database for West Garfield
Center for Economic Policy Analysis	Development of criteria for evaluating the quality of Chicago Transportation Authority service
Center for Law and Human Services, Inc.	Study to initiate year-round tax counseling project for low-income, single-parent families
	Investigation of homeless access to earned income credit

Organization	Project Description
Center for Neighborhood Technology	Documentation of discriminatory effects of current U.S. energy policies
Center for New Horizons	Examination of ways to aid residents to become self-reliant, enhance quality of life, and revitalize community
	Feasibility study to establish a Blues Historic District (Theresa's Bar) as a cultural development piece of local economic development
Centro Sin Fronteras	Study to address health care problems facing Mexican residents of Westtown
	Research action project to encourage participation of elementary school students in lead testing
Chicago Algebra Project	Study to improve the math preparation and achievement of public school students
Chicago Area Committee on Occupational Safety and Health (CACOSH)	Examination of the occupational safety and health of immigrant workers in the Chicagoland area
	Research action project to unite employees in the prevention of workplace injuries
Chicago Coalition for the Homeless	Research into the use of public funding and tax increment financing in the South Loop
Chicago Coalition for Immigrant and Refugee Protection	Documentation of workplace hazards experienced by immigrant workers
Chicago Institute on Urban Poverty	Study to determine effect of regional transportation plan on low-income residents
Chicago Legal Clinic (formerly the South Chicago Legal Clinic)	Research on cumulative contamination in multiple sites in Calumet region
Chicago Mutual Housing Network	Development of a comprehensive research study on affordable housing cooperatives in Chicago

Organization	Project Description
Chicago Rehab Network	Study to promote community empowerment and development without displacement
Chicago Urban League	Survey of Grand Boulevard area businesses on the employment potential of inner-city enterprises
Chicago Women in Trades	Survey of young girls to determine interest in a training workshop and development of the curriculum for that training
Citizens Information Service	Research in support of a comprehensive employment and training program designed to move long-term unemployed adults permanently into the workforce
Community Workshop on Economic Development	Analysis of Chicago enterprise zones, which was used to formulate legislation and influence enterprise zone policy
Covenant Development Corporation	Documentation of the costs of social services that property management staff perform; development of accounting system to build in these costs
East Edgewater Chamber of Commerce	Study to establish databank profile of area businesses
Erie Neighborhood House	Creation of a career preparation plan for Latinos and assessment of their utilization of such a program
	Inventory of city-owned lots to be used for the planning and implementation of a land acquisition strategy in order to develop and implement an affordable housing program for low-income residents
Galewood-Montclare Community Organization	Examination of insurance redlining in Austin/Galewood-Montclare neighborhoods

Organization	Project Description
Grand Cal Task Force	Creation of a computer bulletin board that links the Grand Cal Task Force with other groups interested in environmental issues
Health and Medicine Policy Research Group	Study on how to recruit and retain physicians within the Medicaid system
Heartland Center	Analysis of the structure of welfare in Indiana and an evaluation of the social assistance programs: according to their overall coherence, the extent to which participation rates matched those eligible in the population, and the extent to which benefit levels met an adequate standard of need
Housing Resource Center of Hull House	Management plan for scattered-site public housing on Chicago's northside
Illinois Caucus for Adolescent Health (formerly Illinois Caucus on Teenage Pregnancy)	Survey of administrators and doctors in organizations concerned with adolescent health on education and support services needed for teenage mothers in order to improve advocacy work
Interfaith Council for the Homeless	Oral history project of the homeless living on lower Wacker Drive
Interfaith Leadership Project of Cicero, Berwyn, and Stickney	Creation and assessment of directory that lists job training and placement programs available to youth
Jewish Council on Urban Affairs	Research on the impact of welfare cutoff for single people in poverty
Kenwood-Oakland Community Organization	Study to enhance links between local residents in need of jobs to area medical centers and local schools
Lakefront SRO Corporation	Compilation of information on housing stock in five target neighborhoods

Organization	Project Description
Latin United Community Housing Association	Examination of insurance redlining and its effect on low-income Latino residents of West Town, Humboldt Park, and Logan Square
Latinos United	Analysis of policies that limit Latino access to housing and related employment
Lawrence Avenue Development Corporation	Development of marketing and development plan for Chicago Transit Authority's Kimball Station to encourage use of public transportation
Lawyers' Committee for Better Housing, Inc.	Analysis of the workings and decisions of the Cook County Eviction Court
Logan Square Neighborhood Association	Study to identify essential social services, education, and recreation needs not being satisfied
Metropolitan Tenants Organization	Determination of the extent of discrimination against tenants with children
Mexican Community Committee of Southeast Chicago	Investigation to determine ways to assist local unemployed Latinos and African American women with employment, training, and education
Mutual Aid Associations of Chicago Collaborative	Study to identify the health and welfare needs of refugee women
The Neighborhood Institute	Study on the decline of local jobs available through a support program for entrepreneurial development
New Cities Community Development Corporation	Analyze the acquisition and rehabilitation of single-family homes and its impact on community
Northside HIV Treatment Center	Evaluation of the efficacy of treatments offered by NHTC

Organization	Project Description
Northwest Neighborhood Federation	Study to determine pattern of lending practices of local financial institutions
Parent Community Council	Study to provide technical assistance support and training for schools within the Chicago public school system
Peoples Housing	Program to promote intercultural relations among Peoples Housing residents
Peoples Reinvestment and Development Effort (PRIDE)	Tracking of families who applied but were not placed in PRIDE housing
Resource Center	Study to document history of demolition of homes and buildings in Chicago
Rogers Park Community Action Network	Compilation of models of pooled security deposit funds
South East Asia Center	Program development to lessen interethnic hostilities and improve school dropout rate
Taylor Institute	Analysis of ways domestic violence can be reduced through community organizing
Uptown Center for Economic Development	Creation of on-line information for use in a community-based economic development process
Uptown Community Learning Center / African American Awareness Project	Survey of African American residents' perceptions of needed services in Uptown, with the aim of supplying the data to a community organizer
Uptown Habitat for Humanity	Evaluation of Habitat for Humanity's support programs for low-income homeowners Exploration of viability of condominium ownership for low-income communities
Vietnamese Association of Illinois	Survey of Vietnamese American businesses

Organization	Project Description
Women for Economic Security	Research to determine ways to provide accurate picture of entry-level job market for low-income women
Women Employed Institute	Study on barriers to women pursuing careers in nontraditional jobs
	Collaboration between education and job-training providers, employers, and community organizations to develop and carry out a strategy to improve job placement for low-income women
Women's Self-Employment Project	Feasibility study to create a system of individual development accounts as an asset-based alternative to the consumption-based welfare system
	Study to raise women's economic status through self-employment
Wrightwood Community Development Corporation	Study to determine ways to promote racial diversity and economic stability

References

Adanri, Bayo, et al. 1991. *Emerson Park Neighborhood Improvement Plan*. Urbana, IL: Department of Urban and Regional Planning.

Ali, Jinat, et al. 1992. *Community Safety Plan for the Emerson Park Neighborhood of East St. Louis, Illinois*. Urbana: Department of Urban and Regional Planning.

Alinsky, Saul. [1946] 1969. *Reveille for Radicals*. New York: Vintage Books.

Akalimat, Abdul, et al. 1986. *Introduction to African American Studies: a People's College Primer*. Chicago: Twenty-First Century Books and Publications.

Alkalimat, Abdul, Douglas Gills, and Kate Williams. 1995. *Job-Tech: The Technological Revolution and Its Impact on Society*. Chicago: Twenty-First Century Books and Publications.

Allen, David G., Lewayne D. Gilchrist, Linda Brown, Gary B. Cox, Jeannette Semke, Mary Durand Thomas, Ron Jemelka, and Ronald D. Perry. 1994. "One System, Many Perspectives: Stakeholders and Mental Health System Evaluation." *Evaluation and Program Planning* 17:47–51.

Alston, Dana. 1990. *We Speak for Ourselves: Social Justice, Race, and Environment*. Washington, DC: The Panos Institute.

American Association for the Advancement of Science (1992). *Project 2061: Education for a Changing Future, Update*. Washington, DC: AAAS.

American Association for the Advancement of Science (1990). *The Liberal Art of Science: Agenda for Action*. Washington, DC: AAAS.

Bender, Thomas. 1996. "Universities and the City: Scholarship, Local Life, and the Necessity of Worldliness." Paper presented at the Urban Universities and Their Cities conference, March, University of Amsterdam, Amsterdam, Netherlands.

Berger, Peter L. 1963. *Invitation to Sociology*. Garden City, NY: Anchor Books.

Blumer, Herbert. 1969. *Symbolic Interactionism*. Englewood Cliffs, NJ: Prentice Hall.

Boomgard, James. 1989. *A.I.D. Micro-Enterprise Stocktaking: Synthesis Report*. Washington, DC: U.S. Agency for International Development.

Boulding, Kenneth. 1985. *Human Detriment*. Beverly Hills: Sage Publications.

Brecher, Jeremy, and Tim Costello. 1991. *Building Bridges: The Emerging Grassroots Coalition of Labor and Community*. New York: Monthly Review Press

Briggs, Charles L. 1987. "Getting Both Sides of the Story: Oral History in Land Grant Research and Litigation." In *Land, Water, and Culture: New Perspectives on Hispanic Land Grants*, edited by C. L. Briggs and J. R. Van Ness. Albuquerque: University of New Mexico Press.

Briones, Carlos. 1992. La Pobreza Urbana en El Salvador: Caracteristic y Difference de los Hogares Pobres (1988–1990). San Salvador: UCA Editores.

Brown, L. David, and Rajesh Tandon. 1983. "Ideology and Political Economy in Inquiry: Action and Participatory Research." *Journal of Applied Behavioral Science* 19:277–294.

Brown, Phil. 1985. *The Transfer of Care*. Boston: Routledge and Kegan Paul.

_____. 1992. "Toxic Waste Contamination and Popular Epidemiology: Lay and Professional Ways of Knowing." *Journal of Health and Social Behavior* 33:267–281.

_____. 1995. "Race, Class, and Environmental Health: A Review and Systematization of the Literature." *Environmental Research* 69:15–30.

Brown, Phil, Desiree Ciambrone, and Lori Hunter. Forthcoming. "Does Green Mask Gray? Environmental Equity Issues at the Metropolitan Level." *International Journal of Contemporary Sociology*.

Brown, Phil, and Faith Ferguson. 1995. "'Making a Big Stink': Women's Work, Women's Relationships, and Toxic Waste Activism." *Gender & Society* 9:145–172.

Brown, Phil, and Susan Masterson-Allen. 1994. "The Toxic Waste Movement: A New Kind of Activism," *Society and Natural Resources* 7:269–286.

Brown, Phil, and Edwin J. Mikkelsen. 1990. *No Safe Place: Toxic Waste, Leukemia, and Community Action*. Berkeley: University of California Press.

Brown, Roxanne. 1991. "AIDS: The Growing Threat to Black Heterosexuals" *Ebony* 84 (January): 86–90.

Bruner, Charles. 1991. *Thinking Collaboratively: Ten Questions and Answers to Help Policy Makers Improve Children's Services*. Washington, DC: Education and Human Services Consortium.

Brunner, Ilse, and Alba Guzman. 1989. "Participatory Evaluation: A Tool to Assess Projects and Empower People." In *International Innovations in Evaluation Methodology: New Directions for Evaluation Methodology*, edited by R. F. Conner and M. Hendricks. San Francisco: Jossey-Bass.

Bryant, Bunyan, and Paul Mohai. 1992. *Race and the Incidence of Environmental Hazards*. Boulder: Westview Press.

Bullard, Robert D. 1983. "Solid Waste Sites and the Black Houston Community," *Sociological Inquiry* 53: 273–288.

_____. 1987. *Invisible Houston: The Black Experience in Boom and Bust*. College Station, TX: Texas A&M University Press.

_____. 1990. *Dumping in Dixie: Race, Class and Environmental Quality*. Boulder: Westview Press.

_____. 1993. *Confronting Environmental Racism: Voices From the Grassroots*. Boston: South End Press.

_____. 1994. *People of Color Environmental Groups Directory 1994–95*. Flint, MI: Charles Stewart Mott Foundation.

Carnegie Corporation of New York. 1992. *Report on the Project for Educational Change*. New York: Carnegie Corporation of New York.

Centers for Disease Control. 1990. "U.S. AIDS Cases Reported Through February 1990." *HIV/AIDS Surveillance Report* (March): 11–18.

The Chicago Empowerment Zone Strategic Plan. 1994.

Christenson, James A., and Jerry W. Robinson, Jr. 1980. *Community Development in America*. Ames: Iowa State University Press.

City of Santa Monica. 1994. *Toxics Use Reduction Program*. Santa Monica: Environmental Programs, City of Santa Monica.

Cohen, Sande. 1993. *Academia and the Luster of Capital*. Minneapolis: University of Minnesota Press.

Cole, Jonathan, and Stephen Cole. 1973. *Social Stratification in Science*. Chicago: University of Chicago Press.

Community Renewal Society. 1993. *Building Communities From Within*. Chicago: Community Renewal Society pamphlet.

Cook County Department of Health. 1993. "Reported Cases of AIDS Through September 1993." Chicago: Cook County Department of Health document.

Cooper, Geoff. 1992. "A Pit Bull for Milwaukee's Central City: Fair Lending Project Uses Attack-Dog Tactics to Change Lending Trends." *The Business Journal* (September 23).

Darnovsky, Marcy. 1991. "Overhauling the Meaning Machines: An Interview with Donna Haraway." *Socialist Review* 21 no. 2: 65–84.

Davies, Scott. 1995. "Leaps of Faith: Shifting Currents in Critical Sociology of Education." *American Journal of Sociology* 100, no. 6 (May): 1448–1478.

Dedman, William. 1989. "Blacks Turned Down for Home Loans from S & Ls Twice as Often as Whites." *Atlanta Journal/Constitution* (January 23).

Dowie, Mark. 1995. *Losing Ground: American Environmentalism at the Close of the Twentieth Century*. Cambridge: MIT Press.

Downs, Anthony. 1981. *Neighborhoods and Urban Development*. Washington, DC: Brookings Institution.

Drucker, Peter F. 1989. *The New Realities*. New York: Harper and Row.

Epstein, Steven. 1991. "Democratic Science? AIDS Activism and the Contested Construction of Knowledge." *Socialist Review* 21, no. 2: 35–64.

Etzioni, Amatai. 1993. *The Spirit of Community: Rights, Responsibilities, and the Communitarian Agenda*. New York: Crown Publishers.

Evans, Sara, and Harry Boyte. 1986. *Free Spaces: The Sources of Democratic Change in America*. New York: Harper & Row.

Fawcett, Stephen B. 1995. *Work Group Evaluation Handbook: Evaluating and Supporting Community Initiatives for Health and Development*. Lawrence, Kansas: Work Group on Health Promotion and Community Development, University of Kansas.

Ferris, Deeohn. 1994. "A Call for Justice and Equal Environmental Protection." In *Unequal Protection: Environmental Justice and Communities of Color*, edited by R. D. Bullard. San Francisco: Sierra Club Books.

Feyerabend, Paul. 1978. *Against Method: Outline of an Anarchistic Theory of Knowledge*. London: New Left Books/Verso.

Fisher, Robert, and Joseph Kling. 1993. *Mobilizing the Community—Local Politics in the Era of the Global City*. Newbury Park, CA: Sage Publications.

Freire, Paulo. 1970. *Pedagogy of the Oppressed*. New York: Seabury Press.

Gardener, Andrea. 1994. *Safe Cleaning Products for Janitorial Service Work*. Los Angeles: UCLA Pollution Prevention Education and Research Center (July).

Gaventa, John. 1991. "Toward a Knowledge Democracy: Viewpoints on Participatory Research in North America." In *Action and Knowledge: Breaking the Monopoly With Participatory Action Research*, edited by O. Fals-Borda and M. A. Rahman. New York: Apex Press.

_____. 1993. "The Powerful, the Powerless, and the Experts: Knowledge Struggles in an Information Age." In *Voices of Change: Participatory Research in the United States and Canada*, edited by P. Park, et al. Westport, CT: Bergin & Garvey.

Geiser, Ken, and Gerry Waneck. 1983. "PCBs and Waxten County." *Science for the People* 15: 13–17.

Gibbons, Michael. 1994. *The New Production of Knowledge*. London: Sage Publications.

Gilchrist, Lewayne, David G. Allen, Linda Brown, Gary B. Cox, Jeannette Semke, Mary Durand Thomas, Ron Jemelka, Ronald D. Perry, and Jan

Sutphen-Mroz. 1994. "A Public-Academic Approach to Designing a State Mental Health Program Evaluation." *Evaluation and Program Planning* 17:53–61.

Glabere, Michael L. 1992. "Milwaukee: A Tale of Three Cities." In *From Redlining to Reinvestment: Community Response to Urban Disinvestment*, edited by G. D. Squires. Philadelphia: Temple University Press.

Goetze, Rolf. 1979. *Understanding Neighborhood Change: The Role of Expectations in Urban Revitalization*. Cambridge: Balinger.

Gottlieb, Robert. 1993. *Forcing the Spring: The Transformation of the American Environmental Movement*. Washington, DC: Island Press.

_____. 1994. "A Collaborative Model for Environmental Research and Education: Linking Analysis With Community Issues and Perspectives." *Policy Currents*, no. 3 (August).

Gottlieb, Robert, ed. 1995. *Reducing Toxics: A New Approach to Policy and Industry Decision-Making*. Washington, DC: Island Press.

Grob, Gerald. 1994. *The Mad Among Us: A History of America's Mentally Ill*. New York: The Free Press.

Gronfein, William. 1985. "Incentives and Intentions in Mental Health Policy: A Comparison of the Medicaid and Community Mental Health Programs." *Journal of Health and Social Behavior* 26:192–206.

Hacker, Andrew. 1992. *Two Nations: Black and White, Separate, Hostile, Unequal*. New York: Charles Scribner.

Hall, Budd. 1992. "From Margins to Center? The Development and Purpose of Participatory Research." *The American Sociologist* 23: 15–28.

_____. 1993. "Introduction." In *Voices of Change: Participatory Research in the United States and Canada*, edited by P. Park et al. Westport, CT: Bergin & Garvey.

Hall, Peter Geoffrey. 1989. "The Turbulent Eighth Decade: Challenges to American City Planning." *Journal of the American Planning Association* 55: 272–283.

Hammonds, Evelynn. 1987. "Race, Sex, AIDS: The Construction of 'Other'." *Radical America* 20, no. 6: 28–36.

Hancock, Lynell, and John McCormick. 1996. "What to Chop." *Newsweek* (April 29): 59–67

Harrop, D. O. 1994. "Environmental Assessment and Incineration." In *Waste Incineration and the*

Environment, edited by R. E. Hester, and R. M. Harrison. Royal Soc. of Chemistry. London, England.

Hazard Communication Standard. 1983. Federal Register V. 48 N. 228, #29 CFR 1910.1200 (November 25) 53,280–53,348.

Hill, Elizabeth. 1995. *Coming Clean: The Potential for Toxics Reduction in the Garment Care Industry.* Los Angeles and Chicago: UCLA Pollution Prevention Education and Research Center and the Center for Neighborhood Technology (January).

Hofrichter, Richard, ed. 1993. *Toxic Struggles: The Theory and Practice of Environmental Justice,* Philadelphia: New Society Publishers.

Holt, Sharon L. 1994. "Transformation Lending: Helping Microenterprises Become Small Businesses." In *The New World of Microenterprise Finance: Building Healthy Financial Institutions for the Poor,* edited by E. Rhyne, and M. Otero. West Hartford, CT: Kumarian Press.

House, Ernest. R. 1978. "Justice in Evaluation." In *Evaluation Studies Review Annual,* vol. 1., edited by G. V. Glass. Beverly Hills, CA: Sage.

Illinois State Board of Education (1986). *State Goals for Learning and Sample Learning Objectives.* Springfield, IL: ISBE.

———. (1990). *Building the Foundations for Change.* Springfield, IL: ISBE.

Indiana Division of Mental Health. 1993. *The Indiana Plan for Moving From Institutional to Community Based Care: Policy and Process, Central State District.* Indianapolis: Family and Social Services Administration.

Isaac, Rael Jean, and Virginia C. Armat. 1990. *Madness in the Streets: How Psychiatry and the Law Abandoned the Mentally Ill.* New York: The Free Press.

Kolp, Paul, Barbara Sattler, Michael Blayney, and Timothy Sherwood. 1993. "Comprehensibility of Material Data Safety Sheets." *American Journal of Industrial Medicine* 23: 135–141.

Kretzman, John P., and John L. McKnight. 1993. *Building Communities From the Inside Out: A Path Toward Finding and Mobilizing a Community's Assets.* Evanston, IL: Center for Urban Affairs and Policy Research, Northwestern University.

Kutz, F. W. 1983. "Chemical Exposure Monitoring." In *Residue Reviews,* vol. 84. New York: Springer-Verlag.

La Pointe, A. E., N. A. Mead, and G. W. Phillips. 1989. *A World of Difference: An International Assessment of Mathematics and Science.* Princeton, NJ: Education Testing Service.

Lavelle, Marianne, and Marcia Coyle. 1993. "Unequal Protection: The Racial Divide on Environmental Law." *National Law Journal* (September 21).

Leana, Carrie R. 1996. "Why Downsizing Won't Work." *Chicago Tribune Magazine* (April 14): 14–16.

Lee, Alfred McClung. 1973. *Toward Humanist Sociology.* Englewood Cliffs, NJ: Prentice Hall.

Lee, Charles. 1992. *Proceedings of the First National People of Color Environmental Leadership Summit.* New York: Commission for Racial Justice.

Lester, Calu, and Larry Saxxon. 1988. "AIDS in the Black Community: The Plague, The Politics, The People." *Death Studies* 12: 563–571.

Levidow, Les. 1992. "Impact Assessment: Whose Rationality? Report on the 11th Annual Meeting of the International Association for Impact Assessment." *Capitalism, Nature, Socialism* 3, no. 1:117–124.

Lewin, Kurt. 1946. "Action Research and Minority Problems." *Journal of Social Issues* 2:34–46.

Logan, John, and Harvey Molotch. 1987. *Urban Fortunes: The Political Economy of Place.* Berkeley: University of California Press.

Lonergan, Bernard. 1993. "Topics in Education." In *Collected Works of Bernard Lonergan.* Vol. 10, edited by R. M. Doran, and F. E. Crowe. Toronto: University of Toronto Press.

Long, J. Scott. 1978. "Productivity & Academic Position in the Scientific Career." *American Sociological Review* 43: 889–908.

Lynch, Jean M. 1993. "Community Participation in Community Needs Assessments," *Journal of Applied Sociology* 10: 125–136.

Lynd, Mark. 1992. "Creating Knowledge Through Theater: A Case Study With Developmentally Disabled Adults." *The American Sociologist* 23: 100–115.

Mattessich, Paul W., and Barbara R. Monsey. 1992. *Collaboration: What Makes It Work.* St. Paul, MN: Wilder Research Center, Amherst H. Wilder Foundation.

McCarron, John. 1988. "Chicago on Hold." Series of seven articles in the *Chicago Tribune* (28 August–4 September).

McDonel, Elizabeth C., Paul A. Deci, Jeannette Semke, Trevor Hadley, Michael Hogan, James K. Dias, Bernice A. Pescosolido, and Eric R. Wright. 1993. "Downsizing State Psychiatric Facilities: Three New Research Efforts to Examine the Quality of Care for Persons With Severe Mental Illness." *Proceedings of the NASMHPD Research Institute Fourth Annual National Conference.* Washington, DC: NASMHPD Research Institute.

McGee, Christine. 1995. *Youth/Adult Alliances: Views From Youth Workers and Youth.* Massachusetts Institute of Technology Community Fellows Program.

McKean, Cressida. 1994. *Export and Investment Promotion Services: Do They Work?* Arlington, VA: Office of Evaluation, Center for Development Information and Evaluation. U.S. Agency for International Development.

McLaughlin, Joseph M. 1977. *Practical Trial Evidence.* New York: Practicing Las Institute.

Mechanic, David. 1989. *Mental Health and Social Policy, Third Edition.* Englewood Cliffs, NJ: Prentice-Hall.

Melaville, Atelia, and Martin J. Blank. 1991. *What It Takes: Structuring Interagency Partnerships to Connect Children and Families With Comprehensive Services.* Washington, DC: Education and Human Services Consortium.

Mollenkopf, John H., and Manuel Castells. 1991. *Dual City: Restructuring New York.* New York: Russell Sage Foundation.

Morey, Marilyn K. 1990. Status of science education in Illinois schools. *Journal of Research in Science Teaching,* 27(4): 387–398.

Morganthan, Tom, and Seema Nayyar. 1996. "$1000 a Week: the Scary Cost of College," *Newsweek* (April 29): 52–56.

Nash, Fred. 1993. "Church-Based Organizing as Participatory Research: The Northwest Community Organization and the Pilsen Resurrection Project." *The American Sociologist* 23: 38–55.

National Community Reinvestment Coalition. 1995. *CRA Dollar Commitments Since 1977.* Washington, DC: National Community Reinvestment Coalition.

New York Times. 1992. "Fed Report Gives New Data on Gains by Richest in 80s." (April 21).

New York Times. 1992. "The 1980s: A Very Good Time for the Very Rich." (March 5).

New York Times. 1996. "The Downsizing of America." (Series of articles from March 3– March 9).

Nyden, Philip. 1991. "Teaching Qualitative Methods: An Interview with Phil Nyden." *Teaching Sociology* (July 1991) 19: 396–402.

Nyden, Philip, and Joanne Adams. 1996. *Saving Our Homes: The Lessons of Community Struggles to Preserve Affordable Housing in Chicago's Uptown.* Chicago: Loyola University Chicago and Organization of the NorthEast.

Nyden, Philip, Joanne Adams, and Maryann Mason. 1992. *Our Hope for the Future: Youth, Family, and Diversity in the Edgewater and Uptown Communities.* Chicago: Loyola University Chicago and Organization of the North-East.

Nyden, Philip, Larry Bennett, and Joanne Adams. 1993. *Diversity and Opportunity in a Local Economy: Community Business in Edgewater and Uptown.* Chicago: Loyola University Chicago and Organization of the NorthEast.

Nyden, Philip, Diane Binson, Sr. MaryPaul Asoegwu, Roger Atreya, Ronald Gullata, Gayle Hoopaw, Vijay Kamath, Maryann Mason, John Norton, Layla Suleiman, and Jerry Vasilias. 1990. *Racial, Ethnic and Economic Diversity in Uptown's Affordable Housing: Its Present Character and Future Possibilitie*s. Chicago: Loyola University Chicago, Organization of the NorthEast, and the Human Relations Foundation.

Nyden, Philip, and Wim Wiewel, eds. 1991. *Challenging Uneven Development: An Urban Agenda for the 1990s.* New Brunswick, NJ: Rutgers University Press.

Nyden, Philip, and Wim Wiewel. 1992. "Collaborative Research: Harnessing the Tensions Between Researcher and Practitioner." *The American Sociologist.* 23, no. 4 (winter):43–55.

Orfield, Gary. 1987. *Fair Housing in Metropolitan Chicago: Perspectives After Two Decades.* A report to the Chicago Area Fair Housing Alliance.

Ormiston, Gayle L., and Raphael Sassower. 1989. *Narrative Experiments: The Discursive Authority of Science and Technology.* Minneapolis: University of Minnesota Press.

Park, Peter. 1993. "What Is Participatory Research? A Theoretical and Methodological Perspective." In *Voices of Change: Participatory Research in the United States and Canada,* edited by P. Park et al. Westport, CT: Bergin & Garvey.

Parry, Anne. 1995. *Caring for Children in Dangerous Times: a Protocol for Responding to Violence.* Chicago Department of Human Services, Children's Services Division and the Institute for Choosing Non-Violence, Rainbow House.

Parry, Anne, Melissa Walker, and Chris Heim. 1990. *Choosing Non-Violence: The Rainbow House Handbook to a Violence-Free Future for Young Children.* Chicago: Rainbow House/Arco Iris.

Patton, Michael Quinn. 1990. *Qualitative Evaluation and Research Methods.* 2d ed. Newbury Park, CA: Sage Publications.

Pena, Devon. 1992. "The 'Brown' and the 'Green': Chicanos and Environmental Politics in the Upper Rio Grande." *Capitalism, Nature, Socialism* 3, no. 1:79–103.

_____. 1994. "Pasture Poachers, Water Hogs, and Ridge Runners: Archetypes in the Site Ethnography of Local Environmental Conflicts." Paper presented at the Annual Meeting of the Western Social Science Association, 26–29 April, Albuquerque, New Mexico.

_____. 1996. "A Gold Mine, an Orchard, and an Eleventh Commandment." In *Subversive Kin: Ecology and Chicana Studies,* edited by D. Pena, I. Talamantez, and V. Kjonegaard. Santa Barbara: University of California Press.

Pena, Devon, and Joe Gallegos. 1993. "Nature and Chicanos in Southern Colorado." In *Confronting Environmental Racism: Voices From the Grassroots,* edited by R. D. Bullard. Boston: South End Press.

Pena, Devon, and Jose Rivera. 1996. "Historic Acequia Communities in the Upper Rio Grande: Policy for Cultural and Ecological Protection in Arid Land Environments," In *Rural Latino Communities: Comparative Regional Perspectives,* edited by R. Rochin, J. Rivera, and C. Torres. Lawrence: University of Kansas Press.

Pollution Prevention Education and Research Center (PPERC). 1994. *Program Description and Summary of Activities, 1991–1994.* Los Angeles: UCLA Pollution Prevention Education and Research Center.

Quimby, Ernest, and Samuel Friedman. 1989. "Dynamics of Black Mobilization Against AIDS in New York City." *Social Problems,* 36, no. 4: 403–415.

Ramasubramanian, Loxmi. 1994. "What Works With Youth?" *Wingspread Journal.* Racine, WI: S.C. Johnson Foundation.

Razeto, Luis. 1990. Economia Popular de Solaridad. Santiago, Chile: PEP.

Reardon, Kenneth M. 1995. "Creating University/Community Partnerships That Work: Lessons From the East St. Louis Action Research Project." *Metropolitan Universities: An International Forum.* (spring) 47–59.

Reardon, Ken, John Welsh, Brian Kreiswirth, and John Forester. 1993. "Participatory Action Research From the Inside: Community Development Practice in East St. Louis." *The American Sociologist,* 24: 69–91.

Richardson, Jeff, Robert L. Dyer, and Bobby Conner. 1993. *Central State Hospital Closure Plan: Commitment to Community Based Care: An Update Report to Governor Evan Bayh.* Indianapolis: Family and Social Services Administration.

Rossi, Peter H., and Howard E. Freeman. 1993. *Evaluation: A Systematic Approach, 5th Edition.* Newbury Park, CA: Sage Publications.

Russell, Richard D., and Ronald M. Farqhuar. 1966. *Lead Isotopes in Geology.* New York: Interscience.

Rutherford, Floyd J., and Andrew Ahlgren. 1990. *Science for All Americans.* New York: Oxford University Press.

Saltman, Juliet. 1990. *A Fragile Movement: The Struggle for Neighborhood Stabilization.* New York: Greenwood Press.

Sarri, Rosemary C., and Catherine M. Sarri. 1992. "Organizational and Community Change Through Participatory Action Research." *Administration in Social Work* 16, no. 34: 99–122.

Sclove, Richard. 1995. *Democracy and Technology.* New York: Guilford Press.

Shiva, Vandana. 1988. *Staying Alive: Women, Ecology, and Development.* London: Zed Books.

Shlay, Anne B. 1993. "Shaping Place: Institutions and Metropolitan Patterns." *Journal of Urban Affairs* 15, no. 5.

Simonson, Lynnell J., and Virginai A. Bushaw. 1993. "Participatory Action Research: Easier Said Than Done," *American Sociologist* 24(1): 27.

Singleton, Royce, Brian Straits, and Margaret Straits. 1993. *Approaches to Social Research,* 2nd edition. New York: Oxford University Press.

Solomon, R. L., and J. W. Hartford. 1976. "Lead and Cadmium in Dusts and Soils in a Small Urban Community." *Environmental Science and Technology,* 10:773–777.

Squires, Gregory D., and Sally O'Connor. 1993. "Do Lenders Who Redline Make More Money Than Lenders Who Don't." *The Review of Black Political Economy* 21, no. 4: 81–107

Squires, Gregory, Larry Bennett, Kathleen McCourt, and Philip Nyden. 1987. *Chicago: Race, Class and the Response to Decline.* Philadelphia: Temple University Press.

Stills, Wendell. 1992. *The Emerson Park Community Development Block Grant Program 1992–1997.* Urbana, IL: Department of Urban and Regional Planning.

Stoecker, Randy. 1994. *Defending Community: The Struggle for Alternative Redevelopment in Cedar-Riverside.* Philadelphia: Temple University Press.

Stoecker, Randy, and David Beckwith. 1992. "Advancing Toledo's Neighborhood Movement Through Participatory Action Research: Integrating Activist and Academic Approaches." *Clinical Sociology Review* 10:198–213.

Teitelbaum, Lee E. 1983. "Law and Oral History." Paper presented at a symposium on Land, Law, and Oral History at the Annual Meeting of the American Society for Ethnohistory, 5 November, Albuquerque, New Mexico.

Thys, Dider, and Judith Painter. 1994. *Village Banking with Catholic Relief Services and Partners: A Case Study.* Baltimore, MD: Catholic Relief Services.

United Church of Christ Commission for Racial Justice. 1987. *Toxic Waste and Race in the United States.* New York: Commission for Racial Justice.

United Way of Chicago. 1990. *Chicago's Community Development: Challenges and Opportunities.* Chicago: United Way of Chicago.

U.S. Department of Commerce, Bureau of the Census. 1990. *1990 Census of Population.* Washington, DC: U.S. Government Printing Office.

U.S. Department of Education and U.S. Department of Health and Human Services. 1993. *Together We Can: A Guide for Crafting a Profamily System of Education and Human Services.* Washington, DC: U.S. Government Printing Office.

U.S. Department of Housing and Urban Development. 1975. *The Dynamics of Neighborhood Change.* Washington, DC: Office of Policy Development and Research.

U.S. Environmental Protection Agency. 1991. *Economic Impact Analysis of Regulatory Controls in the Drycleaning Industry.* Washington, DC: U.S. EPA.

U.S. Environmental Protection Agency. 1992. *Environmental Equity: Reducing Risks for All Communities.* Washington, DC: U.S. EPA.

U.S. General Accounting Office. 1983. *Siting of Hazardous Waste Landfills and Their Correlation With Racial and Economic Status of Surrounding Communities.* Washington, DC: U.S. GAO.

Warren, Roland. 1971. *Truth, Love and Social Change, and Other Essays on Community Change.* Chicago: Rand McNally.

Whyte, William Foote. ed. 1991. *Participatory Action Research.* Newbury Park, CA: Sage.

Wright, Eric R., Jonathan B. Miller, Bernice A. Pescosolido, and Elizabeth C. McDonel. 1994. *The Central State Hospital Discharge Study: Tracking Report January 1994.* Technical report to the Indiana Division of Mental Health, Indianapolis, IN. Bloomington, IN: Indiana Consortium for Mental Health Services Research.

Zúñiga-Urrutia, Ximena. 1992. Views and Issues in Action Research. Ph.D. diss., University of Michigan.

Index